THE VICTORIA
CROSSES
OF THE
CRIMEAN WAR

THE VICTORIA CROSSES OF THE CRIMEAN WAR

THE MEN BEHIND THE MEDALS

JAMES W. BANCROFT

FRONTLINE
BOOKS

THE VICTORIA CROSSES OF THE CRIMEAN WAR
The Men Behind the Medals

This edition published in 2017 by Frontline Books,
an imprint of Pen & Sword Books Ltd,
47 Church Street, Barnsley, S. Yorkshire, S70 2AS

ISBN: 978-1-52671-061-1

For more information on our books, please visit
www.frontline-books.com,
email info@frontline-books.com
or write to us at the above address.

Printed and bound by TJ International Ltd, Padstow, Cornwall
Typeset in 10.5/13.5 point Palatino

Great Britain has produced a race of heroes who, in moments of danger and terror, have stood as firm as the rocks of their own native shores, and when half the world has been arrayed against them have fought the battles of their country with heroic fortitude.

Sergeant Major Timothy Gowing, 7th Royal Fusiliers

Contents

Introduction

For the first time in the history of the coveted medal all 111 recipients of the Victoria Cross for the Crimean War have been brought together exclusively in a single publication; to tell the stories of who they were, how they gained the Victoria Cross and what happened to them afterwards.

Most of the information for this project is taken from the J.W.B. Historical Library, compiled over four decades, and the narratives of the Victoria Cross actions are based on the recipient's own account if they left one, the citations in the *London Gazette* and regimental archives and histories. The J.W.B. files concerning biographical details are more comprehensive; however, I decided only to include information that I believe presents interesting anecdotes and informative stories to the general reader and historian about the men who did the fighting, as opposed to the politics of the war and tedious facts and figures. It is not definitive – no individual can make such a claim for a publication of this nature, but it is a project that needed to be attempted and time will tell if I should have been the person who did so!

I have cross-referenced my files with up-to-date official sources to the best of my ability, and I have given a great deal of attention to checking the correct spelling of the names of people and locations, burial places and new memorials, and dates of awards and promotions. I made every effort to contact museums and other establishments to get up-to-date information on the whereabouts of medals and their accessibility.

The men recorded here displayed valour resulting in many deeds of exceptional courage which are a regular occurrence in the illustrious annals of the British Army. Among them are heroes who had the guts to put themselves in mortal danger by picking up live shells that could have exploded and blown them apart at any moment, gallant troopers who took part in a cavalry charge that they knew was doomed before it began and they were about to be cut to pieces, and valiant individuals who had the audacity to sneak into unknown territory to take the conflict into the enemy's back yard and risk capture and ill-treatment. Many men performed more than one act that was considered worthy of the award of the Victoria Cross, and Sergeant John Park of the 77th

Regiment is the only man ever to have five actions mentioned in his citation for the Victoria Cross in the history of the medal. Seven men gained the Distinguished Conduct Medal in addition to the Victoria Cross, and of the twelve awards of the naval Conspicuous Gallantry Medal six men also won the Victoria Cross. Six men who received the Victoria Cross for the Crimean campaign were born in Devon, more than in any other county. At the time of the campaign my home town of Eccles was in Lancashire and not a district of the City of Salford, as it is today, and my research suggests that it is the only small town of its kind which can boast of being the birthplace of two men who became recipients of the Victoria Cross for the Crimean War.

Most of the rank-and-file soldiers and ordinary sailors who took part in the campaign were rough-and-ready lads from the coal mines, farms and dark satanic mills in and around the tough city slums, and their staunch loyalty to their regiment and comrades gave them formidable fighting abilities. Unfortunately, in a time when post-traumatic stress disorder was not even recognised let alone treated with consideration, many men who survived were affected badly by their injuries and what they had witnessed. Some came back to Britain to face a struggle for survival equal to that which they had endured in the Crimea, and they never recovered. Several committed suicide, and some died in destitution. Some died while still serving with the colours and others under unfortunate circumstances after the war, five of these being buried or lost at sea. In contrast to this, sixteen men were knighted for their distinguished careers. Many men were the sons of Peninsular and Waterloo veterans.

News of the fall of Sebastopol was received with immense excitement and enthusiasm, and many cities celebrated victory in the Crimea with displays of illuminations, fireworks and victory processions, and there was 'general feasting and rejoicing' to celebrate the final peace. However, 20,000 men lost their lives, the majority from disease, and most of the men who had fought in the East found little to celebrate.

Although he was not a recipient of the Victoria Cross, an example of how men became unstable and found it difficult to cope with life after the Crimea was Lieutenant Richard Molesworth of the 19th (1st Yorkshire, North Riding) Regiment. He received a severe wound during the final attack on Sebastopol, when a piece of shrapnel hit him and embedded itself in the crown of his head. Surgeons had failed to remove it completely and it caused him terrible stress. He became engaged to Mary Louisa Stewart, who was a prominent Victorian children's writer under the name of Mrs Molesworth. However, she noticed that soon after his return from the Crimea he had shown signs of mood swings and 'a very violent temper', which had given her mother cause for concern. Louisa played it down and trusted that their love for each other would help to keep it under control, and they married in 1861. Richard became a major, and they had several children, but he eventually became too unstable and had to retire from the military. Their domestic problems worsened, Richard became irresponsible and financially inept, and with the approval of his family Louisa was forced to take their children away from him and live in France. She eventually filed for a divorce.

The Crimean War has been described as the first 'modern war'. Newspaper correspondents reported from the front so the public at home could read about what was happening – including the difficult conditions in which British troops were suffering. It was the first war to be photographed, use telegraph and to take advantage of the relatively new mode of transport provided by the railways. The textile industry's winter clothing order books also gained a boost with the Balaclava helmet, the Cardigan, and the Raglan sleeve.

Alfred Lord Tennyson's poem *The Charge of the Light Brigade*, published in 1855, brought attention to that particular action, and many men who took part in it kept in contact. On 25 October 1875, a Balaclava reunion banquet was held at the Alexandra Palace in London, and from it a Balaclava Commemoration Society was formed in 1877, which in 1879 restricted its members to those who had taken part in the Light Brigade action. On the occasion of Queen Victoria's Golden Jubilee in 1887 the survivors signed a Loyal Address which was presented to her.

A number of Crimea and Indian Mutiny Veterans' Associations were established in cities such as Liverpool, Manchester, Bristol, and Nottingham, and after Rudyard Kipling published *The Last of the Light Brigade* on 28 April 1890, to highlight the plight of many of the survivors who were destitute, the British people responded, and numerous benefit concerts were produced, including one in Manchester on 21 May 1890. On 25 October 1890, a first annual dinner was held at the Alexandra Palace, and these continued on the anniversary of the battle until 1913, by which time there were few survivors left.

In 1897, T. Harrison Roberts, a London journalist and publisher, invited seventy-three survivors of the Charge of the Light Brigade to an all-expenses-paid visit to his offices in Fleet Street to watch the Diamond Jubilee procession on 22 June. Queen Victoria stopped her carriage to acknowledge the party of proud veterans. Mr Roberts was shocked to learn that many of them lived in poverty and he decided to start a public fund. Survivors received a weekly pension and no recipient of the T.H. Roberts Relief Fund had to enter a workhouse or have a pauper's burial.

Such is the value of people power, but a man who has risked his life for his country should never need to have to rely on any kind of sustenance.

Chapter 1

The Victoria Cross

The Distinguished Conduct Medal was instituted on 4 December 1854, for gallantry in the field performed by 'other ranks' of the British Army, and the Conspicuous Gallantry Medal was established on 13 August 1855, as the naval equivalent of the DCM, but there was no universal medal that could be awarded for all ranks of the British armed forces. However, stories of the gallantry being performed by her soldiers in the Crimea, set against reports from the first war correspondents of their neglect and suffering which was causing discontent among the British public, prompted Queen Victoria to try to do something within her power to give them recognition. Consequently, the Victoria Cross was instituted by her royal warrant on 29 January 1856, and 111 men who fought in the Crimean campaign became the first recipients for: 'Conspicuous bravery and devotion to country in the presence of the enemy.' Rank, long service or wound was to have no special influence on who qualified for the award.

Queen Victoria took a great interest in the establishment of the award and in the design of the medal. Prince Albert suggested that it should be named after her, and the original motto was to have been *For the Brave*, but Victoria was of the opinion that this would lead to the inference that only those who have got the cross are considered to be brave, and decided that *For Valour* would be more suitable. The design was not to be particularly ornate and not of high metallic value. All the medals have been cast from the bronze cascabels believed to be from two guns, said to be of Chinese origin, which the British had captured from the Russians at Sebastopol. The original ribbons for the medal were blue for the navy and crimson for the army. Queen Victoria thought that 'the person decorated with the Victoria Cross might properly be allowed to bear some distinctive mark after their name'. She pointed out that at that time 'VC' meant Vice-Chancellor, and she suggested 'DVC' (Decorated with the Victoria Cross) or 'BVC' (Bearer of the Victoria Cross). However, just 'VC' was finally agreed on. On its institution it carried an annuity of £10. Many rank-and-file soldiers who gained the Victoria Cross are known to have felt great satisfaction from the fact that military regulations state that all officers must salute a man of any rank who passes by them wearing the Victoria Cross on his breast.

The first man to perform a deed which would be rewarded with the Victoria Cross was Mate Charles Davis Lucas on 21 June 1854, while serving aboard HMS *Hecla* during the bombardment of Bomarsund in the Baltic Sea. The first eighty-five recipient announcements were published in a supplement to the *London Gazette* for 24 February 1857, most of them extremely understated, and the first named was Lieutenant William Buckley of HMS *Miranda*, Royal Navy. The first investiture took place at Hyde Park in London, on 26 June 1857, when sixty-two Crimean veterans received the medal from the Queen herself, in a ceremony which is said to have taken only about 10 minutes. She performed the deed in the rather awkward position of side-saddle on a horse, presumably because most of the men were tall and it would be easier for her to reach them, and she actually pinned the medal to the skin of Commander Raby, who was first in the queue and therefore became the first man ever to wear the Victoria Cross – literally! It seems she didn't get much better with practice, as she did it again to Lieutenant Graham who was twenty-fourth in line. Some men were dressed in plain clothes, another as a gatekeeper and Constable George Walters was wearing his police uniform. The Queen recorded in her diary: 'It was indeed a most proud, gratifying day.' However, even after seeing men in the line with limbs and eyes missing, and other disfigurements, it is unlikely that she or any British civilians really understood what horrors they had witnessed and experienced to gain the award.

The last act of heroism to be rewarded with the Victoria Cross for the Crimean War was performed by Commander John Commerell and Quartermaster William Rickard, both of the Royal Navy, on 11 October 1855, in the Sea of Azov. The last act of heroism performed at the main theatre of war around Sebastopol is not certain. Corporal John Ross of the Royal Engineers crept to the Redan on the night of 8 September 1855, where he witnessed the evacuation of Sebastopol and reported what he had seen, and this seems to have been the last Victoria Cross action.

However, in September 1855, Private George Strong of the Coldstream Guards threw a live shell over the parapet where he was stationed, and saved many lives. An exact date was not recorded, but if this was after 8 September 1855, this was the final act to be rewarded with the Victoria Cross at Sebastopol.

At that time the Victoria Cross was not awarded to men who did not live to wear it, or this publication would have included tributes to names like Thistlethwayte, Tryon, Egan, Woods and Geoghegan, and many more. *The Times* reported on the day after the investiture:

> As they stood in a row, awaiting the arrival of Her Majesty, one could not help feeling an emotion of sorrow that they were so few, and that the majority of the men who would have done honour even to the Victoria Cross lie in their shallow graves on the bleak cliffs of the Crimea.
>
> Where were the men who climbed the heights of Alma, who hurried forward over the plain of Balaklava to almost certain death, who, wearied and outnumbered yet held their ground on that dismal morning when the valley of Inkerman seethed with flames and smoke like some vast hellish cauldron? Where are the troops who during that fearful winter toiled through the snow night after night, with just sufficient strength to drag their sick and wasted forms down to the trenches which became their graves? Let not these men be forgotten at such a time, nor while we pay all honour to the few survivors of that gallant little army omit a tribute to the brave who have passed away forever.

Men who had seen active service in the Crimean War also variously received other medals. The Crimean War Medal was issued to all personnel who had taken part in the campaign, with clasps added for those who had been present at the Alma, Balaclava, Inkerman, Sebastopol and Azov. The Baltic Medal was awarded for those who had taken part in the expedition to that region in 1854–5. The French Legion of Honour was France's highest award for excellent military conduct during the Crimean War. The Turkish Order of the Medjidie was presented in various classes to British and French personnel who came to the aid of the Ottoman Empire during the Crimean crisis as a reward for distinguished service before the enemy. The Turkish Crimea Medal was usually awarded together with the British version to all men who had taken part in the campaign. The Sardinian Medal of Military Valour was especially authorised by Victor Emmanuelle II in 1856 to

3

reward British military personnel for their distinguished service during the Crimean War. The Bentinck Medal was awarded to thirteen men for distinguished conduct during the Crimean campaign. It was first presented by Major General Sir Henry Bentinck, KCB, formerly of the Coldstream Guards and Commander of the Guards Brigade in the Crimea. It was sometimes confused with the Distinguished Conduct Medal.

Chapter 2

The Baltic Fleet

By the middle of the nineteenth century the Turkish Ottoman Empire was falling apart, prompting Tsar Nicholas to refer to it as: 'The sick man of Europe.' Britain and France were suspicious of Russia's expansionist intentions in the Balkans, and this was seriously inflamed when the Tsar began to interfere in Turkish affairs, and the Sultan appealed to Britain and France for guidance. However, there was a lack of co-operation on both sides, and Turkey declared war on Russia on 5 October 1853. Russian forces destroyed a Turkish fleet at Sinope on 30 November, which caused a wave of international hostility.

The Allied Fleet entered the Black Sea on 4 January 1854. A British peace deputation went to see the Tsar on 10 February, but diplomacy broke down, Britain drifted into war, and 'The Long Peace' which had prevailed for Britain in Europe since the Battle of Waterloo ended on 27 March 1854, when Queen Victoria issued the Declaration of War against Russia. A British Expeditionary Force under General Lord Raglan had already begun to set sail for the Balkans on 23 February, and British war ships under Admiral Sir Charles Napier set sail from Spithead on 11 March heading for the Baltic Sea, the north-west frontier of the Russian Empire, where they could threaten the Russian capital at St Petersburg. The Russians could not have imagined the type of gallant and determined men who were coming to wage war against them.

The forty-nine-gun screw frigate HMS *Arrogant* was among the ships. *Arrogant's* first action came on 15 April 1854, when she took part in the capture of a Russian ship. On 18 May 1854, *Arrogant* and the six-gun steam frigate HMS *Hecla* came under fire from Russian troops situated behind a protective sandbank. The Russians were soon dispersed and next morning the two ships proceeded along a narrow channel to the town of Ekness, where they faced determined opposition

5

from two enemy gun batteries. The British ships bombarded the enemy batteries and put them out of action. *Hecla* had to use its superior speed to get away from Russian frigates on several occasions.

On 21 June 1854, HMS *Hecla* was involved in the bombardment of Bomarsund, a fort on the Åland Islands guarding the entrance to the Gulf of Bothnia. The fire was returned from the fort, and at the height of the action a live enemy shell landed on *Hecla*'s upper deck and rolled among the men, hissing and fizzing, and all hands were ordered to fling themselves flat on the deck. One man realised that they were all still in great peril, and with great coolness and presence of mind, Mate Charles Lucas ran forward, picked up the shell with the fuse still burning and, well-aware that it might explode and blow him to pieces at any moment, carried it across the deck and hurled it over the side of the ship and into the sea, where it exploded with a tremendous roar before it hit the surface. It was thanks to Mate Lucas' swift and decisive action that no one on board was killed or seriously wounded by the shell. (Some sources say that two men were slightly wounded from the blast.)

On 21 July 1854, HMS *Arrogant* was one of four British ships that silenced the Russian guns at the fortress on Gogland, while the Allied Fleet went on to attack Sveaborg. On 9 August 1854, *Arrogant* received intelligence that an aide-de-camp of the Emperor of Russia had landed on Wardo Island in charge of mail and despatches to be forwarded to the Russian general on Bomarsund, and it would be favourable to the British if these despatches were intercepted. Lieutenant John Bythesea pointed out to his captain that a large force would attract too much attention and obtained permission for himself and Stoker William Johnstone, who spoke Swedish, to proceed to the shore with a view to seizing the mail bags in a Special Forces-type mission.

They rowed into a small bay, where they hid their boat, but they were seen as they landed and made their way inland, and being informed that a party from the British fleet was on the island, Russian search parties had been sent out to capture them. They were concealed in the cottage of a local farmer, and disguised as peasants they were able to reconnoitre during the dark hours until the night of 12 August, when the farmer informed them that the mail bags had landed and would be sent down to the fortress at Bomarsund. With this information they went out and hid in some bushes on the route and waited for their chance. The mails were accompanied by a military escort, which passed so close to them that a Russian actually brushed against Lieutenant Bythesea's sleeve, and as soon as the escort believed that the road ahead was clear they took their departure and left five unarmed men to carry on along the path.

Taking the opportunity to pounce, Lieutenant Bythesea drew his flintlock pistol, the only weapon they had, and ambushed the men. Johnstone threw a rope around the group while Bythesea provided cover with the pistol. Two of them dropped their bags and ran for their lives, and the remaining three were taken prisoner. They got back to their hidden craft and forced the captives to row back to HMS *Arrogant* with the pistol pointed at them, and the mission was declared a success.

Charles Davis Lucas

Charles Davis Lucas was born on 19 February 1834, at Druminargal House, 29 Poyntzpass, Scarva, County Armagh, Ireland. He was the son of Davis Lucas of Clontibret, County Monaghan, Ireland, and his wife Elizabeth (formerly Hill). He was descended from a well-known former English family of Castle Shane.

Probably prompted by the devastating potato famine, Charles was only 14 when he joined the Royal Navy in 1848 as a mate on HMS *Vanguard*. He subsequently served on HMS *Amazon* in the Mediterranean, and in 1849 he joined HMS *Dragon* under Captain William Hall for service around the coasts of Ireland in the suppression of the Smith O'Brien rebellion. He then joined the frigate HMS *Fox* for service in the Second Anglo-Burmese War of 1852, landing with storming parties for the capture of Rangoon, Pegu, Dalla, Prome and Meaday, for which he received the Indian General Service Medal with *Pegu* clasp. The local newspaper reported that at this time:

> Admiral Lucas also took part in Captain Lock, R.N.'s, unsuccessful attack on the stronghold of the chieftain Mya Toom, in which Captain Lock, being killed, and most of the other senior officers being either killed or severely wounded, the force was obliged to retreat, the command of the rear-guard devolving on Admiral Lucas, then a midshipman of nineteen years of age. The retreat lasted nine hours, during which the rear-guard was warmly engaged in keeping back the enemy. During the said years 1852–53, Mr. Lucas was almost continually employed in command of an armed boat up the River Irrawaddy, in a most unhealthy climate.

Having transferred to the new HMS *Hecla*, again under command of Captain Hall, he left the dock at Hull on 19 February 1854 for active service to reconnoitre the Baltic region.

He became the first man to perform a deed for which the Victoria Cross was awarded when it was announced in the *London Gazette* on 24 February 1857, and he received the medal during the first investiture. He also received the Baltic Medal, 1854–5. After a meeting of the Royal Humane Society held on 12 July 1854, he was awarded their Life Saving Medal.

He was promoted lieutenant immediately after his Victoria Cross action, and was appointed commander on 19 February 1862, being second-in-command of the frigate HMS *Liffey* from 18 August that year for service in the Mediterranean. He became commander of the armoured gunboat HMS *Vixen* on 17 June 1867, for comparative trials, and he was promoted captain on 25 October 1867. He was appointed captain on the retired list from 1 October 1873, and retired as rear admiral on 1 January 1886.

He was brigadier general commanding the Ballachulish Corps of the 1st (Argyllshire Highland) Rifle Volunteers in Scotland from 1873–83, where his home was at Lismore and Appin in Argyllshire.

It is believed that sometime around 1878–9 he was travelling by train from London to Scotland, and when he reached the station in Appin he got off and left his medals behind. There are other less innocent stories of how he lost his medals, but he was issued with a duplicate set.

In early June 1879 in Kensington, he married Frances Russell Hall (1854–1925), the only child of the captain of the *Hecla* and her mother, Hilaire Caroline, the daughter of Admiral George Byng, 6th Lord Torrington. They had three daughters named Hilaire Caroline (Matheson), Frances Byng (Stamper) and Caroline Louisa Byng (1886–1967), who became an artist and established Miller's Gallery in Lewes, Sussex, with Frances. They were important supporters of the visual arts in Wales in the 1930s, and they were the subject of a portrait painted by Sir Cedric Morris entitled *Two Sisters* which they considered to be unflattering. Charles' wife has been described as 'arrogant and violent tempered', although he was described as 'generally loved and esteemed . . . for his benevolent and winning personality'.

The Lucas family lived at 48 Phillimore Gardens, Kensington, London, until the turn of the century, when they settled at the twenty-one-roomed Great Culverden House in the Mount Ephraim district of Tunbridge Wells. It was later demolished to make way for the Kent and Sussex Hospital. Charles was a JP for Argyllshire and Kent, and a trustee for the Amy and Navy Club in London, having been a member since 1868. He was an anti-Home Ruler, and in 1904 he held the position of president of the Ulster Association.

After a three-week illness, Charles died at his home aged 80, on 7 August 1914, three days after Britain declared war on Germany. He was buried at St Lawrence's Church in Mereworth, near Maidstone in Kent. There is a memorial at St Lawrence's, a tablet in the hall at the Poyntzpass Royal British Legion and a blue plaque was unveiled at the house of his birth in 2007. Having become a club member in 1868, he is one of four Crimean VCs named on the memorial in the corridor of the Royal Naval and Royal Albert Yacht Club in Portsmouth, which was unveiled by the Duke of Edinburgh in 2007. He and Matthew Charles Dixon are the Crimean War Victoria Cross recipients commemorated in the Victoria Cross Grove at Dunorlan Park who had connections to the borough of Royal Tunbridge Wells. His duplicate medals are in the National Maritime Museum at Greenwich, along with those of William Peel, William Hewett and John Sheppard.

John Bythesea

The Bythesea family were originally clothiers, who lived at The Hall in Freshford near Bath in Somerset, for a hundred years, and it was there that John Bythesea was born on 15 June 1827, the fifth and youngest son of the Revd George Bythesea, rector of St Peter's Church in Freshford for twenty years, and his wife, Mary (formerly Glossop). John was educated at Grosvenor College in Bath. His four brothers were all in the army, and his eldest brother, Lieutenant George Bythesea of the 80th (Staffordshire) Regiment, had been killed in action at Ferozeshah during the Sikh War in the Punjab in 1845. However, John decided to break with tradition and joined the navy in 1841, as a first class volunteer. Between February and June 1848 he served on board HMS *Victory*. He was promoted lieutenant on 12 June 1849, while serving on HMS *Pilot* in the East Indies, and he joined HMS *Arrogant* in September 1852. The disaster to HMS *Birkenhead* had occurred on 23 February 1852, and John was noted for giving 10s. subscription towards the dependants of those who had lost their lives. After his Victoria Cross exploit he was appointed lieutenant in command of the three-gun HMS *Locust* in the Baltic Fleet, becoming commander in May 1856.

He became the first Englishman to be awarded the Victoria Cross when it was announced in the *London Gazette* on 24 February 1857, and he received the medal during the first investiture. He also received the Baltic Medal, 1854–5.

9

He was promoted captain in March 1858, and served aboard the screw steam sloop HMS *Cruiser*, first at the south-east America station and then in operations on the River Yangtse, the Peiho Forts and Nankin during the Second China War of 1859–60, for which he received the Second China War Medal, 1857–60. He was promoted captain on 15 May 1861, and served in Canada during the Fenian Raid, being appointed to the commission which inquired into the state of the defences of Canada. He was appointed to the sloop HMS *Archer*, being invalided home from her in February 1864. He became naval attaché in Washington from 1865–7. From May 1867 he commanded the frigate HMS *Phoebe* in the flying squadron which sailed around the world in 1869–70.

In 1871 he was appointed captain of the battleship HMS *Lord Clyde* in the Mediterranean Sea, and in March of the following year she went to the assistance of a paddle steamer which had gone aground on the island of Pantelleria near Malta, and the *Clyde* ran aground herself. Captain Bythesea was court-martialled, severely reprimanded and dismissed from the ship. He was never employed at sea again, and from November 1874 he was consulting naval officer to the Indian government, and was largely responsible for the restructuring of the Indian Navy.

He married Fanny Belinda, daughter of Colonel G.N. Prior, in 1874, the year he became consulting naval officer to the Indian government. He retired from the navy on 5 August 1877, being promoted rear admiral on the retired list. He was appointed Companion, Order of the Bath (CB) in the same year. He became Companion, Order of the Indian Empire (CIE) in 1878 and retired as consulting naval officer in 1880.

John died at 22 Ashburton Pace in South Kensington, West London, on 18 May 1906, a month before his 79th birthday, and he was buried in Bath Abbey Cemetery. A party of petty officers from HMS *Victory* formed a guard of honour at his funeral, and his hat, sword and belt were placed on his coffin. His wife died in 1926. There is a memorial to the five Bythesea brothers in St Peter's Church at Freshford, and there is a Bythesea class at the local primary school. His Victoria Cross was purchased at auction in 2007, and is now displayed on rotation at the Lord Ashcroft Gallery, as part of the 'Extraordinary Heroes' exhibition at the Imperial War Museum in London.

William Johnstone

William Johnstone was born on 6 August 1823. He is believed to have enlisted with the name of John, and gave his place of birth variously as Hanover in Germany and Sweden. His home address was 10 Daniel Street at Portsea in Hampshire. Other sources suggest he was one of the foreign nationals picked up by Napier in Stockholm on his way to the Baltic, and his surname may have been Johanssen.

His award of the Victoria Cross was announced in the *London Gazette* of 24 February 1857, and the medal was apparently sent to him by registered post. He also received the Baltic Medal, 1854–5.

However, while in the West Indies working as a cook on HMS *Brunswick* on 20 August 1857, William suffered what was described as 'a fit of insanity', severely cutting Leading Stoker Charles Wood across his face, back and hands, before cutting his own throat with the same knife. He died from his injury at 9 o'clock that morning. He was aged 34, and was buried at sea in the St Vincent Passage.

He is named on a memorial stone at Bomarsund in south-west Finland, and his medals are with the County Museum of Natural History in Los Angeles.

Chapter 3

The Passage of the River Alma

The Allied expeditionary force arrived at Varna in Bulgaria in the summer of 1854. As they waited for orders to proceed their numbers were seriously depleted by the ravages of a cholera epidemic. The Crimea was invaded on 14 September 1854 at Calamity Bay near Eupatoria, and the troops marched south down the coast, escorted by the ships of the fleet out to sea, the objective being to attack the strategic Black Sea port of Sebastopol.

On 19 September 1854, they had the first encounter with the Russians at the River Bulganek, and as they marched over the crest of a hill on the following day they came in sight of the River Alma, and met with Russian forces massed along a high causeway on top of rugged steep cliffs beyond the river. It was a formidable obstacle, and one of the Russian commanders stated that it was such a strong position that they could hold it for three weeks or more. However, one of their officers later stated: 'We did not think it possible for men to be found with such firmness of morale to be able to attack in this apparently weak formation our massive columns.' The British were victorious within 3 hours, and an officer later remarked: 'Effectual people are the English.'

The principal position was an earthwork known as the Greater Redoubt, and at mid-afternoon Lord Raglan gave the order: 'The infantry will advance.' The 1st Battalion, Scots (Fusilier) Guards was among the units ordered to storm the redoubt with bayonets fixed and with colours flying. They came under heavy bombardment and rifle fire as they advanced over rugged ground, crossed the river and passed ruined buildings, burning huts and other obstacles, but they pressed on and up towards the redoubt.

'Could human courage stand the fire from the very muzzles of the weapons and afterwards face the steel of the defenders? Could human strength, taxed so heavily by the desperate advance across the open that men could scarcely speak, survive that final call to mount the heights and drive the brave and sullen grey-coats off?'

When shot and shell from the enemy batteries forced some of the troops of other units to fall back, they came through the ranks of the Scots Guards and threw their line formation into disorder, and it became something like a human triangle with one corner pointing at the foe. However, the Scots Guards continued to advance on the entrenchment, 'though little better than a mob'. The enemy fire was tremendous, and volleys cut down three colour parties in succession. When within about twenty paces of the Russian positions not more than a company was up with the colours, and the odds seemed hopelessly against them.

At the front angle of the triangle, Captain Robert Lindsay, whose father was a veteran of the Peninsular War, stood firm and waved the Queen's colour, while Lieutenant Arthur Thistlethwayte waved the regimental colour. They came under a tremendous fire, during which Captain Lindsay's hand was smashed and the pole of the Queen's colour was broken in half, and there were at least twenty bullet holes through the silk. The captain fell down and disappeared under the colour, and many men around him thought he was lost. However, he suddenly reappeared and got to his feet again, and immediately commenced waving the colour triumphantly in the air. Lieutenant Thistlethwayte did the same with his busby and an enemy bullet went right through it. Sergeant James McKechnie also stood firm alongside Captain Lindsay, and raising his weapon, called out: 'by the centre, Scots, by the centre. Look to the colours and march by them.' Exposing himself in such a way attracted the attention of Russian riflemen and he received a contusion wound.

'The conduct of Lieutenant Lindsay and Lieutenant Thistlethwayte is highly spoken of.' A few weeks later, at a very trying moment during the Battle of Inkerman, Captain Lindsay charged a party of Russians, driving them back and running one through the body. Lieutenant Thistlethwayte died of disease at Scutari on 26 November 1854, which almost certainly deprived him of the Victoria Cross.

As the men of the Scots Guards were falling back down the hill, Captain Scarlett shouted to Sergeant John Knox to assist him in trying to reform the ranks around the colours. The sergeant and Private William Reynolds were conspicuous in their efforts to follow the order, 'in a very cool, gallant and admirable manner'. This was the turning point of the battle for the Great Redoubt, and the re-formed British ranks pushed on to gain their objective. Sergeant Knox was later seriously wounded at the first assault on the Redan.

Luke O'Connor was one of the centre sergeants of the 23rd (Royal Welsh) Fusiliers, and advanced between the officers as they rushed the enemy entrenched in the Great Redoubt, with colours flying. As they approached the position with bayonets fixed, a teenage ensign named Henry Anstruther raced forward with the Queen's colour and got to within about thirty paces of the redoubt when he fell mortally wounded. 'Would his followers waver? Would they rally? For already the 23rd had suffered terribly, and there is a limit to endurance!'

The colour was taken up by Corporal Luby. Sergeant O'Connor was shot in the breast at the same time, and he too fell, nursing two broken ribs; but, recovering himself, he snatched the colour from the corporal and rushed to the redoubt and planted it there as a token of victory. He continued to carry it until the end of the action, although urged by Captain Granville to relinquish it and go to the rear on account of his wounds. He would show gallantry again during the final assault on the Great Redan.

The Tsar had ordered that no guns should be captured by the British, so when the battle seemed lost the Russians had started to limber up their guns to try to get them away. Captain Edward Bell of the 23rd (Royal Welsh) Fusiliers, the son of a soldier and a relation of Lawrence of Arabia, shouted out to his company, 'take that gun, lads!'. He dashed forward as he spoke, and outran his men in his eagerness. He pointed a pistol at the leading driver's head, and he immediately dismounted and ran off. Captain Bell grabbed his horse, and led the team around the shoulder of the earthwork and down to the river – from where it found its way to Woolwich and eventually to Wales. All thirteen of his senior officers had been killed or wounded, so he succeeded to the command of his regiment and brought them out of action. He was reprimanded by his senior officer for having left his position with his regiment, but higher authority recognised his gallantry and he was duly rewarded.

In a subsequent engagement at Sebastopol on 22 April 1855, Captain Bell was complimented in general orders for distinguished conduct while in command of a working party which came under heavy fire.

Private John Park of the 77th (East Middlesex) Regiment was noted for conspicuous bravery during the fighting at the Alma (*see 5 November 1854, 19 April, 18 June and 8 September 1855*).

The Allied armies were totally victorious, but their casualties were such that it took two whole days for them to tend to their wounded and bury their dead. An officer with the Highland Brigade suggested that the battle would be named 'The Passage of the Alma'.

Robert James Lindsay

Robert James Lindsay was born on 16 April 1832, at Balcarres House near Colinsburgh, in the east Neuk of Fife, Scotland. He was the second son and youngest of four children of Lieutenant General The Honourable James Lindsay of the Grenadier Guards, and Anne, daughter of Sir Coutts Trotter, Bart. His great-grandfather was James Lindsay, the 5th Earl of Balcarres. His father had served in the Peninsular War and inherited the house in 1836. The family spent several years in France before Robert went to Eton College in 1846, where he was educated until 1850. The winters of 1851–2 were spent in Rome and Naples with his family, when they befriended Samuel Jones-Loyd, 1st Baron Overstone, one of the richest men in England, and Lady Overstone, and their daughter, Harriett Sarah, caught his eye.

He had blue eyes and golden hair, and was considered by many to be a very handsome man. After contemplating entering the Civil Service with the East India Company, he decided to follow his eldest brother into the Guards Brigade and took up a commission with the 3rd Battalion, Scots (Fusilier) Guards in December 1850. He embarked for active service in the Crimea on 1 March 1854, and on 15 June he was reported as seriously ill with dysentery; but unlike thousands of others he survived.

In March 1855 he was made aide-de-camp to General James Simpson, a friend of his father, and in August he was appointed adjutant of the Scots Guards. These appointments gave him more opportunity to see the broader picture of how the campaign was being mismanaged and he spoke out about the conditions being suffered by the rank-and-file soldiers. During his work in this capacity he became a great friend of Florence Nightingale. A devout Christian, he held Bible classes for soldiers.

The Duke of Cambridge had personally witnessed the events that day, and before he died in Genoa in December 1855, he wrote to Captain Lindsay's father stating: 'I can tell you general, your son is a very fine fellow, a most gallant soldier among gallant men, for they are a fine set of fellows. How we escaped has been a marvel to me.' In the following month he joined the Duke's mother in Florence to console her in her grief. He returned to the Crimea, but the Treaty of Paris was signed on 30 March 1856, and Robert left for home on 11 June.

His award of the Victoria Cross was announced in the *London Gazette* of 24 February 1857, and he received the medal at the first investiture. He also received the Crimea Medal with *Alma, Balaclava, Inkerman* and *Sebastopol* clasps, the French Legion of Honour, the Turkish Order of the Medjidie (5th Class) and the Turkish Crimea Medal.

Shortly after his return from the East he was selected by Albert, the Prince Consort, to be Equerry to the young Prince of Wales. He married Harriet on 17 November 1858, and they settled at Lockinge House, near Wantage in Berkshire (now in Oxfordshire), which Lord Overstone had given them as a wedding present. From then on he assumed the name Loyd-Lindsay.

He left the army in 1859 with the rank of lieutenant colonel, to concentrate on improving his estates. However, there was great fear at that time of an invasion by French forces, so he became a pioneer of the Volunteer Movement. He became colonel commanding the Berkshire Regiment, and colonel of the Honourable Artillery Company at the request of the Prince of Wales in 1866, remaining in that position until 1881.

Soon after the Crimean campaign a series of pictures were produced by the artist Louis Desanges, which included the Victoria Cross actions of Lord Wantage, Sir Charles Russell and Colonel Goodlake. They were on display at the Crystal Palace for many years but were eventually put up for sale. Not wishing them to be dispersed, Lord and Lady Wantage purchased them and presented them to the town of Wantage. The picture of Lord Wantage at the Battle of the Alma is now on display at Wantage Civic Hall. A commissioned bust depicting him was completed by Sir Joseph Boehm and was unveiled in 1869, which can now be seen at Wantage Library.

He entered Parliament in 1865, when he was one of three politicians elected as Members for Berkshire, serving with Sir Charles Russell VC, from 1865–8. He was head of the poll with 2,227 votes. He was re-elected in 1868, and in 1871 he was active in Parliament in debates for army reforms. He was returned again in 1874. In August 1877 he was appointed financial secretary to the War Office, being involved in the decision to allocate £6 million for military expenditure. He held the post until the Liberals were elected in 1880. The Tories returned to power in 1885, and he was offered the position of surveyor general at the War Office but declined on health grounds.

Prompted by the sufferings during the Franco-Prussian War of 1870, he was a founder member of the British Red Cross Society in August that year and he went on to become chairman. In October he visited Versailles and Paris during the siege to distribute aid. His life was in danger on at least one occasion, when he was escorted through the lines in besieged Paris to present aid funds and was seized by the mob who suspected him of being a Prussian spy.

By 1873 his estate comprised 20,000 acres and was the largest in Berkshire and one of the largest in England. Despite his many other commitments, he spent much of his time introducing modern methods to his farms and in the welfare of his workers.

He was appointed Knight Commander of the Bath (KCB) in May 1881, and was raised to the Peerage in 1885. He became Lord Lieutenant of Berkshire in 1886, and he was a Grand Master of Freemasons in Berkshire. He was created Baron Wantage of Lockinge in July 1885, and he received the Queen's Golden Jubilee Medal in 1887. He was a good shot and an enthusiast of rifle shooting, and as chairman of the council of the National Rifle Association from 1887–91 he presided over its move from Wimbledon to Bisley, where the new range opened in July 1890.

He had proven himself to be brave and dutiful, and he was stated by many to have been honest and philanthropic. He once tasked himself: 'I must do something to justify my existence', and Florence Nightingale qualified this after his death when she stated: 'He was a great gain . . . All are better than if he had not lived.'

Lord Wantage died on 10 June 1901, aged 69, at his beloved Lockinge House, and he was buried in the family vault within Holy Trinity Church at Ardington near Wantage. There was no heir to the title. His name appears on the 'For Valour' memorial in the cloisters at Eton College, and Lady Wantage had a monument erected to his name on the Ridgeway ancient footpath in the south of England. In 1908 she opened Wantage Hall, the first hall of residence at Reading University. Lady Wantage died in 1920.

John Simpson Knox

John Simpson Knox was born on 30 September 1828, at King Street in Calton, Glasgow, of a yeomanry family. He was the son of John Knox, late of the 90th (Perthshire) Light Infantry, and his second wife. He was big for his age at 14, and apparently ran away from an unhappy home and enlisted at Glasgow into the 3rd Battalion, Scots (Fusilier) Guards on 15 May 1843.

He kept a scrapbook into which he pasted letters, cuttings and pictures, which were kept by his family. He took to the army well, being promoted corporal on 11 June 1846, sergeant on 9 July 1851 and acting sergeant major and drill sergeant on 7 July 1853, thus becoming one of the youngest senior NCOs in the army. He was described as a man of magnificent physique, 'a formidable and conspicuous figure' and the numerous recommendations he received from high-ranking officers made him well-known throughout the army, and beyond.

The gallantry of the three battalions of Foot Guards during the Battle of Inkerman had so impressed Prince Albert that he placed a commission at the disposal of General Lord Rokeby in the Rifle Brigade. Sergeant Knox had transferred to the 2nd Battalion, Rifle Brigade, and his selection for this honour gave widespread satisfaction among his colleagues. As a consequence he was appointed ensign in March 1855 and lieutenant on 11 May 1855. The Russian canister ball that struck him during the first attack on the Redan and caused the loss of his arm was picked up by another soldier and given to him.

His award of the Victoria Cross was announced in the *London Gazette* on 24 February 1857, and he received the medal at the first investiture. He was one of three men Queen Victoria mentions in her diary when she wrote it that night. He also received the Crimea Medal with *Alma, Balaclava, Inkerman* and *Sebastopol* clasps, the French Legion of Honour and the Turkish Crimea Medal.

He was promoted to brevet major, but the loss of his arm curtailed his army career and he was invalided in 1872. He became the governor of Cardiff Gaol from 1872–6, before moving to Kirkdale Prison in Liverpool from September 1886 until January 1892. He had received an appointment as governor of Hull Prison in October 1891, but he could not take it on because of ill-health and was forced to retire. He was noted to be a stern disciplinarian, he maintained perfect order, but at the same time 'showed the utmost kindness to the prisoners'. Soon after his wife died he left Kirkdale for Cheltenham on 25 April 1892.

In a letter home he had stated: 'The enemy endeavoured to drive us back, however, we stuck to them until we were masters.' However, in later life he seemed to scorn the various reunions that took place, and on learning of 'another' Crimean dinner in 1894, he wrote to an old comrade: 'My presence would make some of our own friends uncomfortable; you must have spotted many of them, as I did, skulking under the banks of the Alma.'

John died on 8 January 1897, aged 70, in his home at 6 Oriel Terrace in Cheltenham, and he was buried in Cheltenham Cemetery; his headstone was refurbished in 2002 after being found badly damaged. His name appears on the Rifle Brigade Memorial at Winchester Cathedral, and on the ledger headstone of his wife, Harriet Louisa, at Anfield Cemetery in Liverpool. His Victoria Cross, and other memorabilia, including the canister ball mounted on a marble plinth, were sold in 2010 and the Victoria Cross is now displayed on rotation at the Lord Ashcroft Gallery, as part of the 'Extraordinary Heroes' exhibition at the Imperial War Museum in London.

James McKechnie

James McKechnie was born in about September 1826, at High Church in Paisley, Scotland. He was a tinsmith before enlisting into the Scots (Fusilier) Guards as 3234 Private McKechnie, at Edinburgh on 11 February 1845, at the age of 18 years and 5 months. He was described as being 5ft 9¾in tall, with a fresh complexion, blue eyes and brown hair. He was promoted corporal on 12 September 1847 and sergeant on 12 January 1853. He saw active service in the East from 28 February 1854–4 July 1856.

His award of the Victoria Cross was announced in the *London Gazette* of 24 February 1857, and he received the medal during the first investiture. He also received the Crimea Medal with *Alma, Inkerman* and *Sebastopol* clasps, and the Turkish Crimea Medal.

He served in Canada from 20 December 1861–18 September 1864, and on 4 September 1865 he was receiving 4 pence a day good conduct pay. He was discharged at his own request on 14 February 1866, having served his country for twenty-one years, although he does not seem to have been awarded the Long Service Good Conduct Medal. He was reported by the regimental board as being 'a very good and sober soldier', and he had been awarded four good conduct badges. He was awarded a pension of 1s. a day for the rest of his life.

James died in Glasgow on 5 July 1886, aged 60, and he was buried in an unmarked grave on common ground at the Eastern Necropolis Cemetery at Gallowgate in Glasgow, where a new turf-stone was erected in 2007. He is named on the Victoria Cross Memorial Stone at Hawkhead Cemetery in Paisley, and his medals are in the Scots Guards Museum at Wellington Barracks in London.

William Reynolds

William Reynolds was born at 5 Jamaica Street in St Stephen's parish in Edinburgh during August 1827. He was a mason prior to enlisting into the Scots (Fusilier) Guards on 2 April 1846, at the age of 18 years and 8 months. He was 5ft 11in tall, with a fresh complexion, grey eyes and black hair. He had a tattoo of an anchor on his left arm. As 3368 Private Reynolds he saw active service in the East from 28 February 1854–4 July 1856.

His award of the Victoria Cross was announced in the *London Gazette* of 24 February 1857, and he received the medal from Queen Victoria at the first investiture. He also received the Crimea Medal with *Alma, Balaclava, Inkerman* and *Sebastopol* clasps, and the Turkish Crimea Medal.

He discharged to pension at his own request on 15 October 1867, aged 40 years and 2 months, and he was described by the regimental board as 'a good and efficient soldier, trustworthy and sober'. He had been awarded two good conduct badges, and he was awarded a pension of 10 pence a day for the rest of his life. His intended place of residence was in London, where he became a banker's messenger.

William died on 20 October 1869, at 59 Stanhope Street, off The Strand in Mayfair, London, aged 42, and he was buried in the Bloomsbury Section of Brookwood Cemetery near Woking. A new headstone was placed at the grave in 2007. His medals are in the Scots Guards Museum at Wellington Barracks in London.

Edward William Derrington Bell

Edward William Derrington Bell was born on 18 May 1824, at Landguard Fort near Felixstowe in Essex, where his father, General Edward Wells Bell, was serving with the 7th Royal Fusiliers. His father was a veteran of the Peninsular War, who became lieutenant governor of Jamaica; and his mother was Mary Anne Battersby (formerly Chapman), who was a great-aunt of T.E. Lawrence – Lawrence of Arabia. The family home was at The Lodge in Kempsey near Worcester, and Edward was educated at Sandhurst School and at the Royal Military Academy in Sandhurst.

He enlisted as ensign in the 23rd (Royal Welsh) Fusiliers on 15 April 1842, being promoted to lieutenant on 17 November 1843, captain on 18 December 1848 and major on 23 March 1855.

He became the first Essex-born man to be awarded the Victoria Cross when it was announced in the *London Gazette* of 24 February 1857, and on his return from India, he received the medal from Queen Victoria at Southsea Common in Portsmouth, on 2 August 1858, along with Henry Ramage, James Mouat, Henry MacDonald, Matthew Dixon, Thomas Esmonde and Howard Elphinstone. He also received the Crimea Medal with *Alma, Inkerman* and *Sebastopol* clasps, the French Legion of Honour, the Turkish Order of the Medjidie (5th Class) and the Turkish Crimea Medal.

He went with the 23rd Regiment for active service during the Indian Mutiny. He was promoted lieutenant colonel on 8 January 1858, being present at the final capture of Lucknow in March 1858, for which he was Mentioned in Despatches, and he received the Indian Mutiny Medal with *Lucknow* clasp. During his military career he was Mentioned in Despatches on seven occasions.

He commanded the 2nd Battalion, 23rd Regiment from 20 June 1858–September 1869, being promoted colonel on 10 August 1862, and received a reward for distinguished service. He was created Commander of the Bath (CB), and he was appointed major general on 6 March 1868.

During the General Election held in October 1868 riots broke out at Newport Town Hall in South Wales. The mayor asked the military to intervene, and Colonel Bell and sixty of his regiment were sent to deal with the situation. The riot act was twice read out, and when the mob began to throw stones in defiant reply, Colonel Bell ordered his men to charge at the mob and disperse them at the point of the bayonet. A woman was bayoneted and killed during the action, but the Royal Welsh were exonerated during the inquest that followed.

He married Charlotte Wadsworth (formerly Bartell) the widow of Surgeon Major John Davies, at St Mary's Church in Cheltenham on 3 August 1869, and they resided at 33 The Promenade in Cheltenham. They had a son and three daughters.

He commanded the Brigade Depot at Wrexham from 1 April 1873, until being appointed General Officer commanding the Northern District in Belfast on 28 February 1875.

Sir Edward died on 10 November 1879, aged 55, at his home, Lisbreen House in Fort William Park, Belfast. He was buried with his parents at St Mary's churchyard in Kempsey. The family tomb was restored in 2007. Bell Court at Hightown in Wrexham is named after him. His medals are with the Royal Welsh Fusiliers Museum in Caernarfon

Castle, where the Russian 12-pounder field piece he captured is on display and known as 'Bell's Gun'.

Luke O'Connor

Luke O'Connor was born on 20 January 1831, at Kilcroy, Hillstreet, near Elphin in County Roscommon, Ireland. He was the son of James O'Connor (1800–39), and his wife, Mary (formerly Gannon). Although the paternal family descended from the O'Conchobhair, who were once Kings of Connacht and the last High Kings of Ireland, his branch of the family were not wealthy, and the family were evicted from their farm because they were unable to pay the rent. They decided to seek their fortune in Canada in 1839. James O'Connor died at sea during the voyage, and his mother and an infant boy died of cholera at Grosse Isle, Quebec. Luke returned to Ireland as a boy, but some of his siblings remained in North America and some of them fought in the American Civil War.

It had been proposed that Luke should become a Catholic priest, but on a visit to Winchester the appearance of a recruiting sergeant, and the name of his regiment, the 23rd (Royal Welsh) Fusiliers, so impressed him that he joined the unit on 21 July 1849, becoming sergeant on 18 May 1851.

He received the thanks of Sir George Brown and Sir William Codrington on the Alma battlefield, and he was recommended for and received a commission as ensign with the 76th Regiment on 19 October 1854, but he returned to the 23rd Regiment on 5 November 1854, the day of the Battle of Inkerman. He was promoted to lieutenant without purchase on 9 February 1855, and during the final bombardment and assault on the Great Redan on 8 September 1855 he behaved with great gallantry and was shot through both thighs.

He became the first man of the army to be awarded the Victoria Cross when it was announced in the *London Gazette* of 24 February 1857, and he received the medal at the first investiture. He also received the Crimea Medal with *Alma* and *Sebastopol* clasps, the Turkish Order of Medjidie (5th class), the Turkish Crimea Medal and the Sardinian Medal of Military Valour.

He went with the 23rd Regiment for active service during the Indian Mutiny, being present at the second relief of Lucknow, 16–22 November 1857 and in the final capture of the city in March 1858, being Mentioned in Despatches and for which he received the Indian Mutiny Medal with *Relief of Lucknow* and *Lucknow* clasps.

He saw service at Gibraltar and Canada, and as a brevet major in the Ashanti War of 1873–4, for which he received the Ashanti Medal and a reward for distinguished service. He became colonel on 17 August 1879, and he was appointed honorary colonel, commanding, 2nd Battalion, Royal Welsh Fusiliers, the name which the 23rd Regiment was given in 1881. He retired on 2 March 1887, becoming honorary major general five days later. He was appointed Commander of the Bath (CB) in 1906 and Knight Commander of the Bath (KCB) in 1913. He was made colonel, Royal Welsh Fusiliers on 3 June 1914.

Sir Luke died on 1 February 1914, aged 84, at Clarges Street in Piccadilly, Central London, and he was buried at St Mary's Roman Catholic Cemetery at Kensal Rise in West London, where the headstone shows his age as 83.

There is a plaque dedicated to him at the Jesuit Church of the Immaculate Conception in Farm Street, Mayfair, London, and his name is inscribed on the baptismal font at St Patrick's Catholic Church at Elphin. There is a plaque at St Giles' Parish Church in Wrexham, and a community centre at Hightown in Wrexham is named Luke O'Connor House. His medals are with the Royal Welsh Fusiliers Museum at Caernarfon Castle.

John Park

John Park was born in February 1835 in Londonderry, Ireland. He joined the 77th (East Middlesex) Regiment, the 'Die Hards', as 2600 Private Park. His award of the Victoria Cross was announced in the *London Gazette* for 24 February 1857, and he received the medal from the General Officer Commanding at Sydney in Australia, in March 1858. He also received the Crimea Medal with *Alma, Balaclava, Inkerman* and *Sebastopol* clasps, the French Legion of Honour and the Turkish Crimea Medal.

John died of heat apoplexy (sunstroke) while still serving with the regiment at Allahabad in India on 16 May 1863, aged 28, and he was buried in an unmarked grave in the Church of Scotland section of Allahabad Cemetery. His medals are at the Newarke Houses Museum in Leicester.

Chapter 4

The First Bombardment of Sebastopol

With no real strategy, the British continued south, and to the astonishment of the unprepared Russians in Sebastopol they watched the Allied army make a flank march past the eastern landward side of the town. Some officers were of the opinion that they could have 'marched straight in' and ended the war, but the Allied command did not commit their forces to an attack and missed the opportunity. They had decided on siege tactics.

They made their base camp at Balaclava, about 10 miles south-east of Sebastopol. It was described as: 'no more than a fishing village . . . a confused aggregation of wrecked houses . . . and mud, dirt and slush everywhere'. When first being shown a 'hospital', in February 1855, a newly arrived medical officer of the 90th Light Infantry was astonished to have pointed out to him:

> a row of bell-tents pitched, like all the others, in the mud. I looked into some of them and found them crowded with sick, ten or twelve men in each tent with their feet towards the pole and their heads towards the curtain. They were lying on the bare ground wrapped in their great coats. It struck me that whatever was the matter with them they had a very poor chance of recovery. The diseases from which they suffered were chiefly dysentery and fever.

The same man stated:

> A walk round the camp revealed a very miserable state of things. Imagine a ploughed field after three days heavy rain followed by a snow storm, and you may be able to form some idea of the ground

on which our tents were pitched; then imagine a cutting wind on an open plain and a temperature of minus twenty-two degrees, no shelter of any kind except a canvas tent, not a house or a wall or tree anywhere within sight, and you may picture the situation.

This gave the Russians time to prepare their defences. On 23 September, under the direction of Eduard Totleben, a talented engineer with the Russian Army, they scuttled their ships across the entrance to Sebastopol harbour, guns from these vessels were brought ashore for use at the inland defences, and fortifications and earthworks were hastily constructed around the southern outskirts of the city. These included the formidable bastion of the Malakoff Tower, which itself was protected by another redoubt called the Mamelon Fort, and the Great Redan (Bastion 3), protected by fortifications called The Quarries. The British sector of the siege was in front of the Redan. They were separated from the French on their left by a ravine, along which ran the Woronzoff Road from Sebastopol Harbour to the valley north of Balaclava in the east, and the French on their right by a vast ravine known as the Dock or Middle Ravine.

The British Fleet launched an attack on the forts around the harbour of Sebastopol on 14 October 1854, and under the direction of the Royal Engineers, working parties of soldiers were ordered to sap with great energy in constructing a series of entrenchments and tunnels leading towards the outer battlements mainly on the high ground on the Right Attack, known as Frenchman's Hill, and between the other side of the Woronzoff Ravine and the French, which was the Left Attack or the Green Hill. They dug into ground that was 'hard as iron and full of stones', while detachments of troops from the same regiment repulsed enemy sorties by night and skirmishes by day, being constantly on the alert. By 16 October the strenuous back-breaking toil was done and they were ready to launch their first bombardment, and 126 guns opened up with tremendous power on 17 October. The siege became the first example of trench warfare which was replicated during the First World War. While the men were working on the siege batteries and trenches the Russians were bombarding and shooting at them.

Troop Sergeant Major George Cruse of the 1st Royal Dragoons, who took part in the Charge of the Heavy Brigade a few days later, stated: 'We have been waiting day after day to hear when the batteries would open, but to every enquiry the answer invariably was, "Tomorrow! Tomorrow!", until I began to be quite tired of asking.' However, a few days later he wrote: 'on 17th we commenced bombarding Sebastopol. This is now the 6th day that the most horrible cannonading ever heard by man has been kept up without cessation. How many hundreds of thousands of shot and shell have been fired it is impossible for me to say, but it is an incessant roar from morning till night.'

An interesting article appeared in the *Liverpool Daily Post* at the time of the death of Edward Tregenza, a Cornishman who had joined the Royal Navy in 1843, and was said to have been present at the passing of the Alma (probably witnessed from his ship sailing off-shore with the Allied Fleet). He was reported to have been one of the first of the Naval Brigade to land at Balaclava as a member of the crew of HMS *Beagle*, and manned the Lancaster battery, which fired the first signal shots from the combined batteries to open fire on the forces defending Sebastopol.

As the British prepared for the first bombardment, Private Francis Wheatley of the Rifle Brigade, and some other Riflemen, were occupying a section of the trenches, when a live Russian shell fell among them. Without hesitation, Private Wheatley approached the shell and tried to knock the fuse out with the butt of his rifle. He was unsuccessful at the first attempt, and so, with great presence of mind and deliberation he seized hold of the shell and managed to somehow heave it over the parapet of the trench. It had scarcely fallen outside when it exploded. Had it not been for his coolness, presence of mind and supreme courage, the shell would have inevitably exploded among the party, causing serious casualties, but instead not a single man was hurt.

Lieutenant Colonel Collingwood Dickson of the Royal Artillery was the grandson of an admiral, and the son of a veteran of the Battle of Waterloo. He had been one of the first men to come face-to-face with the Russians at the Bulganac, and had already distinguished himself at the Alma, when he was on Lord Raglan's staff. When Raglan rode forward to a knoll on the Russian flank and asked for guns to be placed there, Dickson immediately leapt into action and brought up two 9-pounders with great skill, which he helped to serve, and directed his men in an admirable manner. The mighty duel continued for some time, and the fire was so effective that the Russian batteries guarding the post-road retired. He was promoted to brevet lieutenant colonel for his service that day, and Lord Raglan, in congratulating him on his skill, remarked: 'Dickson, my brave fellow. You are your father's better.'

The action for which Colonel Dickson was awarded the Victoria Cross occurred at daylight on 17 October 1854, when a 126 guns of all calibres opened up the first bombardment of Sebastopol, which shook the ground all around the combatants. He was in command of the siege train on the Right Attack. The batteries had run short of powder, so several wagons of the field battery were brought up to the trenches to supply the want. The wagons immediately came under fire from the enemy, but Colonel Dickson displayed the greatest coolness and contempt of danger in directing and offloading them and personally assisting in carrying the barrels into the battery.

During the Battle of Inkerman, Colonel Dickson brought up two 18-pounder field guns. He chose the site for them in a position which dominated the Russian guns and maintained them there, though he was urged by French officers to withdraw them. When the Russians retreated, Lord Raglan said to him: 'you have covered yourself with glory'.

Midshipman Edmund St John Daniel of HMS *Diamond* was among the sailors which formed a Naval Brigade of over a thousand men under Captain Stephen Lushington from HMS *Albion*, which came ashore to help with the siege, and he wrote home to his family on 16 October 1854:

> We are encamped with a thousand of our blue jackets and we have twenty of our guns ashore. We have had a good many shots fired at us, but none of our men have been wounded. I am the Captain's aide-de-camp. I have been obliged to provide myself with a horse as we are six miles from Admiral Lyons and very often I have to go to him twice a-day, and after that to go in the trenches all night with the Captain. Thank God, our battery will be completed by daylight tomorrow. I am very much obliged to you for the pistols.

The captain he spoke of was William Peel, a son of the former Prime Minister, who suggested to his two teenage aides-de-camp: 'disregard fire in the battery, by always walking with head up and shoulders back and without undue haste'. Midshipman Wood remembered: 'He himself was a splendid example. I know that he felt acutely every shot which passed over him, but the only visible effect was to make him throw up his head and square his shoulders.'

On 18 October, Captain Peel was with some men working at one of the Naval Brigade cannon. As several men were passing cases of gun powder into the magazine, a 42-pounder Russian shell smashed through the parapet, and with the fuse still burning it rolled into the middle of a gun's crew, who immediately threw themselves to the ground – but they were still in great peril. Seeing the danger, Peel sprang into action.

At the greatest possible risk he stooped down and picked up the heavy shell and clasped it to his chest as he carried it back to the parapet. He heaved it over the edge, and it had barely rolled down the outside when it exploded. He thus saved the magazine and the lives all the men around it (*see 5 November 1854 and 18 June 1855*).

On the same day Midshipman Daniel saw that a pack of horses bringing supplies of ammunition to a battery came under heavy fire, and after some poor animals had been disabled the others were spooked and refused to move. The wagon was in an exposed position, but Daniel and Midshipman Wood took it upon themselves to try to empty it. A destructive fire sent bullets whizzing over their heads, or smashing dangerously into the boxes and ricocheting in all directions, but they took on the advice of Captain Peel and disregarded the fire, and when they scrambled over the parapet for the last time with their arms full of the last of the ammunition they were met by cheers from their comrades (*see 5 November 1854 and 18 June 1855*).

On 18 October, Private Thomas Grady of the 4th (King's Own) Regiment was among a detachment of men of his unit told off to supply ammunition to the Sailor's Battery on the Left Attack, which was precariously overlooked by two Russian batteries. After long exchanges of fire the defensive embrasures became badly damaged, and the officer commanding was considering abandoning the position. He called for volunteers to repair the damage, but none of his men responded. As a last resort he decided to ask the officer in charge of the 4th Regiment to appeal to his men and Private Grady and a man named P. Egan volunteered to go out to try to repair the defences. It was a particularly dangerous task because they came under heavy fire from the enemy batteries. However, they spent several hours dodging bullets and occasionally being thrown off their feet by the explosions of shells landing too close for comfort, as they filled sandbags and built up the ramparts bit by bit until they completed the task successfully. Unfortunately, Private Egan was killed in action later in the campaign, which deprived him of being awarded the Victoria Cross.

On 22 November Private Grady again showed gallant conduct during the repulse of a Russian attack on the advance trench of the Left Attack. He received a gunshot wound to his left arm, which went through the muscle of the limb but grazed the bone, but with a show of determined bearing he refused to quit the front, which encouraged the weak force engaged with the enemy to fight harder and maintain the position.

Sergeant William McWheeney of the 44th (East Essex) Regiment had volunteered as a sharpshooter at the start of the siege. On 20 October 1854, Private John Keane of his regiment was outside the front of an advance trench when he came under fire and was dangerously wounded. Sergeant McWheeney got together a party of volunteers and led them out to where their comrade was lying. They came under the same heavy enemy rifle fire, so with no time to lose, Sergeant McWheeney lifted Keane onto his back and carried him for a long distance until he could place him in safety.

On 5 December a corporal of the 44th named William Courteney was shot in the head and severely wounded, and was lying in the open outside the front of the trenches. On being informed of the situation, Sergeant McWheeney again ran out of the trenches to the assistance of a comrade. They came under such fire that it was too dangerous to move, so the gallant sergeant dug a dirt cover with his bayonet, where they both sheltered, and when darkness fell they made their escape (*see 18 June 1855*).

Francis Wheatley

Francis Wheatley was born at Ruddington near Nottingham, and he was baptised on 10 August 1821. His father, also named Francis, was a framework knitter, who married Martha Thompson at Ruddington parish church on 21 December 1821. Some sources say Francis was born in 1822. Francis took up the same work as his father until enlisting into the 1st Battalion, Rifle Brigade, at Daventry on 5 November 1839.

He spent the first five years of his service at Malta and the Ionian Islands. He served in South Africa, taking part in the Cape Frontier Wars of 1846–7 and 1852–3, for which he received the South Africa Medal, 1834–53, before receiving orders for active service in the Crimean War.

He became the first Nottinghamshire man to be awarded the Victoria Cross when it was announced in the *London Gazette* on 24 February 1857, and he received the medal at the first investiture. He was awarded the Distinguished Conduct Medal, believed to be for gallantry on 11 October 1854, and he also received the Crimea Medal with *Alma, Inkerman* and *Sebastopol* clasps, the French Legion of Honour (5th Class) and the Turkish Crimea Medal. On his retirement from the army he received the Long Service Good Conduct Medal.

Francis became a lodge-keeper at Bramshill Park at Winchfield in Hampshire, the estate of Sir William Cope, a former officer in the

Rifle Brigade, who wrote a history of the regiment. He was admitted to the Westminster Hospital in London, suffering from acute myelites (inflammation of the spinal cord), and he died of asphyxia on 21 May 1865, aged 43. He was buried in a common grave at Brompton Cemetery in south-west London. He is one of twelve holders of the Victoria Cross buried at Brompton, including Sam Parkes, William Hope and Sir Frederick Maude. A memorial headstone was placed at his grave by the Royal Green Jackets in 2001. His name appears on the Victoria Cross Memorial, which was unveiled at Nottingham Castle in 2010, on the Rifle Brigade Memorial at Winchester Cathedral and Wheatley Close in Ruddington is named after him. His medals are with the Royal Green Jackets Museum in Winchester.

Collingwood Dickson

Collingwood Dickson was born at Valenciennes in France on 23 November 1817, the third son of Major General Alexander Dickson, GCB KCB, who commanded the Duke of Wellington's artillery during the latter stages of the Peninsular War, and was present at the Battle of Waterloo in 1815. His grandfather was a Scottish admiral. His mother was Eulalia, daughter of Don Stefano Briones of Majorca. He was educated at the Royal Military Academy in Woolwich, and followed his father into the Royal Field Artillery as second lieutenant on 18 December 1835, becoming lieutenant on 21 November 1837.

In February 1837, he travelled to Spain with the artillery detachment of the British Legion for active service in the First Carlist War, which lasted from 1833–9. British forces supported the Christinist cause of Queen Isabella II. He distinguished himself in operations before San Sebastian and in Catalonia, and he was present at the defeat of the Carlists at Berga on 6 July 1840. For his distinguished service in the conflict the Queen awarded him the Order of Charles III, the Royal Military Order of San Fernando, the Order of Isabella the Catholic, and he was awarded the Gold Cross for the capture of Morella and Berga (1840).

His father died in 1840, and he married Harriet Burnaby, the daughter of a Northamptonshire vicar, on 14 January 1847. He was described as 'a good linguist, speaking French, Spanish, and Turkish fluently, a ready writer, and a man of "downright commonsense". Dickson had an intimate knowledge of the traditions of his regiment, and an ardent affection for it. He left a portrait of himself to it.'

While still serving in the Crimea, Colonel Dickson was wounded on 4 February 1855, but took part in the bombardments of 9 April and 17 June and in the expedition to Kertch. He was Mentioned in Despatches on several occasions. He commanded the siege train up to 21 July 1855, and from September 1855 until the end of the war he was employed with the Turkish contingent, first as brigadier general, and from 15 February 1855 with the temporary rank of major general.

He became the first man born outside the British Isles to be awarded the Victoria Cross when it was announced in the *London Gazette* of 23 June 1857, and he became the first member of the Royal Regiment of Artillery to wear the medal when he received it during the first investiture three days later. He also received the Crimea Medal with *Alma, Inkerman* and *Sebastopol* clasps, the French Legion of Honour (5th Class), the Turkish Order of the Medjidie (3rd Class) and the Turkish Crimea Medal.

He was made aide-de-camp to Queen Victoria on 29 June 1855, was appointed Companion of the Bath (CB) on 5 July 1855, KCB in 1871, inspector general of Artillery, 1870–5, colonel commandant, Royal Regiment of Artillery, 1875, being promoted general in 1877. He was appointed Knight Commander, Order of the Bath (GCB) in 1884.

Collingwood and his wife had three sons who predeceased him, and Harriet died in 1894, after which he lived a retired life at 79 Claverton Street, Pimlico, south-west London. Sir Collingwood died on 28 November 1904, aged 87, and he was buried in St Mary's Roman Catholic Cemetery at Kensal Green, London, where there is a headstone. He is named on the Royal Artillery VC Memorial at the Royal Garrison Church of St George in Woolwich, and on the Memorial Board at the Royal Military College in Sandhurst. His medals are with the Royal Artillery Museum in Woolwich. He presented the Dickson Manuscripts to the Royal Artillery Institution, written or collected by his father, which provide valuable material for the history of the Peninsular War.

William Peel

William Peel was born on 2 November 1824, at 12 Great Stanhope Street in Mayfair, London. He was the third son and fourth child of the statesman and ex-Prime Minister Robert Peel, who was famous for establishing the metropolitan police force, and his wife, Julia, daughter of Sir John Floyd. He was educated at the Revd Francis Joseph Faithfull's boarding school at The Parsonage in Hatfield, and then like his father he was sent to Harrow School, 1837–8; he would become the first Old Harrovian to gain the Victoria Cross. His grandfather had become Member of Parliament for Tamworth in 1790, and the family home was at Drayton Manor in Tamworth.

His father stated that he had wanted to go to sea from the age of 3, and at the age of only 13 he entered the Royal Navy, joining his first ship HMS *Princess Charlotte* as midshipman on 7 April 1838. After serving on several ships in the Mediterranean he took part in the Turko-Egyptian War of 1839–41, being present at the bombardment and capture of Acre in November 1840, for which he received the Naval General Service Medal with *Acre* clasp, and the St Jean D'Acre Medal. He then spent some time with the royal yacht *William and Mary*.

Britain wished to expand its commercial influence in China, but the Chinese authorities resented the use of opium by the merchants of the 'Fan Kwei' – foreign devils, and they destroyed about £2 million pounds worth of the crop. This led to a declaration of war with China, and Captain Peel joined the *Cambrian 36* for service in the First China War in June 1840. The British eventually reached the outskirts of the ancient city of Nankin on 9 August 1842, where a demonstration of force was enough to bring the Chinese to see reason, after which most of the main Chinese ports were opened to British trade and Hong Kong was ceded to Britain.

After returning to London he enrolled in the Gunnery School at HMS *Excellent* on the Thames in Woolwich, for a fourteen-month course. However, he finished the course in only four months and his father had to make statements to prove that he had not used his influence to gain any advantages for his ambitious son. He received his commission as lieutenant on 13 May 1844 – a week after he passed.

He was in the government steam yacht *Black Eagle* that brought Tsar Nicholas to the UK on a state visit. When the *America 50* was sent to investigate unrest between American and Canadian settlers in the Oregon Territory, Peel went with her and carried out the survey for the Hudson Bay Company to try and determine the dispute. He was promoted commander on 27 June 1846, and was given command of the twelve-gun sloop *Daring*, in which he went to South America. He was promoted captain on 10 January 1850. He applied unsuccessfully to join the expedition to try to find Sir John Franklin, and he published *A Ride through the Nubian Desert* in June 1852, which chronicles his travels there in 1851.

He purchased a somewhat neglected estate which stood between the villages of Sandy and Potton in Bedfordshire, where he oversaw the renovation and enlargement of the house, brought land under cultivation and laid out gardens. When the Great Northern Railway opened nearby in 1850 he decided to finance the construction of a new Sandy and Potton Railway branch line.

He commissioned the frigate HMS *Diamond* in October 1852, which was attached to the Mediterranean Fleet, and when the Crimean War broke out the ship was sent to join the Black Sea Fleet.

One of his aides-de-camp, Midshipman Evelyn Wood of HMS *Queen*, who fought alongside Captain Peel in the Crimea, stated in his memoirs: 'I was evidently much struck with Captain Peel's appearance and manners, for I recorded in boyish language, "Captain Peel, very intelligent, sharp as a needle; I never saw a more perfect gentleman. His looks and bearing were greatly in his favour, for both in face and figure there was an appearance of what sporting men, in describing well-bred horses, call 'quality'".' Wood went on to win the Victoria Cross during the Indian Mutiny, and rose to the rank of field marshall, being knighted for his military service.

Captain Peel was sent to the Therapia Hospital, but his wound would not heel and he was invalided home, where he was given a civic reception at Tamworth Town Hall. During this time the Sandy and Potton Railway, known locally as Captain Peel's Railway, was opened by his mother in 1857, and William named one of the steam engines *Shannon* after his ship.

He was the first of nineteen Old Harrovians to be awarded the Victoria Cross when it was announced in the *London Gazette* for 24 February 1857. He was also entitled to the Crimea Medal with *Inkerman* and *Sebastopol* clasps, the French Legion of Honour (4th Class), the Turkish Order of the Medjidie (3rd Class), the Turkish Crimea Medal and the Sardinian Medal of Military Valour. He was also appointed Knight Commander, Order of the Bath (KCB). However, he did not live to wear the medals.

The fifty-one-gun steam frigate HMS *Shannon* had been launched at Portsmouth in 1855, and she sailed for service in the China War under Captain Peel. However, she was diverted to Calcutta, where Peel formed a Naval Brigade from its sailors for active service during the Indian Mutiny, now usually referred to as the Sepoy Rebellion. British forces had marched to the relief of the Lucknow garrison in September 1857, only to find that enemy forces were too strong and as they could not break out again they too came under siege.

A second relief force was sent in November, including Peel's unit, armed with eight heavy guns and two rocket-launchers mounted on carts. They fought their first action at Kujwa on 1 November, and as the British advanced through Lucknow they battered several strong masonry fortresses. This included a large stone compound known as the Sikandar Bagh, which contained about 2,000 rebels. Captain Peel's unit played a major part in breaching the thick walls of the defences, and four members of Peel's Brigade received the Victoria Cross for their valour. The total number of Victoria Crosses gained for the storming of the Sikandar Bagh was seventeen, which is only surpassed by the twenty at the first assault on the Redan. Peel's Brigade followed Sir Colin Campbell's Oudh campaign, and at the final capture of Lucknow in March 1858 Captain Peel was severely wounded when a musket ball shattered his thigh and upper leg.

He was transported to Cawnpore on a dhoolie that had previously been used to carry a smallpox victim and in his weakened state he too contracted the disease. He was taken to the house of the Revd Moore, where he and his wife did all they could to keep him comfortable. He said mournfully: 'If I were in England the Queen would send her own physician to look after me; here I can scarcely get any attention.'

Sir William died on 27 April 1858, aged 33, and he was buried in the Old British Cemetery at Mirpur, Cawnpore (Kanpur). The inscription read:

> To the memory of William Peel. His name will be dear to the British inhabitants of India, to whose succour he came in the hour of need. He was one of England's most devoted sons. With all the talents of a brace and skilful sailor, he combined the virtues of a humble, sincere Christian. This stone is erected over his remains by his military friends in India, and several of the inhabitants in Calcutta.

The walls and the gate of the cemetery still exist, but most of the interior has been built on.

His name is recorded on the family headstone in Deansgrange Cemetery in Dublin, where there is also a memorial to HMS *Shannon*. He has a statue at St Swithun's Church at Sandy, where there is also a Sir William Peel public house; copies of this statue are in Flagstaff House at Barrackpore in India, and in the National Maritime Museum at Greenwich. A plaque placed at the headquarters of the RSPB at The Lodge in Sandy in 2008 commemorates the 150th anniversary of Captain Peel's death. There is a memorial to Captain Peel and the Naval Brigade of HMS *Shannon* on the seafront at Southsea. There is an anchor and chain inside one of the entrances to Tamworth Castle which is said to have been brought back from the Crimea by Sir William. The *Shannon* locomotive is preserved at the National Railway Museum in York. His Victoria Cross was sent home to his brother, Sir Robert Peel, and his medals are now displayed at the National Maritime Museum, the ribbon of his Victoria Cross being badly worn. The medals of Charles Lucas, William Hewett and John Sheppard are also at the museum.

In 2006 the Victoria Cross of Edward Daniel was brought from the Imperial War Museum to the National Maritime Museum for the filming of a BBC Television documentary. Thus it was the first time the medals had been together since they were originally struck and sent to India for presentation.

Edward St John Daniel

Edward St John Daniel was born in the family home of 1 Windsor Terrace at Clifton in Bristol, on 17 January 1837, the first child of well-known Bristol solicitor Edward Daniel and his wife, Barbara (formerly Bedford), the daughter of a baron. His distant maternal ancestry included Henry Tudor, King Henry VII. Edward was known by his middle name of St John (pronounced Sinjun). He had a younger brother named Henry, and three sisters named Barbara, Adele and Lucy. Their mother died of phlebitis (inflammation of a vein) soon after Lucy was born in 1850, and their father married a younger woman named Darkey Knight Cox, with whom he had another seven children, although two died in infancy.

Ten days before his 14th birthday Edward enrolled as a cadet in the Royal Navy with HMS *Dauntless*, and it has been reported that he initially trained on Lord Nelson's former flagship, HMS *Victory*. A year later he served briefly on HMS *Blenheim*.

In March 1852 he joined the flagship, HMS *Winchester*, with which he got his first taste of naval action in the Second Anglo-Burmese War of 1852–3. An expedition was sent to Burma (now Myanmar) to redress the grievances of British subjects in Rangoon. When Rangoon was occupied, an expedition was sent to Pegu (now Bagu), which was captured on 21 November 1852, and the province was annexed to the British Crown. For his service he received the Indian General Service Medal with *Pegu* clasp. During his time in Burma Edward developed chronic leg ulcers which affected him for the rest of his life.

He joined HMS *Contest* in March 1853, and he began his long association with Captain William Peel when he joined HMS *Diamond* on 7 September 1853, and on the following day he was appointed midshipman. The young teenager became devoted to his leader, and when the war with Russia broke out HMS *Diamond* was sent to join the Black Sea Fleet, where both he and Midshipman Evelyn Wood became Peel's aides-de-camp. On the ship's arrival off the Crimean Peninsula the two midshipmen joined the Naval Brigade with their captain.

Having been recommended for the Victoria Cross himself, Captain Peel put Midshipman Daniel's name forward too, and he was the youngest recipient of the medal at that time, and the first Bristol-born man to be awarded the Victoria Cross when it was announced in the *London Gazette* on 24 February 1857. The medal, along with Captain Peel's, was forwarded from Hong Kong to India, where he received it from Captain Francis Marten, the new commander of the Shannon Brigade, during a special parade of the troops at Gyah in Bengal on 13 July 1858. He also received the Crimea Medal with *Inkerman* and *Sebastopol* clasps, the French Legion of Honour, the Turkish Order of Medjidie (5th Class), the Turkish Crimea Medal and the Sardinian Medal of Military Valour.

He sailed to the East with Captain Peel on HMS *Shannon*, where he served with distinction during the Indian Mutiny, for which he received the Indian Mutiny Medal with *Relief of Lucknow* and *Lucknow* clasps. However, when Captain Peel died of smallpox in 1858 it had a devastating effect on him.

He was promoted to lieutenant on 15 September 1859, and in April 1860 he was presented before Queen Victoria at St James's Palace, where the sovereign is said to have been 'much impressed' by him. However, his career declined drastically from then on.

On 24 May 1860, while serving on HMS *Wasp*, he was severely reprimanded for going absent without leave, and two weeks after that he faced a court martial after being found drunk and incapable while on duty. On 25 June 1861, while serving on HMS *Victor Emmanuel* in the Mediterranean, he was taken into custody again for an unspecified offence which was described by the Secretary of War as 'disgraceful', and Captain Clifford stated that he had been arrested for 'taking indecent liberties with four of the subordinate officers'. He was due to be court-martialled at Corfu, but on the following evening he went missing from the ship and was designated a deserter.

In the following month his name was removed from the navy list, and in accordance with Clause 15 of the Royal Warrant, on 4 September 1861, Queen Victoria signed the warrant which made Edward St John

Daniel the first man to be stripped of the Victoria Cross, the official reason being given as desertion. Seven other men have forfeited their Victoria Crosses since, but Edward was the only officer and the only member of the Senior Service.

Having somehow got back to Blighty undetected, on 16 September 1861, he boarded a clipper at Liverpool bound for Melbourne in Australia, where he is believed to have found work as a miner in the gold fields. In January 1864, he signed up at Melbourne for three years' service with the Taranaki Military Settlers, and arrived in New Zealand in the following month. He spent most of his service engaged in fighting the Maoris in South Taranaki. He was arrested in August 1864 and sentenced to intensive labour, and soon after serving his sentence he was arrested again and a court martial sentenced him to two weeks in confinement. His unit was disbanded in May 1867.

Edward enlisted as a constable in the New Zealand Armed Constabulary in November 1867, and seventy members of his division were sent to Hokitika on the South Island, to deal with disturbances among the Irish Protestants and Catholics in the West Canterbury goldfields.

Edward remained in Hokitika, and on 16 May 1868, after being ill for some time, he was admitted to the Hokitika Hospital. He died of 'delirium tremens' on 20 May 1868, aged 31, and he was buried with military honours at the Hokitika Municipal Cemetery. Cemetery records list his age as 37. A headstone was erected in 1972, and there is a plaque at the foot of a flagpole in the cemetery. A commemorative plaque was placed at his birthplace in Bristol in 2001.

His Victoria Cross was on display at the United Services Institute in Whitehall for some time, and then came up for auction in 1930. It was the first to appear at auction after the Second World War, on the anniversary of the assault on the Redan, 18 June 1947. It was purchased in 1990, and is now displayed on rotation at the Lord Ashcroft Gallery, as part of the 'Extraordinary Heroes' exhibition at the Imperial War Museum in London.

In 1981 a petition sought the restoration of his award, which was rejected on the grounds that: 'the restoration of forfeited awards may only be made on a petition to the Sovereign from the former recipient himself. In Daniel's case this is not possible. Furthermore, as your proposal relates to events so long ago it is considered inappropriate to reverse the decision made in 1861 by Queen Victoria.'

A twist in the story of his life – and death – suggests that the man who died in New Zealand in 1868 may not have been him, and some historians believe that he was living a destitute life in London in 1902.

In his book *The People of the Abyss* published in 1903, the famous American author Jack London, writer of the classic book *The Call of the Wild*, which was published in the same year, tells of his experiences among London's poor people in 1902, and the seventh chapter is entitled 'A Winner of the Victoria Cross'. He says that as he waited in the queue to get into Whitechapel Workhouse he met two men, one of whom he described as a short and stout old man (Daniel would have been in his 65th year if he had still been alive). The man seems to have kicked up a bigger fuss about his plight than anyone else in the line, and eventually began to tell the tale of his service in the same theatres of war as Daniel, and that he had won and lost the Victoria Cross. He also states that a lieutenant had enraged him by calling him a bastard – a terrible degrading insult at the time – and he had attacked him with an iron bar and knocked him into the sea, after which he dived in and tried to drown both the officer and himself. For this he lost all his privileges and his Victoria Cross.

On reading the account I find it difficult to ignore a feeling of embellishment to the story, as if the man was well-rehearsed, and Jack London stated that he 'recited his sentence word for word, as though memorised and gone over in bitterness many times'. There are some obvious discrepancies, such as the fact that he says he was aged 87, which made him twenty-two years older than Edward would have been, he had served for two score years and more, which is over forty years, and Edward died when he was only 31, and he had received fifty lashes and served a two-year prison sentence, which Edward had not. Jack London does not indicate any kind of West Country accent, which would have been noticeable to an American; as Charles Beresford did when listening to the accent of Henry Curtis (see his biography). For all his grievances the man did not mention the severe leg ulcers caused by his naval service, and he did not know the correct word for 'a sea trial', which is strange after being in the navy for so long. The story of Edward's service and downfall would have been well-known among the navy, and possibly the incident the man related, although Captain Clifford states that the problem was with four lieutenants and not just one. He may have even known Edward.

The man was not the only one to claim he had won the Victoria Cross when he had not, and it was common for Victorian ex-servicemen to romance about their battle and seafaring exploits. For instance, just in Liverpool alone there is a gravestone dedicated to 'A Hero of Rorke's Drift' for a man who was not there, and a Liverpool cab driver became quite famous in the city for saying that he rode in the Charge of the Light Brigade when he did not. Respectively, one may well have been with the force that relieved the Rorke's Drift garrison on the following day, and the other may have been at Balaclava on the fateful day of the charge, and a subtle twist in a tale was enough to get a man a free pint.

It was a time when the plight of many surviving Crimean War and other veterans who had fallen on hard times was being highlighted in the media, and several benefit concerts and charity organisations had been set up to give them financial assistance. The man was aware that Jack had some money with him, and it may have simply been an attempt by two down-and-outs to try to dupe the writer for a hand-out. The story of James Gorman is testament to how gullible writers and journalists were in the pursuit of a good story.

In recent times a photograph of a man in civilian clothes has come to light which is said to be Edward Daniel. It is believed to have been taken in London after 1865, and was compared to a known picture of Edward in uniform by a forensic pathologist who was of the opinion that the two are the same person. It is said that Edward may have stolen another man's identity so as not to be tracked down by the authorities on returning to England sometime around 1866 to 1868. If the switched identity is true, the other man is believed to have been a Robert Daniels, who enlisted at Melbourne on the same day as Edward, and apparently there is evidence in the New Zealand National Archives that information concerning the two men may have become mixed up. The pictures do look like the same man, although the one in civvies looks a bit older than Edward would have been at the time. However, the traumatic life Edward had led and his alcohol problem might well have aged him. Nevertheless, I believe Edward is the man buried in New Zealand – but I leave it to the readers to make their own decision!

Thomas Grady

Thomas Grady was born with the surname 'O'Grady' on 18 September 1831, at Claddagh, County Galway, Ireland. He left Ireland and travelled to Liverpool, where he originally attested for the 99th (Lanarkshire) Regiment on 18 June 1853, and transferred to the 4th (King's Own) Regiment on 4 February 1854, as 3319 Private Grady, for active service in the Crimea. He was just over 5ft 5in tall, with a fresh complexion, blue eyes and dark-brown hair.

He is recorded as having had a child named Mary Ellen, born in Liverpool in 1851. He married Catherine Deveney at St Peter's in Liverpool on 6 August 1855, and they had a son named Martin John, born in Liverpool in 1862.

His award of the Victoria Cross was announced in the *London Gazette* of 23 June 1857, and he became the first member of a Regiment of Foot to wear the medal when he received it three days later at the first investiture. He also received the Crimea Medal with *Alma, Inkerman* and *Sebastopol* clasps, the Distinguished Conduct Medal (probably for his gallantry on 22 November) and the Turkish Crimea Medal.

His injury caused numbness and loss of power to his arm, and he could not use his musket properly or lift any weight with it. Consequently, he was discharged as unfit for service at Chatham on 21 September 1858.

He travelled to Western Australia on board the transport *Norwood* as an assisted immigrant, departing at Portland on 16 March 1862, and arrived at Fremantle on 9 June 1862. He then boarded the *Gem* on 17 November 1866, and travelled to Melbourne in a party of three people.

He was in the habit of wearing his four medals proudly pinned to his grey coat, but one day as he was coming out of the Melbourne Post Office having just collected his gratuity a thief tore all the medals but his Victoria Cross off his breast and they were never seen again. He was stated to have told the *Traralgon Record* reporter that he had pawned his medals, and that he had a married daughter living in Collingwood.

The *Geelong Advertiser* for 4 June 1890 reported: 'Thomas Grady is at present obtaining a precarious subsistence in Melbourne, and, for the last three weeks has been indebted for nightly shelter to the excellent Society of St Vincent de Paul, which maintains a "Home" for men in St David's Street, Fitzroy. He had nearly died the other day in the brick kiln at Simpsons Road Sheds in Collingwood'. He had been in the Home of the Little Sisters of the Poor at Northcote, but chose to leave, and in January 1891 he was found asleep in a doorway for which he was charged with vagrancy at the Collingwood Court.

A reporter for the *Traralgon Record* in Victoria on 9 January 1891 stated under the heading 'The Victoria Cross in the Gutter' that he found Thomas lying in a right-of-way in Fitzroy, and during a conversation the hero told him he had arrived in Australia on the *Norwood* convict ship, which might explain why he never returned to Britain, and that he had been working as a gardener.

Not surprisingly, Thomas was said to be suffering with bronchitis, asthma, rheumatism and heart disease, and he was to have been the first inmate of the Old Soldiers' Home at Drysdale, but he was found dead after having suffered an asthma attack on 18 May 1891, aged 59, at the Immigrants Home, St Kilda Road, Drysdale, South Melbourne, and he was buried at the Roman Catholic section of the Melbourne General Cemetery in Springvale, Victoria. The headstone shows his name as Grady, but O'Grady in the burial register, and in his obituary in several Australian newspapers.

His is commemorated on a plaque in Lancaster Priory, and his Victoria Cross was presented to the Hall of Valour in the Australian War Memorial at Canberra by his great-great-grandson in 1985.

William McWheeney

William McWheeney was born in 1830, at Bangor in County Down, Northern Ireland. He entered the 44th (East Essex) Regiment as 2802 Private McWheeney. The award of the Victoria Cross to Sergeant McWheeney was announced in the *London Gazette* of 24 February 1857, and he received the medal at the first investiture, thus becoming the first holder of the Victoria Cross of the Essex Regiment. He also received the Crimea Medal with *Sebastopol* clasp, the Turkish Crimea Medal and the Distinguished Conduct Medal, for his action on 5 December 1854.

At the end of the Crimean War the 44th Regiment disembarked at Spithead on the steamship *Colossus* on 18 July 1856, and a special train was laid on to take them to Aldershot, where Sergeant McWheeney was among about 800 men of all ranks to be inspected by Queen Victoria and Prince Albert on 31 July 1856.

He later sailed for active service in the Second China (Opium) War of 1860, as part of the Anglo-French expeditionary force. The 44th Regiment took a major part in the capture of the North Taku Fort on 21 August 1860. The attacking force had to cross a series of ditches and bamboo-stake palisades under heavy enemy fire. When an attempt to gain entry by the main gate failed, the 44th were in the vanguard of an assault party which climbed the wall to an embrasure and forced entry into the fort. The 44th Regiment gained two more Victoria Crosses during this engagement, and Sergeant McWheeney received the China War Medal with *Taku Forts* clasp.

Having been promoted to colour sergeant, and stationed at Dover Citadel, William was only 36 years old when he died on 17 May 1866. He was buried in the consecrated section of St James' Cemetery, where the headstone reads: 'In Honoured Memory of C/Sgt William McWheeney VC, 44th Regiment of Foot. Died 17th May 1866, aged 36 years. The First VC of the Essex Regiment.' His name is one of four which appear on the Dover War Memorial, a project commemorating Victoria Cross recipients who are buried in Dover.

His Victoria Cross was sold for a record amount of £50 on 17 June 1893, and the *Dover Express* for 16 February 1894 reported:

> Perhaps it cannot be otherwise, but there is something incongruous about selling the Victoria Cross; yet two of these decorations were offered in auction in London the other day. The first offered was that presented to Sergeant McWheeney, 44th Regiment, by the Queen, and was earned by valour in three actions in the Crimea – on 20 October and 5 December 1854, and June 18, 1855. With the cross were included the same soldier's Crimea, Taku Fort, Distinguished Conduct in the field, and Turko-British Crimea medals. The lot sold for £50.

His medals are with the Essex Regiment Museum in Chelmsford. There is a cannon displayed in Oaklands Park, Chelmsford, described as 'The Sevastopol Cannon, 1855'.

Chapter 5

The Battle of Balaclava

It was mid-morning at Balaclava, on 25 October 1854, as Lord Raglan looked from his vantage point on the Sepoune Heights, where he had a panoramic view of the region to the east, and Sebastopol was behind him to the west. There was a plain 600ft below him which was divided into a north and south valley by the Causeway Heights, which carried the main track up to the plateau, and where the British had built six redoubts, installed some naval guns, and manned them with Turkish troops.

At dawn that day the Russians made a threatening advance towards the harbour at Balaclava; only 2 miles south of the causeway. After an hour Turkish troops had fled from the redoubts, leaving British naval guns behind, and the Russians occupied the three most easterly. A large force of Russian cavalry entered the south valley and four squadrons broke off making directly for Balaclava. Suddenly, a 'Thin Red Line' of 93rd (Sutherland) Highlanders, led by the dominant figure of Colin Campbell, appeared from behind a hill and blocked their way. Volley fire from the Highlanders checked the Russian advance and unnerved them, and they were soon put in reverse.

The five regiments of the Heavy Brigade, made up of the 1st Royal Dragoons, the 2nd Dragoons (Royal Scots Greys), the 4th and 5th Dragoon Guards, and the 6th (Inniskilling) Dragoons, had been ordered to support the Highlanders but they had not had chance to do so before the Russian cavalry advance was almost upon them. The enemy's leading line was about three times as long and deep as the British and behind that was another line of the same strength. As the Russians came to within about 200 paces they suddenly halted. General James Yorke Scarlett, late of the 5th Dragoon Guards, and now the commander of the Heavy Brigade, at once decided to take advantage of this tactical error and ordered his trumpeter to sound the Charge.

As they totalled only 300 horsemen, the British tried to create the image that their numbers were more by extending into one line as they thundered into action, having to negotiate several obstacles as they did so. They brushed their way through a vineyard, scaled two fences then rode up a hill and leaped over a ditch which left them little space to gather the momentum for an all-out charge and they had not formed up in good order when they reached the Russian front line. The Royal Scots Greys gave out a low moan which echoed across the valley as they were the first to cut their way into the Russian ranks and their large cumbersome chargers barged the enemy horses out of the way as they slammed headlong into them, and the rest of the Brigade followed. They slashed left and right but in many cases the swords just deflected off the thick Russian greatcoats, so they changed their tactic and used a thrusting action with their sabres. Some simply grabbed at loose reins and pulled at them to try to unhorse the Russians or used their fists to punch them out of their saddles. Against all the odds they got the better of the Russians through sheer guts and determination and found themselves in the vulnerable open space between the two lines of enemy cavalry.

They were completely surrounded and some units of Russian horsemen fell back from the ranks and tried to overwhelm them. They now needed some strong leadership and Lieutenant Miller, who was famous for his howling voice, galloped out of the confused jostling mass and roared at the Greys to rally on him.

As the men responded, Sergeant Major John Grieve of the Royal Scots Greys saw that one of his officers was surrounded by Russian horsemen, and with gallant conduct he rode to the rescue. He cut off the head of one Russian and slashing left and right with his sabre he disabled and dispersed all the others.

Sergeant Henry Ramage of the Royal Scots Greys saw that Private McPherson of his regiment had been severely wounded and was in great peril from an attack by as many as seven Russians, so he spurred his horse and galloped into action. He hit out at every rider who was wearing a Russian greatcoat with such ferocity that they all quickly dispersed.

Those that could do so formed up preparing to charge the second line of the advancing enemy. With little time to gather momentum the Greys led a second charge into the Russian cavalry, and there was the clashing sound of steel against steel as they fought their way through to the other side, and then with their adrenaline high and their eyes glaring with rage they wheeled about and re-entered the entangled mass of desperately fighting cavalrymen. Against all the odds the Russian nerve broke down and they began to fall back and retreat from the battlefield in hopeless disorder.

As they did so, Sergeant Ramage saw the opportunity to capture a Russian, but his horse would not leave the ranks. He dismounted and brought in the enemy prisoner on foot.

Eight men of the Heavy Brigade had been killed in action and seventy were wounded, and as they congratulated themselves on a job well done, Colin Campbell rode up in triumph and called out to his fellow Scots: 'Greys, gallant Greys, I am 61 years old, and if I were young again I would be proud to be in your ranks!'

All this time Lord Cardigan, commanding the British Light Cavalry, had been seated on his charger in front of his Brigade, which he had kept standing to horses in ranks across the end of the north valley below the Sepoune Heights, and the men were becoming frustrated with being deliberately held back. The 11th Hussars (Prince Albert's Own), 13th Light Dragoons and 17th Lancers (Duke of Cambridge's Own) formed the front line of the Brigade, while the second line consisted of the 4th Light Dragoons and the 8th Hussars. His officers had urged him to allow them to attack the flank of the retreating Russians, but Cardigan would take nothing from his subordinates and refused. About 670 Light Cavalrymen were on duty. They had taken little part in the battle so far, and they were furious that 'The finest cavalry brigade that ever left the shores of England' had not been used in an independent action.

At his observation post Lord Raglan had his attention brought to the distant high ground to the east where there seemed to be movement in the captured redoubts, and it was suggested that the Russians were limbering up the British naval guns to take them away. This was the equivalent of an infantry regiment losing its colours and he was alarmed. He wrote a hasty note, and gave it to Captain Lewis Edward Nolan of the 15th (King's) Hussars, to take to Lord Lucan, the cavalry commander. Nolan was a cavalry fanatic, who was agitated by the inaction of the Light Brigade. But he was a good horseman and he arrived safely with the message.

Lord Lucan was sitting on his horse between the two Brigades. Nolan had little respect for the senior officer who he had nicknamed 'Lord Look-on!' and he thrust the note at him. Lucan opened it and read: 'Lord Raglan wishes the cavalry to advance rapidly to the front, follow the enemy, and try to prevent the enemy carrying away the guns.

Troop Horse Artillery may accompany. French cavalry is on your left. Immediate.'

Lord Lucan did not have the extensive range of view that Lord Raglan had up on the ridge. He could see no significant enemy activity, except in the distance at the far end of the valley, where an eight-gun Russian battery was situated, and he was bewildered by the order. Nolan impatiently urged him to attack, but Lucan retorted angrily, 'Attack, Sir! Attack what? What guns, sir?' Nolan pointed eastward, and replied sharply, 'There, my Lord, is your enemy; there are your guns.' Lord Lucan shrugged his shoulders. It would seem that he must order the Light Brigade to attack the Russian guns at the other end of the valley. He cantered towards Lord Cardigan, while Nolan took up a position in front of the 17th Lancers, fully intending to take part in the action.

Lord Lucan and Lord Cardigan were brothers-in-law and apparently disliked each other 'like poison'. However, on hearing the orders, Lord Cardigan kept his nerve and maintained military courtesy and remarked, 'Certainly, sir, but allow me to point out to you that the Russians have a battery in the valley to our front, and batteries and riflemen on each side!' Lord Lucan reminded Lord Cardigan that they had no choice but to obey. Cardigan's coolness was commendable considering what he was being asked to do. He brought down his sword in salute, wheeled his horse about, and said, 'Well, here goes the last of the Brudenells.' That being his family name and he was the only male sibling. He took his place ahead of his men, and gave the order, 'The Brigade will advance. Walk, March, trot.' The 11th Hussars dropped back, and they moved down the valley in 3 lines about 200 paces across and 400 paces apart.

As the pace quickened the first Russian barrage thundered across the valley. At the same time Captain Nolan spurred his horse forward, and galloped across the advancing line from left to right, with his sword waving in the air. He was seen to turn and shout back, just before a shell burst close to him. A piece of metal ripped into his chest and tore it apart. He gave out a terrible cry, and his horse bolted with his body trapped in the saddle. He was dragged for a considerable distance before he fell to the ground.

The Brigade broke into a gallop as they came into a shower of shot and shell from the Russian guns that were situated to the right on the Causeway Heights, and to the front of them. Still Lord Cardigan, rigidly facing ahead, led them forward through the heavy acrid smoke and the dust kicked up by their horses' hooves. The roar of cannon was deafening, and there was a continuous whine of musket-balls in the air. Russian shells ripped up the ground, sending men and horses sprawling over each other. Limbs were torn from bodies, heads blown from shoulders and there was a horrible thud and slush as groups of troopers were blasted out of existence. Men struggled to free themselves from beneath their fallen horses, or writhed in agony among the carnage left behind as the wave of British cavalry, their adrenaline in full flow, raced forward.

The Brigade began to take echelon shape, and as the shocked onlookers began to realise Lord Cardigan's objective, the French general, Bosquet, remarked emotionally: 'It is magnificent, but it is not war. It is madness.' They were almost at the Russian battery when a cannonade from most of the guns at once almost annihilated the front line.

The Russian drivers tried to limber up the guns to get them away as the British plunged headlong in at them. The momentum of the pace took the leading rank right through the line of enemy guns and into the stunned Russian cavalry standing to horses at the rear. The 4th Light Dragoons and the 11th Hussars then came in and engaged the Artillerymen, while the 8th Hussars veered to the right in order to take them in the flank and rear. A desperate hand-to-hand struggle ensued.

The panic-stricken Russian gunners tried to defend their field pieces by fending off the attackers with their rammers, but flashing British sabres cut many of them down, hacking mercilessly at those who tried to get away. The Brits had quite a free hand for several minutes, during which time they spiked the guns. They were attempting to try to pull some away when the officers saw that the enemy cavalry were re-forming, so the call to rally was sounded. Some troopers managed to locate each other amid the gun smoke and re-formed in groups, but they found the way back blocked by a body of Russian Lancers who had ridden down from the hillside. Sections of British horsemen were brought into formation, wheeled about and charged. Once again Russian nerve failed against British grit, and the Light Brigade broke through them.

When his unit reached the Russian guns and engaged the Artillerymen, Private Samuel Parkes of the 4th Light Dragoons, noticed that Lord Paget's sabre was still in its scabbard and called out: 'C'mon my Lord, it's time you were drawing your sword, we are on top of the guns!' His commander drew the weapon at once and immediately thrust it through the neck of a gunner. Private Parkes needed to stay close to and protect both Lord Paget and Trumpeter Crawford, who relayed the commander's orders to the troops. However, his horse was shot from under him and he had to fight on foot, which caused him to become detached from them. He shouted anxiously, 'Where's my chief? Who's seen the Colonel?' Fortunately Paget was not too far away and was able to reassure Parkes that he was alright. Sam became surrounded by the enemy and fought with gallant determination, and he was about to attack a Russian when one of his officers shouted: 'Spare him, Sam!', but he ignored this curious request and killed the man with his sabre.

As he was returning to the British lines he came upon Trumpeter Crawford whose horse had collapsed from exhaustion and he was about to be attacked by two mounted Cossacks. With complete disregard for his own safety, he ran to the trumpeter's rescue and, raising his sword, he placed himself between Crawford and his assailants and helped his comrade to his feet, supporting him with his arm as he warded off the enemy horsemen with his sword. The Russians were kept at a safe distance until being driven off.

As the two men moved cautiously up the valley trying to keep to areas that were thick with smoke to shield them from the view of marauding Russians, they came upon Major Halkett, second-in-command of their regiment, dangerously wounded and collapsed on the ground. They were joined by Private Edden, and Private Parkes got his comrades to lift the officer onto his back, and they carried on as best they could. A party of Cossacks suddenly appeared, and realising that he had little chance of survival and his burden was too great, Halkett told them to leave him and try to save themselves, requesting that they put a sabre in his hand so he could die fighting.

Having placed the officer on the ground they struggled to make a retreat, but Crawford could only limp slowly and Sam had to fight desperately to keep the enemy at a distance. A Russian officer approached them and shouted in English: 'If you will give yourselves up you shall not be harmed!' Sam refused, and raised his sword for a last stand, but a bullet hit him in his right arm and caused him to drop his weapon. They made one last effort to escape but only Edden succeeded. Suspecting that they might be treated roughly by the Cossacks, Parkes requested the protection of his officer. As they were being taken away they passed Major Halkett's body, which had been stripped of everything but his jacket.

The survivors were still in great danger, and it was every man for himself as they tried to get back to the British lines. Russian artillerymen had returned to their cannon and riflemen sent volleys up the valley, bringing down horses and men as they tried to get out of range. At the same time they were in danger from Cossacks who had moved in to pillage the dead and finish off the wounded. Other survivors were taken prisoner. The Russian battery and riflemen on the hills opened fire again, but an attack by the French horsemen of the 4th Chasseurs d'Afrique put them out of action. At last the blood-spattered remnants of the Light Brigade began to get back from the mouth of hell, many of them terribly maimed.

As the 11th (Prince Albert's Own) Hussars were making their way back to the British lines several horses began to slow down with fatigue and their riders could not keep up with the unit, among them being Sergeant William Bentley and Private Robert Levett, who both happened to be Yorkshire men. Cossacks began to move in on the stragglers and Sergeant Bentley was attacked from behind and wounded as he tried to fend them off. Private Levett was also being assaulted and both men were in grave danger.

Lieutenant Alexander Dunn dropped back from the main body of men to offer assistance. He charged at the enemy and smashed into them wielding his powerful sabre. A thrust to the body knocked a Cossack off his horse, and two others suffered similar fates. As a fourth Russian came near he raised the sword above his head, and brought it down with such force that it split his skull and almost cut the man in half. Turning his attention to Private Levett, who was being attacked by a lancer, he charged at the man, and with one stroke of his sabre he almost cut his head off. Unfortunately, Levett had been mortally wounded.

On reaching the Russian guns a round shot broke the leg of the horse of Sergeant John Berryman of the 17th (The Duke of Cambridge's Own) Lancers, and caused it to stop, and when he dismounted he realised he too had received what he considered to be only a slight wound in his leg. He was about to mercifully shoot his charger when Captain Alexander Webb of his regiment rode up, and he noticed a gaping wound where the officer's right shin had been shattered, so they decided to make their way back up the valley. Sergeant Berryman managed to catch a loose horse but almost at once an enemy shell hit it and the force of the missile drove the breastplate into its chest and it stumbled to the ground. He continued on foot, at one point running between units of 11th Hussars for protection.

In the confusion he came upon Captain Webb again, who was still mounted but in so much agony from his wound that he could not carry on. Sergeant Berryman asked Lieutenant Smith of his regiment to hold the horse steady while he assisted the officer out of the saddle and onto the ground. Lieutenant Smith went to look for something they could use as a stretcher, during which time Berryman was joined by Sergeant John Farrell of the 17th Lancers, and Corporal Joseph Malone of the 13th Light Dragoons, who were making their way back up the valley on foot. Corporal Malone had been riding with E Troop when his horse was shot and he was trapped under the body of the dead animal until Corporal James Nunnerley of the 17th Lancers dragged the horse off him and set him free.

The officer was crying out for a drink of water, and was continually telling them to leave him and save themselves, but they refused to do so. Private James Lamb of the 13th Light Dragoons joined them for a short while, and searched the dead bodies all around them and found a canteen of water with which to quench the officer's thirst. The two Lancers made a chair with their arms, as Corporal Malone supported his legs, and they succeeded in carrying him from the battlefield.

The French General Morris said to Sergeant Berryman, 'Sergeant, if you were in the French service I would make you an officer on the spot.' Captain Webb was transported to Scutari hospital where he had his leg amputated, 'partly under the influence of chloroform'. However, the trauma proved too much for him and he lost his fight for life.

A message was received by the 17th Lancers that their commanding officer, Captain Morris, had been seriously wounded and had collapsed from loss of blood and lay on the battlefield in a dangerously exposed situation. Surgeon James Mouat of the 6th Inniskilling Dragoons, the son of a military doctor, volunteered to go to attend to him and struck out under murderous enemy fire and at the mercy of marauding Cossacks who were plundering the dead and finishing off the wounded. On reaching the stricken officer he found that Sergeant Charles Wooden of the 17th Lancers, who had his horse shot from under him, had been making his way back up the valley when he stopped to help and together they managed to bind the officer's wounds and succeeded in stopping a severe haemorrhage which would almost certainly have proved fatal. They then managed to carry the captain to a place of safety and he consequently survived the terrible ordeal.

As the Scots Greys were covering the retreat of the Light Brigade, Sergeant Ramage saw Private William Gardner of the 13th Light Dragoons in difficulties. He had been disabled by a severe fracture of his leg by a round shot. The sergeant went to his assistance, and on dismounting he helped Gardner from his horse, slung him over his shoulder, and carried him to the rear under a very heavy cross-fire. The spot where the trooper would inevitably have fallen was immediately afterwards covered by Russian cavalry.

Lord Cardigan addressed fewer than 200 men who managed to answer the roll call, with the promise: 'Men you have done a glorious deed. England will be proud of you, and grateful to you. If you live to get home, be sure you will be provided for. Not one of you fellows will have to seek refuge in a workhouse.' The final casualty list was believed to be 113 killed and 134 wounded, with the loss of 475 horses.

The Light Brigade action at Balaclava was ill-fated before it began, and had little effect on the outcome of the battle. However, contrary to popular belief the men who took part were proud of what they had achieved, and would have done it again had they been ordered to do so. It had a devastating effect on the enemy cavalry, who were reluctant to face the British for the rest of the conflict, and it is still considered by many to be, as Lord Raglan was to state later: 'The finest thing ever done.'

John Grieve

John Grieve was born on 3 May 1821, at Musselburgh near Edinburgh. Not much is known of his early life but a descendant wrote: 'As a young man he ran through a small fortune.' He entered the 2nd Dragoons (Royal Scots Greys) as 774 Private Grieve, and had achieved the rank of sergeant when he received orders for active service in the Crimea.

His award of the Victoria Cross was announced in the *London Gazette* of 24 February 1857, and he became the first cavalryman to wear the medal when he received it during the first investiture. He also received the Crimea Medal with *Balaclava, Inkerman* and *Sebastopol* clasps, the French Military Medal and the Turkish Crimea Medal.

Charles Dickens wrote about his heroic deed in one of the first issues of his journal *All The Year Round*. He was appointed adjutant of the Scots Greys on 18 February 1859.

John died at the age of 52 on 1 December 1873, at 26 New Bigging, Inveresk, Midlothian, and he was buried in an unmarked family grave at St Michael's churchyard, Old Inveresk. A memorial stone was erected at the grave by representatives of the 2nd Dragoons and the Royal Highland Fusiliers in 2003. His medals are housed at the Art Gallery of South Australia in Adelaide.

Henry Ramage

Henry Ramage was born in 1827 in the Morningside district of Edinburgh. There is little known about his life.

His award of the Victoria Cross was announced in the *London Gazette* of 4 June 1858, and he received the medal from Queen Victoria at Southsea Common in Portsmouth on 2 August 1858, along with Edward Bell, James Mouat, Henry MacDonald, Matthew Dixon, Thomas Esmonde and Howard Elphinstone. He also received the Crimea Medal with *Balaclava*, *Inkerman* and *Sebastopol* clasps and the Turkish Crimea Medal.

Henry was aged only 32 and was still in military service when he died on 29 December 1859, at Newbridge, County Kildare, Ireland. He was buried in an unmarked grave at Newbridge Cemetery. His medals are with the Royal Scots Dragoon Guards Museum housed in Edinburgh Castle.

James Mouat

James Mouat was born on 14 April 1815, at Chatham in Kent, the son of Surgeon James Mouat who had served with several cavalry and infantry regiments, who died on the voyage home from India in 1848. His younger brother, Frederick John, who was born in Maidstone just over a year after James, was a prominent chemist and general surgeon, and his uncle had a distinguished career with the Indian Medical Service.

James and Frederick were educated in Paris, and at the University College Hospital in London, from where he became a member of the Royal College of Surgeons in 1837, becoming a Fellow in 1842. He joined the 44th (Essex) Regiment on 14 December 1838, transferring to the 4th (King's Own) Regiment in 1839, and the 9th (East Norfolk) Regiment in 1848. He became attached to the 6th (Inniskilling) Dragoons on 15 August 1854, for medical service in the Crimea, and he was placed in charge of the field hospital of the 3rd Division for most of the campaign.

Surgeon Mouat was the first Kent-born man, the first medical man and the only man of the 6th Inniskillings to be awarded the Victoria Cross, when it was announced in the *London Gazette* of 4 June 1858, and he received the medal from Queen Victoria at Southsea Common in Portsmouth on 2 August 1858, with Edward Bell, Henry Ramage, Henry MacDonald, Matthew Dixon, Thomas Esmonde and Howard Elphinstone. He also received the Crimea Medal with *Balaclava, Inkerman* and *Sebastopol* clasps, the French Legion of Honour, the Turkish Crimea

Medal and in 1856 he was appointed Commander of the Bath. He was promoted surgeon major on 9 February 1855, and he was appointed Deputy Inspector General of Hospitals on 1 October 1858. He went on active service in New Zealand in 1861 and served throughout the Maori Wars until 1865, for which he received the New Zealand Medal, 1845–7, and the thanks of the New Zealand government for his valuable service.

Known throughout his life for his immaculate appearance, James Mouat retired from military service in 1876. He lived with his wife, Adela, at 108 Palace Garden Terrace in Kensington, London. He received the Queen Victoria Jubilee Medal in 1887, and became Honorary Surgeon to the sovereign in 1888. He was appointed Knight Commander of the Order of the Bath in 1894. Sir James died at his residence on 4 January 1899, aged 83, and he was buried in Kensal Green Cemetery, where there is a memorial stone erected at the grave. There is a plaque dedicated to him at the National Arboretum in Staffordshire. His medals are with the Royal Army Medical Corps Museum in Aldershot.

Samuel Parkes

Samuel Parkes was born in the year of the Battle of Waterloo, on 6 September 1815, at Wiggington, near Tamworth in Staffordshire, and he was baptised at St Editha's Church, Tamworth, on 24 December 1815. He was the son of Thomas and Lydia Parkes and had at least two sisters, Elizabeth, who was baptised in 1812, and Mary, who was baptised in 1819.

He had been a general worker when he joined the 4th Light Dragoons on 28 July 1831, being described as 'six feet two inches tall with a powerful frame'. 635 Private Parkes took part in the Afghanistan campaign of 1839 and for his services he was awarded the Afghanistan Medal with *Ghuznee* clasp, for his part in the storming of the fortress of the same name. He was confined in cells in Ireland in 1848, after which he was convicted and sentenced by a district court martial to fifty-six days in Galway Prison. It is unusual for a soldier not to have been promoted after so many years of service which suggests a chequered military career, and although he received four good conduct badges, the last being issued to him on 18 November 1857, the cavalry required twenty years of 'irreproachable character' so he was not awarded a Long Service Good Conduct Medal.

He received orders for active service in the Crimean War, where he acted as orderly to his CO Lord Paget, taking part in the Battle of the Alma. Lord Paget had a couple of narrow escapes on the morning of the battle but he seemed to have fate on his side. He was ahead of the Brigade watching the movement of the enemy as they advanced towards Balaclava when a shell burst right in front of him and a stray splinter hit his stirrup. He asked Private Parkes what it was and Sam replied: 'It was a piece of shell, my Lord, and it nearly took your foot off!' Paget ordered Parkes to pick it up and look after it because he intended to send it home to England as a souvenir of war. Soon afterwards a spent cannon ball came bounding towards Lord Paget and as fortune would have it yet again it passed right under his horse. Private Parkes found this funny and laughed: 'Haha, it went right between your horse's legs.' However, Paget was not quite so amused and complained at Sam's audacity.

Private Parkes also had a lucky escape when he returned to the cavalry lines. He was standing at the side of his charger's head holding a flame inside his helmet to shield it from the breeze ready to light his pipe when an enemy shell came bounding towards them and thumped into the head of the horse behind which Sam was sheltering and took it clean off. The body of the poor animal was left standing upright for a short while before its legs folded and it crashed to the ground, leaving Sam looking dazed but unharmed.

Private Parkes had become one of about sixty men who were prisoners of war. While in captivity he saved the life of Private Farquharson of his regiment who had become so annoyed at being frequently ill-treated at the hands of his captors that he got drunk one night and wanted to fight with some Russians who were trying to search him. When the situation became serious Private Parkes simply picked him up, threw him over his shoulder and carried him away from his tormentors. During a march to Simferopol they came upon a man who they suspected of being a Russian spy so Sam took it upon himself to knock the man senseless with a punch on the nose! A fellow trooper of the 4th Light Dragoons recalled that Parkes told them: 'he and others were taken to St Petersburg, treated well, and were allowed eight pence a day for food, which was very cheap'. He also remarked to Lord Paget: 'My Lord, the officers were not ashamed to be seen walking along with us.' When he was released a year later he was court-martialled for desertion but as the full facts became known he was cleared of all charges.

He was the first Staffordshire-born man to be awarded the Victoria Cross, and the oldest for the Crimean campaign when it was announced in the *London Gazette* of 24 February 1857, and he received the medal at the first investiture. He also received the Crimean Medal with *Alma, Balaclava* and *Sebastopol* clasps and the Turkish Crimea Medal. He is the only Victoria Cross holder of the 4th Light Dragoons.

He was discharged on 1 December 1857, becoming a warder at Hampton Court Palace, and a Chelsea out-pensioner. He married Ann Jeffrey on 13 February 1858, at St George's Church, Hanover Square, London. They were both living in Oxford Street at the time, and by the spring of 1861 they were living at West Lodge, Marble Arch, London, where Sam was employed as a Hyde Park Constable.

On 23 May 1863, he swore an affidavit, along with other Light Brigade survivors, in the libel case of Cardigan v. Calthorpe. He recalled that he saw Cardigan come from the Heavy Brigade and give orders to Lord George Paget that the Light Brigade should advance. Later, when confronted by Russian Lancers, he added that Paget enquired as to the whereabouts of Lord Cardigan and Captain Lowe, to which he was told that: 'Lord Cardigan has gone back some time.'

He lost his original Victoria Cross and a duplicate was issued. Eventually the original turned up and was purchased by the officers of the 4th Light Dragoons and presented to the regiment on Balaclava Day 1954. The duplicate was destroyed.

Sam suffered a stroke and died on 14 November 1864, at Stanhope Lodge in Hyde Park, apparently penniless. His death was registered on the same day, stating he was 49 years old and an Inspector of the Park Constables. The official cause of death was recorded as 'apoplexy-five days'. He was buried in a pauper's grave at Brompton Cemetery in west London. He is one of twelve holders of the Victoria Cross buried at Brompton, including, Francis Wheatley William Hope and Sir Frederick Maude. His wife died in London in 1885. A memorial stone was laid on his grave in 1999, and plaques were placed at the family grave and inside St Editha's Church in Tamworth in 2004. An obelisk memorial was unveiled at Wiggington in 2011. His medals were sold by the Queen's Royal Irish Hussars Museum at Eastbourne in 2016, to offset the cost of the Queen's Royal Hussars Museum in Warwick, and they are now displayed on rotation at the Lord Ashcroft Gallery, as part of the 'Extraordinary Heroes' exhibition at the Imperial War Museum in London.

Alexander Roberts Dunn

Alexander Dunn was born on 15 September 1833, 'in an old-fashioned mansion' in Catherine Street, Dunstable, York (now Toronto), which his father had built when newly arrived in Canada from England in 1820. He was the second son of John Henry Dunn, who served as receiver general of Upper Canada from his arrival in the country until 1841, and represented Toronto in the first Canadian Parliament from 1841–4. His mother was Charlotte Roberts, and he was given her maiden name as his middle name. Alexander was educated at Upper Canada College, and at Harrow School in England. Although only an average student, he was a keen sportsman and a good horse rider, becoming a formidable swordsman and a good marksman. Said to be an impressive-looking man, standing 6ft 2in tall, he was known to have an easy-going nature.

On the death of his mother, his father moved back to England, and Alexander was commissioned as cornet in the 11th (Prince Albert's Own) Hussars, on 12 March 1852, being promoted lieutenant on 18 February 1853. He had been away on leave when his regiment received orders for active service, and returned to his unit in time to sail with them to the East. He gave his regimental sword away and acquired one in England which was much larger than the regulations allowed. He was present at the Battle of the Alma, and he took part in the Light Brigade action at Balaclava.

He became the first Canadian-born recipient of the Victoria Cross and the only officer to gain the award for the Battle of Balaclava when it was announced in the *London Gazette* of 24 February 1857, and he received the medal at the first investiture. He also received the Crimea Medal with *Alma, Balaclava, Inkerman* and *Sebastopol* clasps and the Turkish Crimea Medal.

A relationship developed between him and Rosa Maria Douglas, the wife of his commanding officer, who eventually asked her husband for a divorce. From then on Alexander's status in the regiment suffered, and he was overlooked for a number of promotions. A troop leader's vacancy he had applied for was given to a man who had not taken part in the Light Brigade action, and when he protested he was told that he was too young for the responsibility. He requested permission to resign his commission, but Lord Cardigan turned him down. However, Lord Lucan intervened, and when permission was granted early in 1855, the couple went to live in Toronto.

On returning from the Crimea he spent two years on the family estates engaged in hunting and shooting, and he helped to raise a body of men named the Royal Canadians to be incorporated into the British Army as the 100th Regiment (Prince of Wales' Royal Canadians) for service in India. He was appointed major of the regiment on 29 June

1858, and took over command while they were stationed at Aldershot. He was appointed Lieutenant Colonel on 25 June 1861, aged only 27, and when the unit was posted to Malta in 1864, he became the youngest Colonel in the British Army. While on the island his brother, John, who was a subaltern in the regiment, died of fever, leaving Alexander as the sole heir to the family estate. The sadness at the death of his brother, and the inactivity of garrison duty prompted Colonel Dunn to seek a transfer, and he became a Lieutenant Colonel in the 33rd Regiment (Duke of Wellington's Own), station at Poona in India. He became known as a strict disciplinarian, and one of the most popular and respected officers of his day.

In late 1867 the 33rd Regiment was ordered for active service with the Abyssinian Expeditionary Force under General Napier, sent to repatriate a number of diplomats who were being held against their will by the defiant King Theodore. Colonel Dunn is said to have had premonitions of death, and during the advance into Abyssinia the force stopped at Senafe. On 25 January 1868, Dunn set off on a hunting trip with the regimental surgeon and two orderlies. Eventually the officers were separated, and when Dunn and his companion stopped to take a drink a freak accident occurred. He is believed to have caught his gaiter on the trigger of his rifle, causing it to go off, and the bullet tore into his chest and killed him. He was aged 34, and he was buried with military honours in a small cemetery on high ground which men of the regiment constructed in Senafe, which is now Eritrea, Ethiopia. A friend writing to his sister stated: 'In no regiment was ever a commanding officer so missed as the one we have so unhappily lost. So perfect a soldier, so fine a gentleman, so confidence-inspiring a leader. He was a friend, and felt to be such by every man in the regiment. The regiment will never again have so universally-esteemed a commander.' A court of inquiry was unsure about the circumstances surrounding his death, and came to the supposition that it was accidental. However, it has been said that he was killed by his servant, who is believed to have confessed to the crime on his death bed in a Liverpool workhouse.

The grave site fell into disrepair, until it was rediscovered and restored, and it is now under the protective eye of the Commonwealth War Graves Commission. A commemorative plaque was placed close to his family home in Toronto in 1966, and a plaque was installed in Clarence Square Park, at Spadina, Toronto. There is also a 33rd Regiment memorial at York Minster. His medals are in the possession of Upper Canada College.

Joseph Malone

Joseph Malone was born at Eccles, near Manchester, on 11 January 1833. His father was of Irish descent, and was probably one of the hundreds of labourers, or 'navvies', drafted into the area to work on the Liverpool and Manchester Railway for the engineer, George Stephenson. Cecil Buckley also came from Eccles.

Joseph left his job as a farrier to enlist into the 13th Light Dragoons at Hulme Barracks in Manchester, on 28 March 1851. He was 5ft 7in tall. The regiment was stationed in Birmingham when it received orders for active service with the Light Brigade of cavalry in the Crimea, and they embarked at Portsmouth in May 1854. He was present at the Battle of the Alma, and four days later he and three other troopers volunteered to go on a reconnaissance, in which they succeeded in capturing an escort of enemy cavalry, along with the baggage they were taking to Sebastopol. The Brits arrived at Balaclava, where, on 14 October 1854, he was promoted corporal. Corporal Malone was also present at the actions of the Bulganak and Mckenzie's Farm and during the expedition to Eupatoria, being promoted sergeant on 20 September 1855.

According to Private Lamb, a Victoria Cross was left at the disposal of the 13th Light Dragoons and he and Corporal Malone simply drew lots to decide who should receive the medal, and Malone won.

He became the first Lancashire-born man to be awarded the Victoria Cross when it was announced in the *London Gazette* of 25 September 1857, and he was presented with the medal by Queen Victoria at a ceremony held in the Quadrangle of Windsor Castle on 28 November 1857, with the whole of the Windsor garrison attending. George Symons, James Craig and Sir Christopher Teesdale received their awards at the same ceremony. He also received the Crimean Medal with *Alma, Balaclava, Inkerman* and *Sebastopol* clasps and the Turkish Crimea Medal.

He was sent to the riding establishment at the Maidstone cavalry depot on 10 August 1857, where he remained until 10 June 1858. He was posted to Dublin, but, described as 'a very intelligent man', it was decided that he would make an efficient riding master, qualified to serve with the 6th Dragoons in India, and on being sent back to Maidstone, he embarked for India with the Inniskillings, being gazetted into that regiment as 450 Riding Master Malone, on 7 September 1858. He, and his father-in-law, Captain Weir, were concerned with giving evidence in the court martial of Paymaster Smales, of the Inniskillings, at Mhow, in 1861, and he held the post of Assistant Paymaster while this was in progress, a position which he apparently did not like. He returned from India on 6 April 1867.

He married Eliza Weir, at Mhow, India, on 3 May 1860. She was the second daughter of Captain Archibald Weir of the 6th Dragoons. There were seven children. Kate Isabella Upton was born at Ahmenugger, India, on 11 March 1861, Joseph Archibald Edwin was born at Mhow, India, on 4 January 1863, Ada Bertha was born at Manchester on 4 July 1868, Edward Joseph was born at Brighton on 17 September 1871, Archibald Weir was born at Cahir on 26 December 1872, Eva Josephine was born at Dundalk on 1 June 1875 and Arthur Philip was born at Edinburgh on 26 February 1875. The 1881 census shows Joseph Malone as being at the Royal Artillery Barracks, Cheriton, Kent, with his family. He attended the first Balaclava reunion banquet in 1875, and was a member of the Balaclava Commemoration Society, 1879.

He was serving at the Canterbury Cavalry Depot when orders were received for active service in South Africa, where a Boer uprising was causing serious problems, and he and his unit embarked at Chatham on 7 November 1882. While he was at the Cape he began to suffer ill-health, but he had only one year of service to complete and he would not be invalided home.

Joseph died suddenly of bronchitis on 28 June 1883 in the Officers' Mess at the Rugby Hotel at Pinetown, Natal, aged 50. He was buried in St Andrew's Old Cemetery, King's Road, also known as Christ's Church, Pinetown, Natal. His name is recorded on a brass tablet in Pietermaritzburg Cathedral. At the time of his death he was described as: 'an excellent, energetic, and hard-working officer'.

His medals came up for auction in June 1972 and bought by the 13th/18th Hussars for their Regimental Museum at Cawthorne in Yorkshire. A replacement Victoria Cross was apparently authorised by the War Office in 1950 and was presented to his great-niece, Florence Malone. Hancocks confirmed in 1999 that the cross was a genuine issue, but it is not the same medal as the one presented in 1857. It was in a private collection in Australia in 2000. The centenary of the Battle of Balaclava was commemorated by a wreath-laying ceremony at his renovated grave.

His son, Joseph, known as Captain Malone, was a respected theatre director in the West End of London during the early years of the nineteenth century, and his great-granddaughter, Sally Ann Howes, was an actress, best known as Truly Scrumptious in the film *Chitty Chitty Bang Bang*.

John Berryman

John Berryman was born on 18 July 1825, in Dudley, which at that time was within the county of Worcestershire, where his father, Edward, was the proprietor of the *Bell Inn*, which still exists in Upper High Street opposite Dudley parish church. His mother was named Elizabeth, but she was known as Betsy, and came from Truro in Cornwall. Cholera was prevalent at that period and claimed the lives of John's two brothers and a sister in 1832. By 1841, his father had died and Betsy lived with her three sons at New Mill Street in Dudley. Edmund was a puddler, Richard was a carpenter and John was a cabinet maker.

John enlisted into the 17th (Duke of Cambridge's Own) Lancers at Birmingham, on 18 October 1843. He was promoted corporal on 21 October 1851, and after sailing for active service in the East in 1854, Sergeant Patrick Brennan 'drowned in the reservoir at Yenibazar' on 1 August, and on the following day John was promoted to sergeant. He received orders for active service in the Crimea.

He was the first Worcestershire (and now West Midlands) man to be awarded the Victoria Cross when it was announced in the *London Gazette* of 24 February 1857, and he received the medal at the first investiture. He also received the Crimea Medal with *Alma, Balaclava, Inkerman* and *Sebastopol* clasps and the Turkish Crimea Medal.

Sergeant Berryman was appointed Troop Sergeant Major on 18 April 1856, and left the Crimea in that month. In 1857 unrest among soldiers of the Bengal Army in India flared up into rebellion, and a British force was sent to deal with it. TSM Berryman sailed with the regiment in October from Queenstown on the troopship *Great Britain*, and although they arrived at Bombay in December, they were not ready for service until May 1858, when they joined the force being prepared by Sir Hugh Rose for service in Central India. Under Sir William Gordon, they fought an extremely difficult campaign, as they pursued the leading rebel named Tantia Topi. For a distance of 1,000 miles, 500 of which were covered in one month, they suffered long forced marches under the constant threat of rebel attack and the ravages of disease, after which they assaulted large, heavily manned masonry fortresses. But they overcame these hardships and the rebel leader was captured and dealt with. For his service in India he received the Indian Mutiny Medal with *Central India* clasp.

He remained in India with the regiment, where on 14 January 1861, he married Eliza (formerly Enright), and they had a daughter named

Florence, born on 21 March 1863. On 12 April 1864 he was promoted lieutenant and quartermaster. Sadly, as his unit were preparing to depart for England, Eliza contracted cholera and died in Bombay. John and Florence returned to England in 1865, and his daughter was initially raised by his sister, Mary, in Dudley.

The British Army invaded Zululand early in 1879 to deal with the defiant King Cetshwayo, and on 22 January over a thousand British troops were massacred at Isandlwana. Reinforcements had to be hurried out to South Africa, and the 17th Lancers were rushed from Hounslow Barracks to the Victoria Docks at Blackwall, to set sail for active service at the Cape. They arrived in mid-April, and after being on escort duty with the troops which witnessed the carnage at Isandlwana in May, they formed part of the British column which advanced on the Zulu capital at Ulundi in June. On 4 July 1879, a British force in classic square formation was attacked by a large army of Zulus and their warriors were killed in their thousands. TSM Berryman was with the Lancers who charged out from the square to finish off the enemy and break their spirit. The Zulu capital was destroyed and Cetshwayo was captured. For his service TSM Berryman received the South Africa Medal with *1879* clasp.

On 19 May 1880 he exchanged into the 5th Lancers, becoming honorary captain on 1 July 1881, and honorary major on 28 July 1883. John Berryman attended the first Balaclava reunion banquet in London on 25 October 1875, and he became a member of the Balaclava Commemoration Society two years later, which restricted its membership in 1879. On the occasion of Queen Victoria's Golden Jubilee celebrations in 1887, he signed a Loyal Address which was presented to the Sovereign. He was able to attend the reunions of 1890, 1892 and 1893, but he was too ill to attend the reunion of 1895.

On 25 June 1886, his medals, one of the finest sets ever to be worn on the chest of a Victorian soldier, were auctioned at Sotheby's. John and his family lived in Richmond Villa at Langley in Buckinghamshire until 1888, before moving to Upper Court at Woldingham in Surrey, being described as a farmer and retired cavalry major. For a few years he was a church warden at St Agatha's Church, where his daughter played the harmonium. In March 1891 the *Strand Magazine* published his own account of the action.

John had an operation on 2 October 1894, for 'epithelioma of the tongue' (a tumour), and he died at his home on 27 June 1896. In addition to the tumour there was 'secondary infection of glands in his neck, severe ulceration, haemorrhage and exhaustion'. John had made a will before he died naming his daughter as sole executor, leaving a substantial amount of about £20,000. There was no military funeral, and John was buried in the south-west corner of St Agatha's churchyard in Woldingham, where the local history society and villagers still tend to his impressive pink granite gravestone.

John Farrell

John Farrell was born in Dublin in March 1826, and he enlisted into the 17th (Duke of Cambridge's Own) Lancers in about 1842. He was known to be about 5ft 7in tall. He had reached the rank of sergeant when the regiment received orders for active service in the Crimea, and he was present at the battles of the Alma and Inkerman, and he took part in the Light Brigade action at Balaclava.

His award of the Victoria Cross was announced in the *London Gazette* on 20 November 1857, and he received the medal from Sir Colin Campbell, the commander-in-chief in India in 1858. He also received the Crimea Medal with *Alma, Balaclava, Inkerman* and *Sebastopol* clasps and the Turkish Crimea Medal.

He was appointed Troop Sergeant Major on 2 May 1856, and later achieved the rank of Quartermaster Sergeant. In 1857 unrest among soldiers of the Bengal Army in India flared up into rebellion, and the 17th Lancers were among a British force sent to deal with the crisis. QMS Farrell sailed with the regiment from Queenstown, Ireland in October 1854. They were ready for service in May 1858, when they joined the force under Sir Hugh Rose which went in pursuit of the leading rebel named Tantia Topi, across Central India. They fought an extremely difficult campaign, but the rebel leader was captured and executed in May 1859. For his service he received the Indian Mutiny Medal with *Central India* clasp.

The regiment were due to return home when John took ill and died from an abscess of the liver at Secunderabad, India, on 31 August 1865, aged 39. He was buried in Secunderabad Cemetery, and the grave has no memorial stone.

Charles Wooden

Charles Wooden was born in Germany on 24 March 1827. Nothing is known of his early life, and it has been suggested that he may have been born in London of German parentage. He enlisted into the 17th (Duke of Cambridge's Own) Lancers in about 1845, becoming a sergeant major.

Sergeant Wooden was something of a character in the 17th Lancers. One night, returning to camp the worse for wear after a drinking session, he was challenged by the sentry on guard duty, but could not remember the password. 'Tish me', Wooden whispered in a slurred voice. 'Who?' asked the sentry. 'Tish me, Tish me!' came the answer. Down came the sentry's lance as he demanded to know just which 'me' it was. By now in a temper, Wooden bellowed: 'Tish me, the Devil.' The sentry, now exercising his better judgement on recognising his sergeant retorted: 'Pass, Tish me the Devil!' The nickname stuck and for the remainder of his service Wooden was referred to as 'Tish me the Devil'.

Apparently Sergeant Wooden was not a popular man in the regiment, possibly because of his odd demeanour and strong German accent. Even the award of his Victoria Cross was controversial. His name was not put forward for the award at first, although Dr Mouat was. Wooden wrote to the doctor saying that if Mouat was to receive a Victoria Cross then so should he, as he had been at Mouat's side during the rescue of Colonel Morris. Luckily for Wooden, Dr Mouat agreed and wrote to the Horse Guards supporting his claim. The reply to his letter reads: 'His Royal Highness feels very unwilling to bring any further claim for the Victoria Cross for an act performed at so distant a period but as the decoration has been conferred on Dr James Mouat for the part he took in the rescue of Colonel Morris, and Sergeant Major Wooden appears to have acted in a manner very honourable to him on the occasion and, by his gallantry, been equally instrumental in saving the life of this officer, His Royal Highness is induced to submit the case.'

His award of the Victoria Cross was announced in the *London Gazette* of 26 October 1858, and he received the medal in India in February 1859. He also received the Crimea Medal with *Alma, Balaclava, Inkerman* and *Sebastopol* clasps, the French Military Medal and the Turkish Crimea Medal.

The Indian Mutiny broke out in May 1857 and he sailed to join the force being prepared by Sir Hugh Rose for active service in Central India. It was an extremely difficult campaign as they embarked on long forced marches under the constant threat of rebel attack and the ravages of disease, after which they assaulted large heavily manned masonry fortresses. But they overcame these hardships and most of the rebel leaders were captured and dealt with. For his service in India he received the Indian Mutiny Medal with *Central India* clasp.

He exchanged into the 6th Inniskilling Dragoons, being promoted lieutenant and quartermaster on 26 October 1860. During his service with the Inniskillings he appeared as a witness in the court martial of a fellow officer at Aldershot in 1863. He exchanged to the 5th Lancers on 21 March 1865, and then into the 104th Bengal Fusiliers on 4 February 1871.

Charles lived on the Dover Heights in Kent, and on 23 April 1875, he complained of severe pains in his head. His wife, Eliza, sent for an army doctor, who found him in a drunken state, and bleeding from his mouth and nose. Wooden pointed to his mouth and was attempting to dislodge an object, stating that he had a tooth that needed removing. The doctor examined him, and discovered that the roof of his mouth was severely damaged. There were two cartridge cases and a Colt pistol lying near him. The doctor attended to him until he died early next morning, St George's Day. It seemed that he had accidently killed him while trying to shoot out an aching tooth. He was aged 47. He was buried at St James' Cemetery in Dover, and a headstone was erected by his brother officers, which has since been renovated. In 1926 his medals were owned by a member of the British Numismatic Society, who displayed them that year at one of their meetings, and they are now with the Queen's Royal Lancers Museum at Thoresby Park, near Ollerton in Nottinghamshire.

Chapter 6

Little Inkerman

At noon on 26 October 6,000 Russian infantry and 4 guns moved out of Sebastopol to mount a powerful sortie against the outposts of the Second Division on the heights of Inkerman, on the exposed extreme right flank of the forward lines, which put the British under pressure. The picket line that day was formed by three companies each of the 30th (Cambridgeshire) and 49th (Hertfordshire) Regiments, and one company each of the 41st (Welsh) and the 95th (Derbyshire) Regiments. The First Division, a division of the Guards, a Rifle battalion and five French divisions marched to their support, and the fire of eighteen guns posted on high ground brought about the collapse of the Russian attack.

A deep and wide feature known as the Careenage Ravine ran south-east from Sebastopol and separated the Victoria and Inkerman Ridges. Lieutenant William 'Bully' Hewett of the four-gun steam sloop HMS *Beagle*, Naval Brigade, was in command of the Lancaster Battery on Victoria Ridge, and as a large force of the enemy was seen to be advancing on their flank, hurried orders were sent to him to spike his gun and retreat. He disregarded the order, stating that he only took orders from his commander, Captain Stephen Lushington, and told off some men to help him to rip down the side parapet and turn the gun on the advancing enemy. He manned the gun and poured devastating fire on them, and his decisive action helped to break up the attack.

While being in an isolated position on Shell Hill, Lieutenant John Conolly and Corporal James Owens of the 49th (Hertfordshire) Regiment, greatly distinguished themselves. Lieutenant Conolly was the only man not wearing a greatcoat, as he led his men in repulsing a strong enemy attack, and Corporal Owens fought a personal encounter with the Russians. Lieutenant Conolly was subsequently wounded while trying to defend the position. He collapsed from loss of blood and Corporal Owens assisted him.

Brevet Major Gerald Goodlake of the 1st Battalion, Coldstream Guards, the son of a cavalry veteran of the Peninsular War, was given the command of a party of very young volunteer sharpshooters of the Guards Brigade, which he did from 17 October–27 November 1854. He was recognised for distinguished gallantry while the sole surviving officer in command of his sharpshooters when they held a position at the bottom of the Windmill Ravine below the piquet house.

One of the sharpshooters under his command was Private William Stanlake, who undertook a dangerous assignment which needed him to get as close to the enemy as he could. Having been warned of the imminent risk he would run during the endeavour, he volunteered to reconnoitre, and crawled to within 6yd of the enemy sentries, bringing back valuable information which enabled Major Goodlake to launch a surprise attack. Encouraged by the major's sole leadership and command during the action, they killed an officer and thirty-seven men, took an officer and two men prisoners, and captured their knapsacks and rifles.

On another occasion his fellow officer named Cameron was wounded and Captain Goodlake had to carry him out of the fight on his back. On one of these sorties he killed 5 men, one of whom he shot through the head at about 300 paces, and 1 officer beating on his men at 30 paces. He and Sergeant Ashton were nearly caught in the Magazine Grotto cave in the Careenage Ravine, but they made a bolt for it (passing the Russian assailants on the way down the ravine) and got off with a bullet through his coat and he was shot in the arm. It was suggested that they got away because they were wearing grey greatcoats and the Russians mistook them for their own men.

As the Russians began to falter from the intense artillery fire, the British infantry advanced from the barrier on Inkerman Ridge, and Colour Sergeant Ambrose Madden of the 41st (Welsh) Regiment led a small party of men which cut off and took a Russian officer and fourteen private soldiers prisoners, three of them solely by Madden himself.

The action which came to be known as 'Little Inkerman' confirmed in the minds of the British infantry that their individual and collective gallantry was superior to that of the Russians, but it also demonstrated to the Russians the weakness of the British positions. They would be back to try again over the same ground just over a week later.

William Nathan Wrighte Hewett

William Nathan Wrighte Hewett was born in Brighton on 12 August 1834; the son of Dr William Wrighte Hewett of Berkeley Square in London, Weston Green in Surrey and Bilham Hall near Doncaster. The hall is now demolished but the ruins of the Belvedere (summer house) can still be seen. His father was surgeon and physician to William IV, and his mother, Susan, was the daughter of the Revd Dr John Maddy Moore, who was Prebendary of Ely, rector of Somerton and chaplain to Queen Victoria, and the three monarchs before her, including William IV. Presumably his parents were introduced while his grandfathers were in the service of the king. They had married in Suffolk in 1824.

William joined the Royal Navy as a cadet on HMS *Ocean*, on 22 April 1847, being made acting mate on HMS *Impregnable* on 26 May 1849. He served as a midshipman during the Burmese War of 1851, and thereafter served on several ships before being posted to HMS *Beagle* as a lieutenant on 26 October 1854.

He became the first Freemason to be awarded the Victoria Cross when it was announced in the *London Gazette* of 24 February 1857, and he received the medal at the first investiture. He was one of three men that Queen Victoria mentioned when she wrote her diary that day. He also received the Crimea Medal with *Inkerman*, *Azov* and *Sebastopol* clasps, the French Legion of Honour, the Turkish Order of Medjidie (2nd Class), the Turkish Crimea Medal and the Sardinian Medal of Military Valour.

Known for his blunt, sometimes offending manner, and a bad temper, he became known as 'Bully' Hewett. He had married on 23 February 1857, the day before his investiture, his new wife being Jane Emily Blackadar, the 14-year-old daughter of J. Wood, consul for the Marea in Greece. They had four sons named Hugh, William Warrington, Edward Matson and Charles (who died an infant), all born between 1858 and 1872, and two daughters named Jane and Emily, born in 1866 and 1874. William and Edward became lieutenants in the Royal Navy. In 1866 they lived at 1 Hamilton Villas on Hamilton Road in Southsea, before moving to 10 Eastern Parade in 1871.

After passing the examination at Portsmouth he was appointed to the royal yacht *Victoria and Albert*, from where he was appointed commander on 13 September 1858. He then successively commanded HMS *Viper* on the west coast of Africa, and HMS *Rinaldo* on the North American and West Indian station. He was made a captain on 24 November 1862.

As civil war was raging in North America, the steam blockade runner, *Condor*, sailed from Greenock under its new captain, Samuel S. Ridge, bound for the United States. On board were the Confederate Commissioner for London and Mrs Rose O'Neal Greenhow, also known as 'Wild Rose', the Confederacy's most renowned spy, who had been in Britain on a diplomatic mission trying to gain support for the Confederacy among the British aristocracy. As the ship was off the coast of North Carolina on 1 October 1864, it ran into a storm, and was spotted by the Union gunboat USS *Niphon*. The captain tried to escape but ran aground at the mouth of the Cape Fear River. Rose jumped into a small rowing boat and tried to escape capture, but the craft was swamped before she could get to shore and she was drowned, apparently weighed down by the European gold she was carrying secreted all over her person. Samuel S. Ridge was the false name being used by none other than Captain William Hewett of the Royal Navy.

He afterwards commanded HMS *Basilisk* on the China station from 1865–9; was flag captain in HMS *Ocean* on the China station from 1870–2; and was captain of HMS *Devastation* from 1872–3. He received the Indian General Service Medal with *Pegu* clasp.

From October 1873–October 1876 he was commodore and commander-in-chief on the west coast of Africa. He was in charge of the naval operations during the Ashanti War, being present at the Battle of Amoaful and the capture of Coomassie. For his services during this campaign he was appointed a Knight, Commander of the Bath (KCB) on 31 March 1874, and he received the Ashanti Medal with *Coomassie* clasp.

In May 1877 he was appointed to HMS *Achilles* and commanded her in the Mediterranean and the Sea of Marmora. He attained his flag on 21 March 1878, and in April 1882 he was appointed commander-in-chief in the East Indies. During the Egyptian War of 1882, he conducted the naval operations in the Red Sea, especially the occupation of Suez and the seizure of the canal in August.

From 1880–4 he lived at 33 South Parade in Southsea. He moved to London, but when he became ill he moved back to Southsea, and resided at St Elmo on Lennox Road, until his death.

Commander Hewett arrived at Saukin in the Sudan on 16 December 1883, in his flagship HMS *Euryalus* and landed with a force of 550 seamen and marines, with 6 heavy guns, for the defence of the town on 6 February 1884, and 4 days later he was formally appointed governor as representative of the Khedive. He was present at the victorious

Second Battle of El Teb on 29 February 1884. In April 1884, he led a delegation to Emperor Yohannes IV which successfully negotiated for access through Abyssinian territory for the evacuation of the Egyptian garrison that had been isolated at Kassala in southern Sudan. For his service he was awarded the Khedive's Bronze Star and the Abyssinian Order of Solomon.

On 8 July 1884 he became a vice admiral, and from March 1886–April 1888 was in command of the Channel Fleet. He was appointed Knight Commander, Order of the Star of India (KCSI).

After being in failing health for some time, Sir William died of kidney disease at the Royal Naval Hospital in Haslar near Portsmouth on 13 May 1888, aged 53. There were six admirals at his impressive military funeral, including John Commerell VC, as he was buried at Highland Road Cemetery in Portsmouth, where there is a maritime headstone. His wife died in 1910 and is buried with him, along with their two naval sons. Having become a club member in 1885, he is one of four Crimean VCs named on the memorial in the corridor of the Royal Naval and Royal Albert Yacht Club in Portsmouth, which was unveiled by the Duke of Edinburgh in 2007. Hewett Close at Tichfield near Fareham is named after him. His medals are with the National Maritime Museum in Greenwich, along with those of Charles Lucas, William Peel and John Sheppard.

Gerald Littlehales Goodlake

Gerald Littlehales Goodlake was born on 14 May 1832, at Wadley House, Shellingford, near Faringdon in Berkshire (now Wiltshire), the second son of Thomas Mills Goodlake and his wife Emilia Maria, the daughter of Sir Edward Baker, 1st Baronet of Radstone in Dorset. His father served with the 5th Dragoon Guards during the Peninsular Campaigns. They also owned Kitemore House at Faringdon, and his brother, Thomas Leinster, became a Justice of the Peace for Berkshire and then Oxfordshire, and his sister was named Olivia (1853–1906). Gerald was educated at Eton College from 1844–9, where he was noted as an excellent runner, a talented boxer and he became a good shot.

On 14 June 1850, he was commissioned by purchase as an ensign in the 23rd (Welsh) Fusiliers, before transferring to the 1st Battalion, Coldstream Guards, on 27 June 1851, becoming a lieutenant. He sailed for active service in the East on 14 February 1854, being appointed captain on 14 July. He left the Crimea on 6 June 1856.

His award of the Victoria Cross was announced in the *London Gazette* of 24 February 1857, and he received the medal at the first investiture. The citation gives the date as 28 October, but in one of his letters he states that his Victoria Cross action was the day after the Battle of Balaclava (25 October). He was also awarded the Crimea Medal with *Alma, Balaclava, Inkerman* and *Sebastopol* clasps, the French Legion of Honour, the Turkish Order of the Medjidie (5th Class) and the Turkish Crimea Medal.

In 1857 he was the subject of a painting by James Edgell Collins which is now held at Newstead Abbey in Nottinghamshire. Although it is frowned upon in modern times, his dog, Meg, was a winner of the three-day hare-coursing event the Waterloo Cup in 1865. He married Margaret Jane (formerly Christian-Curwen) on 5 January 1870, and they lived at 42 Grosvenor Place in Belgravia, London.

He was promoted to brevet colonel on 30 April 1869, and became aide-de-camp to Queen Victoria until 11 August 1879, when he was promoted to major general, and he rose to the rank of honorary lieutenant colonel on 1 July 1881.

Gerald died on 5 April 1890, aged 57, at The Fishery, Dedham, Middlesex (now Buckinghamshire), and he was buried at St Mary the Virgin churchyard, Church Hill, Harefield, Middlesex. His name appears on the 'For Valour' memorial in the cloisters at Eton College, and his medals are with the Guards Museum at Wellington Barracks in London.

Apparently, a party visiting the battlefield in 1998 found his name scratched on a wall of cave, presumably the one in which he must have hidden.

William Stanlake

William Stanlake was born at Uppacott Farm in Halwill near Okehampton in Devon, and he was baptised on 31 October 1830. He attested for the 1st Battalion, Coldstream Guards as 3968 Private Stanlack, at Totnes on 27 July 1852.

He was the first Devonian of six to be awarded the Victoria Cross for the Crimean War when it was announced in the *London Gazette* of 24 February 1857, under the name of Stanlock. Apparently, he had not been allowed to receive the Victoria Cross at the first investiture because he had recently been punished by his commanding officer for theft, so it was presented to him in July 1857. He was also awarded the Distinguished

Conduct Medal, the Crimea Medal with *Alma, Inkerman* and *Sebastopol* clasps, the French Military Medal and the Turkish Crimea Medal.

William died on 24 April 1904, aged 73, at Blue Anchor Lane in Peckham, Camberwell, south-west London, and he was buried in Camberwell Old Cemetery, where a headstone was erected in 1987. His medals are with the Coldstream Guards Museum in London.

Ambrose Madden

Ambrose Madden was born at Cork in Ireland in 1820. He was a labourer prior to enlisting into the 2nd Dragoon Guards at Cahir on 24 May 1838, and he transferred to the 1st Battalion, 41st (Welsh) Regiment at Dublin on 31 October 1845. He was appointed colour sergeant on 1 May 1853. He married Bridget Furlong at Tuam, County Galway, on 10 September 1947, and they had two daughters.

His award of the Victoria Cross was announced in the *London Gazette* of 24 February 1857, and he received the medal from Major General Edward W. Bell, the Lieutenant Governor and General Officer Commanding at Jamaica, on 7 August 1857. He also received the Crimea Medal with *Alma, Inkerman* and *Sebastopol* clasps, the French Military Medal and the Turkish Crimea Medal.

He returned from the Crimea as a sergeant major, but reverted to colour sergeant, and voluntarily transferred to the 2nd West India Regiment in October 1858, gaining a commission as ensign on 13 December 1858. He served in the Biddiboo War in West Africa in 1861, where he suffered a severe attack of fever. He transferred to the 3rd West India Regiment in April 1861 as garrison adjutant at Gambia in West Africa, and was promoted lieutenant on 20 August 1861. He finally transferred to the 4th West India Regiment on 7 April 1862.

Ambrose was still serving with the regiment when he died of fever in Jamaica on 1 January 1863, aged 42, and it is believed that he was buried at Up Park Military Camp Cemetery in Kingston, which was the only official British cemetery at the time. His medals are with the Welsh Regiment Museum in Cardiff Castle, and he is named on a framed memorial in the regimental chapel at Llandaff Cathedral in Cardiff.

John Augustus Conolly

John Augustus Conolly was born on 30 November 1829, at Cliff House in Ballyshannon, County Donegal (some sources give Castletown

House, Celbridge, about 13 miles west of Dublin but in County Kildare.) He was one of a family of ten children to Lieutenant Colonel Edward Michael Conolly of the Donegal Militia, who was Tory Member of Parliament for Donegal from 1831 until his death in 1849, and his wife, Catherine Jane, daughter of Chambre Brabazon Ponsonby Baker MP. Colonel Conolly was magistrate in the counties of Kildare, Dublin and Donegal and a deputy lieutenant in Donegal and Kildare, for both of which shires he served as sheriff.

Most members of the Conolly family went into politics and administration, but John entered the 49th (Hertfordshire) Regiment, and later transferred to the 1st Battalion, Coldstream Guards. His brother, Captain Arthur Wellesley Conolly, entered the 30th (Cambridgeshire) Regiment and was killed in action at Inkerman.

His award of the Victoria Cross was announced in the *London Gazette* of 5 May 1857, and he received the medal at the first investiture. He was also awarded the Crimea Medal with *Alma* and *Sebastopol* clasps, the Turkish Order of the Medjidie (5th Class), the Sardinian Medal of Military Valour and the Turkish Crimea Medal.

On 4 August 1864, he married Ida Charlotte, daughter of Edwyn Burnaby, a brother of the famous Victorian adventurer, Colonel Fred Burnaby, and they had four daughters and a son. Their youngest daughter, Oonagh Edwina, was aged 93 when she died in 1960.

On leaving the army in 1877 John joined the Dublin Metropolitan Police. He died on 28 January 1889, aged 59, at the Magistrate's House in Curragh Camp, County Kildare, and he was buried on Cypress Walk at Mount Jerome Cemetery in Dublin, where there is a headstone. He is also named on his daughter's memorial stone at All Saints' Church in Branston, Lincolnshire. His medals are with the Coldstream Guards Museum in London.

James Owens

James Owens was born in 1827, at Killain, Bailieborough, County Cavan, Ireland. He entered the 49th (Hertfordshire) Regiment.

His award of the Victoria Cross was announced in the *London Gazette* of 24 February 1857, and he received the medal at the first investiture. He also received the Crimea Medal with *Alma, Inkerman* and *Sebastopol* clasps and the Turkish Crimea Medal. The date given on the citation was 30 October 1854, but it is more likely to have been on 26 October.

James became a Yeoman Warder at the Tower of London, and died at Romford in Essex on 20 August 1901, aged 74. He was buried in Christchurch Cemetery at Warley, Brentwood in Essex, where there is a headstone. His medals are with the Duke of Edinburgh's Regiment Museum in Salisbury.

Chapter 7

The Battle of Inkerman

On 4 November 1854, Florence Nightingale and her team of thirty-eight nurses arrived at the hospital in Scutari, and when they eventually got past most of the red tape and petty jealousy they began to make life better for the soldiers. The timing could not have been better, for on the very next day one of the bloodiest battles in British military history was fought.

The Russians tried to relieve pressure on Sebastopol by launching an attack on British positions at Inkerman, with 40,000 men advancing from three directions, supported by 135 guns. Their main objective was the Inkerman Ridge, held by just under 3,000 men of the 2nd Division, and 12 field guns. The mighty force intended to drive the Allies into the sea. The morning of 5 November was cold and wet, and the fierce combat was fought to gain features such as Shell Hill, Home Ridge and the Inkerman Caves, across large areas of mist-shrouded rough terrain. Units did not know how other units were doing, and it was more like several separate battles than just one. Because of this it came to be known as The Soldiers' Battle.

During the early stages of the fighting General Henry Adams and 700 men of the 41st (Welsh) Regiment, and the 49th (Princess Charlotte of Wales' Hertfordshire) Regiment captured the Sandbag Battery, and by 8 o'clock they found themselves defending it against heavy odds. The general had his horse shot from under him, and he received a wound in the ankle which proved fatal. Sergeant George Walters of the 49th Regiment saw his old commanding officer in difficulties, and highly distinguished himself as he charged forward and single-handedly attacked the Russians swarming all around the stricken man. He killed one and drove off the rest, and carried the officer back to the British lines.

Captain Hugh Rowlands of the 41st Regiment showed gallant exertions in holding the ground occupied by his advanced picket against the enemy at the commencement of the battle. One of the advance pickets was Private Thomas Beach of the 55th (Westmoreland) Regiment, who saw Lieutenant Colonel George Carpenter of the 41st Regiment being plundered and stabbed with bayonets by five Russian soldiers as he lay wounded on the ground, having previously received three bullets to his body. Private Beach showed conspicuous gallantry as he ran forward and attacked the Russians, killing two assailants. He then stood over the officer and protected him until some men of the 41st Regiment arrived to offer assistance. However, Colonel Carpenter died of his wounds on the following day.

Having come under fire from enemy grapeshot, Colonel William O'Grady Haly of the 47th (Lancashire) Regiment had been forced to retire gradually with his men, but on the arrival of reinforcements he had galloped his horse forward and led his men in a gallant counter-attack against the foremost Russians, three of whom he cut down, but he was wounded in the leg and unhorsed, and was lying on the ground disabled and unable to move, with a party of Russians moving in to finish him off. Captain Rowlands, Privates Kelly and John McDermond of the Light Company, 47th Regiment, and an unknown bugler of the 30th Regiment, saw that the officer was in great peril and showed intrepid conduct by rushing to his rescue. Private McDermond killed the man who had disabled his officer, and together they held off his assailants and got him to safety. Private Kelly was killed later in the battle.

The men of the 41st and 49th Regiments were eventually overwhelmed by superior numbers and forced out of the position, and the enemy entrenched themselves. They manned the embrasures and parapets of the battery, from where they kept up a most severe fire of musketry.

The 3rd Battalion, Grenadier Guards were among the units which advanced to try to regain the Sandbag Battery. Colonel Hugh Percy had been shot through the arm during the passage of the Alma, but he charged single-handedly into the battery, followed immediately by the Guards. However, he found himself with many men of various regiments, who had charged too far, nearly surrounded by the Russians, and without ammunition. Colonel Percy had been wounded, but using his knowledge of the ground he extricated these men, and passing under a heavy fire from the Russians then in the Sandbag Battery, brought them safe to where ammunition was to be obtained, thereby saving some fifty men, and enabling them to renew the combat. He received the approval of his Royal Highness the Duke of Cambridge for this action on the spot.

A fierce hand-to-hand fight ensued, and a desperately outnumbered party of Grenadiers found themselves pinned down and cut off from the main force. Captain Charles Russell offered to dislodge the party of Russians which had them pinned down and ran forward calling out for volunteers. Sergeant Norman and Privates Anthony Palmer and Bailey responded. As they advanced Major Russell was met by an enemy soldier. The officer aimed his pistol at the Russian and pulled the trigger, but the weapon misfired. The Russian thrust his bayonet forward, but Private Palmer came to his aid and stunned the Russian with a sharp blow to his head. Major Russell re-loaded and shot the enemy soldier dead. The attack was a success, although Russell, wearing no overcoat was a prominent mark for the enemy. He was a man of slight build, yet he was able to tear the rifle from the hands of a Russian soldier.

Captain Peel had joined the officers of the Grenadiers, with ever faithful Midshipman Daniel remaining alongside him. Peel insisted on helping to defend the colours of that regiment, and led seven charges. Captain Russell then rushed forward calling out for volunteers to attack the Russians. Their example of gallantry inspired the ranks of the Guards and they eventually broke out and saved the colours of the battalion from capture (*see 18 October 1854 and 18 June 1855*).

Later Private Palmer moved forward at the head of a band of men who made a desperate charge against superior numbers and saved the colours of the battalion from capture. Even later, the Guards section of the trenches was enfiladed by enemy fire from a farmhouse overlooking them, and ten men were hit. Private Palmer was among a number of men who charged across open ground under heavy fire and succeeded in killing the snipers inside the house. He was later wounded in the head.

Sergeant Knox was present at the battle, and wrote in his diary:

> We Guards immediately formed line and advanced, meeting a warm reception as we closed in, in the form of shot, shell and bullets. The force opposed to us was five-to-one, so the bayonet was levelled and on we rushed, but no stand was made by the enemy. At them we went, loading and firing as quickly as possible, and the foe were in such numbers that one could not miss very easily. The scene that met my gaze was the most awful description, it made

me shudder. The bodies of our opponents were so thick on the ground that for some distance I had to go on tiptoe to pass without touching the bodies.

When the alarm was given by the pickets, the men of the 30th (Cambridgeshire) Regiment advanced in two battalions, the right under Major James Thomas Mauleverer and the left under Major James Patullo; Lieutenant Mark Walker, the son of a Waterloo veteran, who had been slightly wounded in the chest by grape shot and had his horse shot from under him at the Alma, was with the right advance, which was sent down the Post Road to the Barrier on the right of Home Ridge, where they moved towards the wall and lay down. Two battalions of the Russian Borodino Regiment suddenly appeared out of the thick fog not far away and the command was given to open fire. However, their rifles had become wet overnight and therefore would not fire, and as the enemy drew even nearer their situation was becoming desperate. A further 2 battalions appeared at the rear, and 2,500 men were advancing towards them.

Major Mauleverer and Lieutenant Walker noticed that the men were becoming nervous and felt that they might panic. Lieutenant Walker took charge of the situation and distinguished himself by jumping onto the wall and presented his bayonet to encourage his men to advance against very heavy odds. Major Mauleverer and the men took heart from his action and followed him as he jumped down from the wall, and led them straight at the enemy, who were shocked by the sudden attack, and could not see that it was an inferior number of men being led towards them. The tables turned and they were the ones who became panic-stricken. Despite the exhortations of their officers their men turned and bolted, with Lieutenant Walker and his men chasing after them for some distance. Colonel Mauleverer was severely wounded during the action, but recovered enough to receive a second less serious wound during the final attack on the Redan on 8 September 1855.

On 9 June 1855, Captain Walker, by then of the 3rd (East Kent) Regiment, the Buffs, was severely wounded by a piece of howitzer shell and had his right arm amputated on the same night.

It was the first time the 57th and 77th Middlesex Regiments had fought together. They were ordered to recapture the Home Ridge, which had already changed hands three times with furious fighting, and the unit was out of ammunition. Nevertheless, they moved up to the position and lay down along the ridge with their bayonets at the ready. The Russians were already in possession of part of the ridge, but when the artillery came forward through the lines of the 77th, they too advanced, and faced with this combined force the Russians retreated.

Lieutenant Henry Clifford of the 1st Battalion, Rifle Brigade (Prince Consort's Own), the nephew of a baron, was part of the first reinforcements to reach the destroyed camp at Home Ridge, where he saw a large force of Russians emerging out of the fog only about twenty paces away. At first General Buller would not identify them as Russians, but Lieutenant Clifford insisted, and shouted: 'In God's name, fix bayonets and charge!' He gave the order, and the lieutenant urged his men: 'Come on, my lads.' And the next moment they dashed in at the astonished Russians and were soon in hand-to-hand combat with them, bayoneting them in every direction. A Russian came up to Lieutenant Clifford and tried to run him through with his bayonet, but Clifford drew his sword and cut off his arm. A second man saw this and was in the act of getting out of the way when Lieutenant Clifford hit him over the back of his head and he dropped dead at his feet. Another action saved the life of a fellow soldier. Lieutenant Clifford recalled: 'I saw one poor fellow's head carried away by a shot, and some ten or a dozen blown into the air by a shell.'

The British gun batteries had been heavily engaged throughout the battle. Lieutenant Hewett acted with great bravery during the fighting around the Lancaster Battery. When a large force of Russian infantry advanced up the Careenage Ravine to attack his position, Seamen James Gorman, Thomas Reeves, Mark Scholefield, John Woods and Thomas Geoghegan of HMS *Albion*, Naval Brigade, mounted the banquette with the help of the walking wounded soldiers in the trench, and under a heavy fire, made use of the disabled soldiers' muskets, which were loaded and handed to them by others under the parapet. The men are supposed to have said that they: 'wouldn't trust any Ivan getting within bayonet range of the wounded', and they kept up such a rapid and withering fire that they drove the enemy back three times when they were within forty paces of the wounded. Seamen Woods and Geoghegan were killed during the action.

Russian sharpshooters occupied the strategically situated Inkerman caves which overlooked the Lancaster Battery, and the Royal Marines were ordered to take them. As they moved into action, an enemy frigate opened fire on them from the harbour, pinning them down and consequently halted the momentum of the assault. Corporal John Prettyjohn of the Royal Marine Light Infantry led his unit forward in spite of the heavy fire and personally killed four Russians as they succeeded in capturing the caves. However, almost all their ammunition had been expended, and superior numbers of enemy infantry were moving up the hillside in single file to attempt to retake them. Corporal Prettyjohn saw them advancing and called out: 'Well, lads, we are just in for a warming, and it will be every man for himself in a few minutes. Look alive my hearties, and collect all the stones handy, and pile them on the ridge in front of you. When I grip the front man you let go the biggest stones upon those fellows behind.' As soon as the leading Russian reached the level ground, Prettyjohns pushed him backwards, and they all fell, tumbling down the slope under a hail of stones. A volley of bullets then forced them to retreat.

After advancing over rough ground in thick brushwood with his P Battery, Lieutenant Frederick Miller of the Royal Regiment of Artillery, who was the son of a Waterloo veteran, had unlimbered the guns to provide fire support, when the 88th Connaught Rangers poured out of the mist and retired through his battery with a large body of Russians in pursuit. He suddenly found himself and his gunners surrounded by the Russians. And with quick presence of mind Lieutenant Miller at once ordered his men to draw swords and attack the enemy. Lieutenant Miller was on horseback, and personally took on three Russians. The guns were captured, but when cannon fire was opened up on the Russians they fell back and Lieutenant Miller's battery was recovered having not been spiked.

Sergeant Major Andrew Henry of G Battery, 2nd Division, Royal Regiment of Artillery, was 'a fine fellow' in charge of number 6 gun in the battery, which had been placed on the western slope of Home Ridge. A mass of Russian infantry moved up the hill to attack them, and as they charged into the battery 'howling like mad dogs', he and Gunner James Taylor stood firm and defended the gun against overwhelming numbers of the enemy, fighting like fiends, and with Henry slashing at them with his heavy sword. Taylor was slain, and they could easily have killed Henry, but they wanted him alive, and waited until he dropped down with fatigue. In this condition they raced forward and disabled him further by stabbing him about the arms and shoulders, until he fell unconscious from loss of blood. The reason for this was the fact that he was wearing a dress tunic and they thought he was an officer and wanted to take him prisoner so they could claim the reward given for every captured British officer. They dragged him away for some distance then dropped him down on the sodden floor to wait for an escort. Seeing what was happening three of his comrades hurried after them, but one was shot dead, so Sergeant Patrick Conway and Jim McGrath ran to the spot where their comrade lay. They surprised the three Russians and killed them with their swords, and got their badly wounded comrade back to the British lines. He was found to have received twelve bayonet wounds.

Later, a company of the 77th Regiment, and other units, was sent forward to help in the capture of the enemy's most western batteries on Shell Hill. When the attack stalled, Lieutenant William Acton called out that he would go by himself and ran forward about forty paces. However, Private James Tyrell advanced and placed himself beside his leader, and after another man went rushing forward too and they lined up beside them, the rest of the men took heart and the line began to advance again. Faced with this, the Russians decided to withdraw their guns, and this turned out to be the last action of the battle.

Lieutenant Graham wrote to his sister two days after the battle making a reference to Guy Fawkes Night: 'we need no longer to be told to remember the 5th November, for it is a day to be marked red in our annals'. It was stated that the enemy left a greater number of killed and wounded on the field of battle than the entire force of British and French soldiers engaged, and they made no more large-scale attempts to defeat the Allies on the battlefield.

Continuing the story of Edward Tregenza, who was at the Battle of Inkerman. It was stated that he used to tell the following: 'In the early morning of 5 November he saw the Russian army advancing over the plains, so he informed Mr Wood, who at first believed that he had been deceived by a cloud just above the horizon. But the cloud turned out to 'deliver a vigorous assault on the British camp'. Just before his death he met Robert Baden-Powell and told him of this incident, which Baden-Powell in turn told to Sir Evelyn Wood. Sir Evelyn wrote to Edward stating that he remembered him well and expressed the hope of his good health.

Edward also met Florence Nightingale, for whom he had performed some service which had enabled her to 'safely view the conflict, and for this she rewarded him with a sovereign'. When the war was over a regatta by the Allied fleets was held in the Mediterranean Sea. Mr Tregenza rode in the cutter race for the British, who were victorious. He was stated to be one of the best known personalities in New Brighton on the Wirral, where he had lived for forty years. He died on 20 August 1910, at 23 Virginia Road, Wallasey, aged 83.

An interesting set of articles also appeared in Liverpool newspapers on 5 September 1940, entitled *'Regimental Dogs of War'*. One concerned a dog found by a Scots (Fusilier) Guards sentry which had been badly beaten after being thrown over a high wall and into the courtyard at St James's Palace one cold winter night. The sentry had left his post to give the dog first aid and was caught and marched off in disgrace to the guard room, with the grateful dog limping loyally behind him. The officer in charge showed some compassion and forgave the breach of regulations and allowed the soldier to adopt the animal as a regimental pet, and they called him Jack.

At the passage of the Alma the dog contrived to save the life of its master, and then made himself useful by trotting from one of the fallen wounded to another with a flask of brandy. He was wounded in the right paw at Inkerman after charging the enemy several times and caused many casualties. Limping back from one of the charges, he found his master dead and remained at his side until the body was removed, later returning to the spot. The dog was apparently not in the same spirit again.

On Jack's return to Britain, Queen Victoria presented him with a miniature Victoria Cross and a Crimea Medal, which she personally placed around his neck. He was found dead in the snow at the camp one morning. The National Museums of Scotland have a stuffed dog that was the regimental pet of the 1st Battalion, Scots Fusilier Guards, and is stated to have sailed to the Crimea with the regiment. However, this animal is named 'Bob'.

James Gorman

James Gorman was born on 21 August 1834, at Islington in north London. He was the son of Patrick James Gorman, a nurseryman, and his wife, Ann (formerly Furlong).

At the age of 13, James was one of the first boys to be accepted into the Royal Navy as an apprentice, being assigned to HMS *Victory* as boy second class on 2 March 1848. He was 5ft 2in tall, with blue eyes, light-brown hair, and he had a ruddy complexion. He had been vaccinated against smallpox. After six months' training he was transferred to HMS *Rolla*, and having impressed his instructors he was kept on beyond his allotted time to act as an instructor to the next intake of apprentices. He was subsequently appointed for short periods on HMS *Dragon*, HMS *Howe* and HMS *Queen*, before joining HMS *Albion* as a boy first class on 13 July 1850. He was appointed ordinary seaman, second class, on 13 May 1852, and two months later to able seaman. The ship received orders for active service in the Crimea.

His award of the Victoria Cross was announced in the *London Gazette* of 24 February 1857, and his medal was sent care of HMS *Elk* in China in 1857. He also received the Crimea Medal with *Inkerman* and *Sebastopol* clasps and the Turkish Crimea Medal.

He left HMS *Albion* on 5 January 1856, with a 'very good conduct' report, and on 17 March 1856, he was admitted to Haslar Naval Hospital in Gosport for six weeks suffering from rheumatism. He discharged from the Royal Navy in May 1856.

After just two weeks ashore he re-enlisted for the Chatham Volunteers for duty on HMS *Elk*. He was awarded a good conduct badge on 26 May 1857, and was made captain of the afterguard on 21 February 1858. He took part in operations along the Canton River from 28 December 1857–5 January 1858, being present at the taking of Fatchan and Canton, for which he received the Second China War Medal, 1857–60, with *Canton* clasp.

HMS *Elk* was one of the first ships of the Royal Navy to become part of the Australia station and Captain of the Afterguard Gorman visited the colony on three occasions. He was paid off at Sheerness on 21 August 1860, and on 7 January 1863 he sailed from Plymouth to seek a new life in Australia.

He resided at 259 Kent Street, overlooking Sydney Harbour, and found work as a sail maker. He moved to a dockside house in Sussex Street, where he met Marianne (Mary Ann) Jackson, and they married in Sydney on 10 November 1864. They had a daughter named Annie Elizabeth, but his wife died of fever in 1866. James gained employment as a drill master and gunnery instructor on the Nautical School Ship *Vernon* on 17 April 1867, being appointed master at arms responsible for the discipline and welfare of 135 boys. He was appointed second mate on 1 April 1878, a position he retained until 7 June 1881.

He became disappointed that HMS *Vernon* ceased teaching nautical skills and he transferred to the ordnance department as foreman of the powder magazines at the naval stores complex on Spectacle Island on the Parramatta River, Sydney. Six weeks after moving to Spectacle Island, James married Deborah King, and he, Deborah and Annie lived in a stone cottage.

James suffered a stroke on 18 October 1882, aged 48, at Spectacle Island, and he was buried in the Pioneers Memorial Park, Leichhardt,

Sydney, which is also known as the first Church of England Cemetery, Balmain. A strong detachment of officers and boys from NSS *Vernon* were present. The original headstone was destroyed as the cemetery was transformed into Pioneers Memorial Park. There is a plaque on the memorial stone archway entrance to the cemetery dedicated to him, and one on the Balmain War Memorial. His Victoria Cross is held privately.

There is a death certificate for a James Devereux Gorman, who died in Southwark, London, in 1889. This man claimed he was James Gorman VC and has sometimes been wrongly confused with him because they served alongside each other during the Crimean War, and James Devereux was present at the engagement for which Lieutenant Hewett was awarded the Victoria Cross at Little Inkerman.

Thomas Reeves

Thomas Reeves was born at 50 King Street in Portsmouth in 1828. He was a baker's apprentice prior to joining the Royal Navy in August 1846.

His award of the Victoria Cross was announced in the *London Gazette* of 24 February 1857, and he received the medal at the first investiture. He also received the Crimea Medal with *Inkerman* and *Sebastopol* clasps and the Turkish Crimea Medal.

He remained on HMS *Albion,* and became gunners mate and captain of the foretop in 1856, before volunteering for an extra ten years and taking a gunnery course on HMS *Excellent.* He was just 32 when he was discharged for age and infirmity in 1860. He had married on his return from the Crimea.

Thomas had suffered from consumption (tuberculosis) for three years and was aged only 34 when he died at his home in King Street on Portsea Island, Portsmouth, on 4 August 1862. He was buried in an unmarked public grave at Portsea General Cemetery, which is now Mile End Gardens, part of the P & O Continental Ferry Port Terminal. His final resting place was marked by a commemorative plaque placed at the port by the Greenwich Royal Naval Association Victoria Cross Memorial Fund in 1999. Thomas Reeves Court in Portsmouth is named after him. His Victoria Cross is now displayed on rotation at the Lord Ashcroft Gallery, as part of the 'Extraordinary Heroes' exhibition at the Imperial War Museum in London.

Mark Scholefield

Mark Scholefield was born in London on 16 April 1828. He joined the Royal Navy as boy second class in 1846, and served on HMS *Tortoise* the guard-ship at Ascension Island. He joined HMS *Albion* as an ordinary seaman in October 1850, and was later coxswain of the barge. He was 5ft 8in tall, with a fresh complexion, fair hair and hazel-brown eyes, with a crown tattooed on his left hand.

His award of the Victoria Cross was announced in the *London Gazette* of 24 February 1857, and he received the medal at the East India station in 1857. He also received the Crimea Medal with *Inkerman* and *Sebastopol* clasps and the Turkish Crimea Medal.

After paying off the *Albion* in January 1856, he joined the sloop HMS *Acorn* for active service in the Opium War in China, spending nine months on the Canton River, taking part as the only sloop in a flotilla of eight ships in the engagement with Chinese junks at Fashtan Creek on 1 June 1857, and the bombardment and capture of Canton and its governor in December 1857. For his service he received the China War Medal, 1857–60, with *Canton* clasp.

Mark gained the rank of quartermaster and petty officer, but he died at sea on board *Acorn*, on 15 February 1858, aged 29, from 'one of numerous perils against which seamen of the day were defenceless'. It is believed he was buried at sea. His Victoria Cross is now displayed on rotation at the Lord Ashcroft Gallery, as part of the 'Extraordinary Heroes' exhibition at the Imperial War Museum in London, although there is no China Medal with the set.

John Prettyjohns

John Prettyjohns was born on 11 June 1823, at Dean Coombe in the parish of Dean Prior, Buckfastleigh in Devon. He worked as an agricultural labourer before enlisting for unlimited service in the 59th Company, Royal Marine Light Infantry, at Stonehouse Barracks in Plymouth, on 10 June 1844. He embarked on HMS *Melampus* on 22 March 1845, and sailed to the southeast coast of America, before moving on to the East Indies. On 28 June 1845 he was flogged for a misdemeanour and his name appeared in the defaulters' book for the only time in his career. He joined HMS *Bellerophon* on 7 November 1850, being promoted corporal on 15 January 1852.

HMS *Bellerophon* was with the Allied Fleet which blockaded Sebastopol Harbour, and began bombarding the town on 17 October 1854.

When a Royal Marine Battalion was requested to go ashore to relieve some of the troops in the trenches, Corporal Prettyjohn volunteered his services, and took part in the naval bombardment of Balaclava. On his return home he was promoted sergeant on 16 January 1856.

He became the first Royal Marine to be awarded the Victoria Cross when it was announced in the *London Gazette* on 24 February 1857, and he was presented with the medal while in China. He also received the Crimea Medal with *Balaclava, Inkerman* and *Sebastopol* clasps, the Turkish Crimea Medal and the Sardinian Medal of Military Valour.

He married his distant cousin, Elizabeth Prettyyjohn, on 10 February 1850, and early in 1857 his first daughter, Elizabeth (Bessie), was born. On 12 March 1857, he sailed for Hong Kong on HMS *Sanspareil*, where he was promoted colour sergeant on 29 April 1857. Soon after his arrival news that the Indian Mutiny had broke out reached the island and he was among a detachment of Royal Marines which joined HMS *Shannon* and sailed for Calcutta on 16 July 1857. He was stationed at Fort William until transferring to HMS *Assistance*, sailing as part of the 1st China Battalion for service in the Second China War, 1857–60. On 28 December 1857, he took part in the capture of Canton, for which he received the China Medal with *Canton* clasp. His last tour of duty was with HMS *Tribune* at Vancouver Island and San Juan Island, returning to England on 17 December 1863. He was discharged on 16 June 1865, having served for just over twenty-one years, and he received the Royal Naval Long Service Good Conduct Medal.

He settled with his family at 13 Hester Street, in the working class district of Chorlton-on-Medlock, Manchester. Being a fit and muscular man, he was able to find work as a coal carter. Afterwards he became the steward at the Whalley Range Golf Club in Withington. His second daughter, Alice Maud, was born in 1865.

John died at his home on 20 January 1887, aged 64, and he was buried with military honours in Southern Cemetery, Manchester. Bessie died two years later and his wife died in 1912. Alice lived to the grand old age of 95. His medals are at the Royal Marines Museum in Southsea, Prettyjohn House at the Royal Marines Barracks in Eastney is named after him, and the Royal Marines hold a procession at the cemetery each autumn in his honour.

Frederick Miller

Frederick Miller was born on 10 November 1831, at Radway Grange in Radway-under-Edgehill, Warwickshire. The area is the site of the famous Battle of Edgehill in 1642, during the English Civil War. He was the youngest of four sons in a family of seven children to Lieutenant Colonel Fiennes Sanderson Miller, CB, of the 6th (Inniskilling) Dragoons, who was wounded at the Battle of Waterloo in 1815, when a cannon ball shattered his thigh, and he became a magistrate and deputy lieutenant for the county of Warwick. His great-grandfather was a well-known architect and landscape gardener. His mother was Sibella, daughter of the Revd Philip Storey of Lockington Hall in Leicestershire (now converted to offices). Two of his brothers became army officers and the other went into the church. Frederick was educated at Rugby School.

He became the first Warwickshire man to be awarded the Victoria Cross when it was announced in the *London Gazette* on 16 May 1859, and he received the medal from Queen Victoria at Buckingham Palace, on 8 June 1859. He also received the Crimea Medal with *Alma, Balaclava, Inkerman* and *Sebastopol* clasps, the French Legion of Honour, the Turkish Order of the Medjidieh (5th Class) and the Turkish Crimea Medal.

He attained the rank of lieutenant colonel, and he was a talented painter in water colours, and a collection of forty-three of his inscribed canvases were sold at auction in 2009. They are dated between May 1869 and October 1871, and include views of the environs of Baroda in India and Jamestown in St Helena.

Frederick died on 17 February 1874, aged 42, at the Star Fort, Castle of Good Hope in Cape Town. He was first interred in St Peter's Cemetery and later his remains were relocated at St Peter's Ossuary Memorial Garden in Observatory, Cape Town. His name appears on the family vault at St Peter's churchyard in Radway. His Victoria Cross was purchased by Lord Ashcroft in 2009, and is displayed on rotation at the Lord Ashcroft Gallery, as part of the 'Extraordinary Heroes' exhibition at the Imperial War Museum in London. His father's uniform and battle notes were passed down the generations of the family until they were sold at auction in 2010 for a record amount for such a set of items. Radway Grange is now a listed building of historic interest.

Andrew Henry

Andrew Henry was born on 1 November 1823, at Woolwich in London. He entered the Royal Regiment of Artillery, where he served as a trumpeter in the Royal Artillery band.

His award of the Victoria Cross was announced in the *London Gazette* of 24 February 1857, and he received the medal at the first investiture.

He also received the Crimea Medal with *Alma, Balaclava, Inkerman* and *Sebastopol* clasps and the Turkish Crimea Medal.

Having been given a commission in the Land Transport Corps on 15 May 1855, he was promoted to captain on 28 November 1855. Henry and Sergeant Conway met again at Aldershot some years later.

Andrew died on 14 October 1870, aged 46, at the Royal Citadel in Plymouth, which is still a military base, and he was buried at Ford Cemetery in Plymouth, where a headstone in the shape of a Victoria Cross was erected in 1952. A wreath-laying ceremony is still held annually at his grave by members of the Plymouth Royal Artillery Association, and he is named on the memorial at the Royal Artillery Chapel in Woolwich. His medals are with the Royal Artillery Museum in Woolwich.

Henry Hugh Manvers Percy

Henry Hugh Manvers Percy was born on 22 August 1817, at Burwood House in Convent Lane, Cobham, Surrey (which has been home to the Notre Dame School since 1937). He was the fifth child and third son of George Percy, Lord Lovaine of Alnwick (later 2nd Earl of Beverley), and his wife, Louisa Harcourt (formerly Stuart-Wortley), the daughter of the Honourable James Stuart-Wortley-Mackenzie, a British politician and soldier, and son of the 3rd Earl of Bute. His ancestor, Major Henry Percy, was the man chosen by the Duke of Wellington to take the news of his victory at Waterloo back to England. He was educated at Eton College.

He entered the 3rd Battalion, Grenadier Guards, as ensign, on 1 July 1836, and on the outbreak of the Crimean War the Grenadier Guards were among the first troops to mobilise.

He became the first Surrey-born man to be awarded the Victoria Cross when it was announced in the *London Gazette* of 5 May 1857, as the most senior officer to be awarded the medal during the Crimean campaign and he was the first Guardsman to wear it when he received it at the first investiture. He was tasked with commanding the sixty-two recipients who were present that day. He also received the Crimea Medal with *Alma, Balaclava, Inkerman* and *Sebastopol* clasps, the French Legion of Honour, the Turkish Order of the Medjidie (4th Class) and the Turkish Crimea Medal.

From 29 June 1855 to 10 February 1865 he was aide-de-camp to the Queen. He became styled as Lord Henry Percy after his father became the 5th Duke of Northumberland in 1865. That year he was elected Member of Parliament for North Northumberland, and served until 1868.

During the Franco-Prussian War of 1870 he was sent to Sedan by the Duke of Cambridge as an observer with the Prussian Army. He was invested Knight Commander of the Bath (KCB) in 1873, and he was appointed a Commander of the Order of the Tower and Sword, the highest award in the Portuguese honours system. He gained the rank of general in 1877.

He remained unmarried, and was found dead in his bed at his residence, 40 Eaton Square, Belgravia, London, on 3 December 1877, aged 60, and he was buried in the Percy family vault, the Northumberland Vault of St Nicholas' Chapel in Westminster Abbey. His name appears on the 'For Valour' memorial in the cloisters at Eton College, and there is a memorial cross dedicated to him on a wall at Alnwick Castle in Northumberland. His medals are also at Alnwick Castle.

Charles Russell

Charles Russell was born on 22 June 1826, at Sothern Hill near Reading. He was the second, but eldest surviving son of Sir Henry Russell, 2nd Baronet, and British 'Resident' at the court of Hyderabad in India. He was the first of the four recipients of the Victoria Cross for the Crimea to be educated at Eton.

He was first commissioned as an ensign in the 35th (Royal Sussex) Regiment, on 25 August 1843, becoming lieutenant on 9 June 1846. He transferred to the 3rd Battalion, Grenadier Guards, in 1847, and was promoted captain on 13 September 1853. He inherited Swallowfield Park, near Reading, from his father in 1852.

At the outbreak of the Crimean War the Grenadier Guards were among the first troops to mobilise, taking part in the passage of the Alma, and took a supportive role in the Battle of Balaclava.

His award of the Victoria Cross was announced in the *London Gazette* of 24 February 1857, and he received the medal at the first investiture. He also received the Crimean Medal with *Alma, Balaclava, Inkerman* and *Sebastopol* clasps, the French Legion of Honour, Turkish Order of the Medjidie (5th Class) and the Turkish Crimea Medal.

He was promoted major on 2 November 1855, while still in the Crimea, and he retired as lieutenant colonel in 1868. He was elected Member of Parliament for Berkshire, with Robert Loyd-Lindsay, from

1865–8; and for Westminster from 1874 until his death. Lord Palmerston appointed him chairman of the Peruvian Bondholders Committee, to overlook a possible crisis between the United States and Peru.

Charles died unmarried on 13 April 1883, aged 56, at Swallowfield Park. He was buried in the family vault inside All Saints' Church at Swallowfield, which has access from the outside next to the church wall. There is also a commemorative stained-glass window inside the church. His name appears on the 'For Valour' memorial in the cloisters at Eton College. A sash he wore during his army career is held in the collection at the National Army Museum in London. His medals are with the Guards Museum at Wellington Barracks in London.

Anthony Palmer

Anthony Palmer was born at Somerford, near Brereton Green, Congleton, Cheshire, on 10 March 1819, and spent his early life at Cheetham Hill in Manchester. His parents were James and Mary Palmer. He began working in the salesroom of a Manchester warehouse, spending his spare time teaching at the local Sunday school.

He enlisted into the 3rd Battalion, Grenadier Guards, as 3571 Private Palmer on 14 March 1838, at Cross Lane Barracks in Salford. He was nearly 6ft tall and stockily built, with a fresh complexion, grey eyes and dark-brown hair. One of his Home duties was as Guardsman at Windsor Castle, where he was several times presented before the royal family.

In his chequered army career he was convicted of desertion, absent without leave or drunkenness on twelve occasions. He was promoted corporal on 15 April 1840, 3 January 1855 and 27 August 1855, but on each occasion he had his stripes taken away.

His award of the Victoria Cross was announced in the *London Gazette* of 24 February 1857, and he received the medal at the first investiture. He also received the Crimea Medal with *Alma, Balaclava, Inkerman* and *Sebastopol* clasps, the Turkish Order of the Medjidie (5th Class) and the Bentinck Medal.

It was the general opinion that his drinking habits prevented him from gaining a commission. In spite of this he was a popular man among his comrades, being 'most dignified and upright in physique'. On leaving the army on 24 March 1863, he was presented with a pocket watch and an illuminated address, having served over twenty-six years, for which he received the Long Service Good Conduct Medal. His intended place of residence was York Street in Westminster, London.

In civilian life he became a total abstainer from drink, and on 18 June 1864 he joined the Victoria Dock Company of London as a clerk. In 1881 he was living in Poplar on the Isle of Dogs and was Chief Constable of the Millwall Docks Police. Fellow ex-Guardsman Alfred Ablett also lived in Poplar and worked for the Docks Police. He married his wife, Susannah, who came from Spoxton in Somerset, and they lived at 1 Dock House in Millwall. He became a volunteer captain in the 5th (Plaistow and Victoria Docks) Essex Rifle Volunteer Corps, on 6 May 1874; a position from which he retired in 1882.

Anthony eventually came back north to settle in Manchester, where he spent the last few years of his life in quiet retirement at a cottage called 'The Glen' in Katherine Street, Higher Crumpsall. His heart began to fail him and he died on 12 December 1892, aged 73. He was buried with military honours in the family grave at Heywood Cemetery, Rochdale. The inscription on the headstone reads: 'An Upright, Valorous, God-Fearing Hero; Much Beloved'. The grave was renovated and a commemoration plaque was erected at the church chapel in 1992. In 2014 Rochdale Council re-named a street in Heywood Pvt Anthony Palmer VC Parade in honour of his bravery.

His Victoria Cross was stolen during a fight in a bar and a replica was struck for him on the instruction of Queen Victoria. The original was later recovered and his medals are now with the Guards Museum at Wellington Barracks in London, where there is a portrait painting of him in the Officers' Mess.

Hugh Rowlands

Hugh Rowlands was born on 6 May 1828, at Plastirion House (the gentle mansion) in Llanrug, Caernarfon (now Gwynedd), Wales. He was the son of John Rowlands, a gentleman landowner and heir to the Plastirion Estate. His father was a deputy lieutenant for Caernarfonshire, a Justice of the Peace and an officer in the Caernarfonshire Militia. His mother was Elizabeth Anne (formerly Hastwell). He had an older brother named John, who became a solicitor, and a sister named Elizabeth. His family claimed descent from Bleddyn ap Cynfyn, Prince of Powys, and Dafydd ap Llywelyn, Prince of Gwynedd. They employed seven servants. Hugh was educated at Beaumaris Grammar School (The David Hughes School) from 1837–42, and at John Taylor's Cramming Academy in Woolwich in 1849.

He was commissioned as ensign by purchase in the 41st (Welsh) Regiment, on 25 September 1849, becoming lieutenant on 21 April 1851.

He served in Ireland, the Ionian Islands and Malta before receiving orders for active service in the Crimea. He became captain by purchase of the Grenadier Company while on active service in the East on 24 August 1854. When an officer was asked to name one person who did more than any other during the campaign he named Hugh Rowlands of the 41st Regiment.

He became the first Welshman and Freemason to perform a deed which was rewarded with the Victoria Cross when it was announced in the *London Gazette* of 24 February 1857, and he received the medal from Major General, Sir Josias Cloete, at the Barbados station in the West Indies, on 5 August 1857. He also received the Crimea Medal with *Alma, Inkerman* and *Sebastopol* clasps, the French Legion of Honour, the Turkish Order of the Medjidie (5th Class) and the Turkish Crimea Medal.

On his return home he received a civic reception from the people of Caernarfon, who presented him with a Mameluke scimitar Sword of Honour in Caernarfon Castle. He married Isabella Jane Barrow in 1867, who was the daughter of Thomas James Raikes Barrow of the Royal Navy, who came from Ryelands in Randwick near Stroud. They had a daughter and a son named Hugh Barrow, who was born on 22 January 1870, and died from wounds he received during the Battal of Daratoleh in Somalia, on 22 April 1903, while serving as a captain with the King's African Rifles.

He served in the West Indies and several Home stations, and he was in command of the 34th (Border) Regiment in 1875, before embarking for India, where he took command of the Welsh Regiment. He was special service officer in South Africa in 1878–9, being appointed commandant of the Transvaal in 1878, and served the colony as a Justice of the Peace. He served as aide-de-camp to Lord Chelmsford, the commander-in-chief of British forces in South Africa, and later he led an expedition to assault the stronghold of Sekhukhuni, chief of the Pedi tribe, which was aborted. He was commander of the town of Pretoria early in 1879, which was under threat of Boers demanding independence, a situation which was resolved without any violence. He served as local brigadier general in charge of a brigade during the latter stages of the Zulu War of 1879. For his service he received the South Africa Medal with *1878–79* clasp.

His latter service was spent in India, where he commanded the Bangalore Division of the Madras Army, taking temporary command of the Madras Army on two occasions. On returning to Britain he was commander-in-chief of the Scotland Division from 1894 until his retirement as general in 1896, and in 1897 he was appointed colonel of the Duke of Wellington's Regiment, which he retained until his death.

Having been appointed lieutenant general in 1890, Queen Victoria appointed him lieutenant for the Tower of London in 1893, and he was a deputy lieutenant and a Justice of the Peace for Caernarfon. For his distinguished service he was appointed Knight Commander, Order of the Bath (KCB) in 1898.

Sir Hugh died at Plastirion on 1 August 1909, aged 81, and he was buried at St Michael's churchyard in Llanrug, also known as the old cemetery Eglwys Mihangel Sant, where there is a headstone. He is named on a framed memorial at Llandaf Cathedral in Cardiff; his father erected a monument of pointed stones in the fields of Plastirion to commemorate his Victoria Cross action. His medals are with the Welsh Regiment Museum in Cardiff Castle, who also have his Sword of Honour and infantry officer's sword, his sash and forage cap.

John McDermond

John McDermond is believed to have been born in 1832, in the borough poorhouse in Glasgow, because that was where he attested for the 47th (Lancashire) Regiment, in October 1846, but his service record states Clackmannan as his place of birth.

His award of the Victoria Cross was announced in the *London Gazette* of 24 February 1857, and he received the medal when he returned from overseas duty, from Major General, Sir James Yorke Scarlett on the parade ground at Southsea Common in Portsmouth on 12 March 1858. He also received the Crimea Medal with *Alma*, *Inkerman* and *Sebastopol* clasps, the French Military Medal and the Turkish Crimea Medal.

He saw further service in the Ionian Islands, Malta, Gibraltar and Canada, before being invalided out of the army in 1862, for an injury which was recorded as being: 'inflammation of the right ankle joint in consequence of a strain received on duty on board ship in passage to Canada, about 1 July 1861.

John is believed to have died of typhus in Glasgow, on 22 July 1868, aged 35. He was described as a 'pensioner', but this probably refers to the army pension he would have received because of his injury. He was buried in an unmarked grave at the Parochial Board Ground, Woodside Cemetery (Paisley Old Cemetery) under the name of John McDiarmid. Because a person of that name died in the poorhouse at Paisley on 9 November 1868, some sources say that this was the Crimean VC holder.

Soon after the Crimean campaign a series of pictures was produced by the artist Louis Desanges, which included John McDermond's Victoria Cross action. They were on display at the Crystal Palace for many years, before coming into the possession of Lord Wantage, and the one depicting John McDermond is now in the Queen's Lancashire Regiment Museum at Fulwood Barracks in Preston. He is commemorated on the Glasgow Victoria Cross Memorial in Glasgow Cathedral. The whereabouts of his Victoria Cross is not known.

George Walters

George Walters was born on 15 September 1829, at Newport Pagnell in Buckinghamshire. He was the third son of seven children to James Walters, an innkeeper in the town, and his wife, Jane (formerly Green).

He became the first Buckinghamshire-born man to be awarded the Victoria Cross when it was announced in the *London Gazette* of 24 February 1857, and he received the medal at the first investiture. He also received the Crimea Medal with *Alma, Inkerman* and *Sebastopol* clasps and the Turkish Crimea Medal.

George married Mary Ann Norman at the Parish Church of St Peter and St Paul in Newport Pagnell, on 8 September 1856. Now with marital responsibilities, he left the army on 5 January 1857, and joined the Metropolitan Police as Constable 444 of R Division in Deptford, where they made their home at 10 Lucas Street. James Isaac was born on 21 June 1857, George was born in the following year and Ephraim Robert a decade later.

After a short period he resigned from the police on 26 October 1857, and joined the Regent's Park Police as a park constable. The family lived at West Lodge House, Park Crescent, Marylebone (the gatehouse to Regent's Park). During the 1871 census George is recorded as a visitor of the Mapley family at North End in Newport Pagnell.

After suffering with phthisis (pulmonary tuberculosis) for several years, George died at West Lodge House on 3 June 1872, aged 43, and he was buried in the City of London Cemetery, now named the East Finchley Cemetery, London. A headstone was erected at his grave by the Royal Berkshire Regiment in 1997. A commemorative plaque was unveiled and a memorial panel displayed at the Newport Pagnell Royal British Legion for 'A Gallant Son of Newport Pagnell'. His medals are with the Rifles (Berkshire and Wiltshire) Museum in Salisbury.

Thomas Beach

Thomas Beach was born in Dundee in 1824. He entered the 92nd Highlanders as 3493 Private Beach on 30 April 1840, and he was posted to several locations. When his unit was serving at the garrison in Gibraltar he answered a request for volunteers for other units for active service in the Crimea and joined the 55th (Westmoreland) Regiment.

His award of the Victoria Cross was announced in the *London Gazette* of 24 February 1857, and he received the medal with Major Elton from General J. Ferguson, the officer commanding at Gibraltar, on 20 July 1857. He also received the Crimea Medal with *Alma, Inkerman* and *Sebastopol* clasps and the Turkish Crimea Medal.

He returned to the 92nd Highlanders. During the rest of his career he was awarded two good conduct badges, however, his name appears twenty-one times in the regimental defaulter's book, and he was twice tried by court marshal, probably due to excessive drinking habits. He was stationed at Perth in 1861, and he left the army in June 1863.

Thomas became a railway labourer, and died from the effects of alcohol poisoning at the Royal Infirmary in Dundee, on 24 August 1864, aged 40, and he was buried in an unmarked grave in poor ground at the extensive Eastern Necropolis burial ground in Dundee, although the exact location of his grave is not known. Commemorative benches dedicated to him and Private Peter Grant were placed at the cemetery in 2003. Private Grant of the 93rd Highlanders was one of seventeen men awarded the Victoria Cross for gallantry during the attack on the Sikandar Bagh at Lucknow on 16 November 1857, the second most Victoria Crosses awarded for a single action after the first attack on the Redan.

A stamp was issued in 2006 by the island of Kiribati in the Pacific Ocean commemorating Private Beach's Victoria Cross action, which had been taken from a sketch which had appeared in the *Illustrated London News* at the time of the Crimean War. His name appears on the Border Regiment Victoria Cross Memorial at Carlisle Castle. His Victoria Cross was purchased on behalf of the Maharaja of Patiala, Bhupendra Singh, in the 1920s and is one of the five Victoria Crosses, including John Taylor and George Fiott Day, kept in the Sheesh Mahal Museum Collection, housed in Patiala, Punjab, India. Apparently, access to view them is difficult.

Mark Walker

Mark Walker was born on 24 November 1827, at Gore Point, Finea, County Westmeath, Ireland. He was the eldest of three sons of Captain Alexander

Walker, who had distinguished himself during the Peninsular War with the 38th (1st Staffordshire) Regiment when he saved the colours of the regiment at Talavera having torn them from the pole and tied them around his waist, and his wife Elizabeth (formerly Elliott). His brother was Sir Samuel Walker, 1st Baronet, who became Liberal Member of Parliament for Londonderry. All three Walker boys were educated at Arlington House in Portarlington. His brother, Sir Samuel Walker, 1st Baronet, became Liberal Member of Parliament for Londonderry, and Alexander Walker joined his father's old regiment.

He was gazetted as ensign in the 30th (Cambridgeshire) Regiment, on 25 September 1846. He was promoted lieutenant on 4 February 1854, and became acting adjutant with the 30th Regiment from 30 December 1854–14 May 1855. Because of his wound he was sent home on 7 July 1855, and later joined the depot at Winchester, being promoted brevet major on 6 June 1856, for his service in the Crimea. After two years in Ireland he joined the Buffs in Corfu.

His award of the Victoria Cross was announced in the *London Gazette* of 4 June 1858, and he received the medal in November 1858, from Major General, Sir George Butler, the general officer commanding the Ionian garrison on Corfu. He also received the Crimea Medal with *Alma, Inkerman* and *Sebastopol* clasps, the Turkish Order of the Medjidie (5th Class) and the Turkish Crimea Medal.

Soon after receiving his Victoria Cross he went with the regiment to India. On 22 November 1859, he proceeded with a wing of the regiment to Canton, for active service in the Second China War, being appointed brigade major of the 4th Brigade. He took part in the capture of Chusan, the Battle of Sinho, and in the assault on the Taku Forts. For his service he was Mentioned in Despatches and received the Second China War Medal, 1857–60, with *Pekin* and *Taku Forts* clasps. He received the brevet of lieutenant colonel on 15 February 1861.

He arrived back in England on 15 April 1862, and was quartered at various depots, being in command of the company depot. He was promoted brevet colonel on 15 February 1869, and on 3 August 1870 he was advanced to a regimental majority in the 1st battalion quartered at Sitapur in Oude. He joined them in January 1871, and served at Benares, Lucknow and Calcutta.

On 10 December 1873, he was appointed to the command of the 45th Sherwood Foresters, stationed at Rangoon, and on leaving the Buffs at Calcutta he was given a rousing farewell by the officers and men. From 4 August 1875–4 November 1879, he commanded a brigade at Kamptu in Madras, being promoted major general on 11 November 1878. He had been appointed Commander of the Bath (CB) on 24 May 1875, which was Queen Victoria's birthday.

In 1881 he married Catharine, the daughter of a barrister, Robert Bruce Chichester, of Arlington Court, Arlington near Barnstaple, who was a brother of the First Baron of Arlington.

From 4 August 1883–31 March 1884, he commanded a brigade at Aldershot, and from 1 April 1884–31 March 1888, he was major general at Gibraltar. He was promoted lieutenant general on 16 December 1888, and was appointed general on 5 February 1893. He retired from the army after forty-six years' service on 1 April 1893. He was appointed Knight, Commander of the Bath on 3 June 1893. On 27 September 1900, he became colonel of the Sherwood Foresters.

Sir Mark lived for many years in retirement at 10 Castle Avenue in Folkestone. He died on 18 July 1902, aged 74, at the home of his wife's parents at Arlington Court, and he was buried at Cheriton Road Cemetery in Folkestone, where there is a headstone. There are commemorative plaques in Canterbury Cathedral and Blackburn Cathedral; and at Castlepollard Church in County Westmeath. There is a portrait of him, and what is said to be a vase he looted from Peking held at the Royal Museum and Art Gallery in Canterbury.

Lady Walker left an oil painting of General Walker, and a set of miniatures of his medals, along with the watch and grey overcoat he wore at Inkerman, to the 1st Battalion, the East Lancashire Regiment. She also endowed a bed at the Union Jack Club in his memory, and there is a small painting of him at the United Services Club in Pall Mall, London. His medals were with the Buffs Regimental Museum in Canterbury, until being transferred to the National Army Museum in London.

Henry Hugh Clifford

Henry Hugh Clifford was born on 12 September 1826, at Irnham Hall near Grantham (now an exclusive hotel and wedding venue). He was the third son of four in the family of six children to Hugh Charles Clifford, 7th Baron Clifford of Chudleigh, and his wife, Mary Lucy, the only daughter of Cardinal Thomas Weld of Lulworth Castle in Dorset. His parents were second cousins, and the family home is Ugbrooke House in Chudleigh near Newton Abbott. He was sent to be educated at Stonyhurst College in Lancashire.

He was commissioned as 2nd Lieutenant in the 1st Battalion, Rifle Brigade (Prince Consort's Own), on 7 August 1846. In the following year he first saw active service at the Cape of Good Hope during the 7th Cape Frontier War against Xhosa warriors, and against the Boers until their submission at Weinberg. He went to the South Africa again for service against the Xhosas in the 8th Cape Frontier War of 1850–3, where he remained until November 1853. For his service he received the South Africa Medal, 1834–53.

The Russian whose arm he had severed was taken prisoner, and Lieutenant Clifford met him again expressing his relief that he had survived, and enquired about his welfare afterwards. He was appointed deputy assistant quartermaster general in May 1855, and remained in the Crimea until the end of hostilities, when he was promoted to brevet major. General Brown later said that he was 'universally admitted to be one of the most gallant and most promising officers in the British army'.

He became the first Lincolnshire-born man to be awarded the Victoria Cross when it was announced in the *London Gazette* of 24 February 1857, and he became the first member of the Rifle Brigade to wear the medal when he received it at the first investiture. He also received the Crimea Medal with *Alma, Inkerman* and *Sebastopol* clasps, the French Legion of Honour (5th Class), the Turkish Order of the Medjidie (5th Class) and the Turkish Crimea Medal.

On 21 March 1857, he married Josephine Mary, the daughter of Joseph Anstice, a professor at King's College in London, and they had eight children. Their sixth child, Hugh Charles, born at Roehampton in 1866, was knighted for his service as a British colonial administrator. His father died in 1858.

He then saw active service in the Second China War as assistant quartermaster general present during the operations from December 1857–January 1858, which resulted in the capture of Canton. For his service he received the Second China War Medal, 1857–60, with *Canton* clasp, and the brevet of lieutenant colonel.

On his return to England he was assistant quartermaster general at Aldershot from 1860–4, held a similar appointment at headquarters from 1865–8, was aide-de-camp to the commander-in-chief from 1870–3 and was assistant adjutant general at headquarters from 1873–5.

He was selected to proceed to South Africa early in 1879, to take charge of the communications of Lord Chelmsford between Durban and the forces in the field, during the Anglo-Zulu War. His task was difficult, but with his administrative and logistic capabilities and his experience of warfare in the region, with untiring energy he soon brought everything to order.

He had been made Companion of the Order of the Bath (CB) on 2 June 1869, and was appointed Knight Commander, Order of St Michael and St George (KCMG) on 19 December 1879. He served as general officer commanding the eastern district in Colchester from April–September 1882. However, he was diagnosed with cancer and was obliged to retire.

Sir Henry died on 12 August 1883, aged 56, at Ugbrooke House, and he was buried in the family vault in the private crypt of St Cyprian's Chapel at Ugbrooke House, where there is a plaque, and there is a marble family plaque at Buckfastleigh Abbey in Devon He is named on the Rifle Brigade Roll of Fame Memorial at Winchester Cathedral. His Victoria Cross and other medals are still held by his family, along with his camp bed and some of the many watercolours he painted on active service in the Crimea. Others are kept in the collection of the Royal Green Jackets in Winchester.

Sir Henry's second son, Brigadier General Henry Clifford DSO, of the Suffolk Regiment, was killed in action on the Somme in 1916, and six of his grandsons were killed in action during the First World War.

Chapter 8

Winter, 1854–5

The Crimean winter of 1854–5 was the most severe for many years, and prompted Tsar Nicholas to remark that the weather produced his three most effective generals – January, February and March – which he expected to break the spirit of the Allied army. A disaster had already occurred on 14 November 1854, when a hurricane devastated the Crimea. Sergeant Major George Smith of the 11th Hussars was sitting in his tent waiting for the coffee, or 'warm, dirty water and sugar' as he described it, 'when all of a sudden, without any warning, came a mighty rush of wind accompanied by driving rain', which increased to a hurricane and blew everything away. Twenty-one British ships were smashed to pieces, many against the rocks in the harbour at Balaclava, and *The Prince* went down with all hands on board, along with the warm clothing, footwear, blankets and medical supplies. Sergeant Major Smith lamented: 'This was a wretched night for tens of thousands.' As the months drew on conditions became almost unbearable, and both armies spent most of their time trying to survive the freezing conditions half-starved in the miserable camps. Hundreds of men and animals weakened by starvation eventually died of exposure. However, the fighting went on!

Russian riflemen had established themselves in some caverns in the side of the hills in front of the left attack, from where they sniped and enfiladed the Allied trenches and inflicted great damage on British and French working parties, so General Canrobert asked Lord Raglan to order some men to dislodge them.

On 20 November 1854, a party drawn from the 1st Battalion, Rifle Brigade (Prince Consort's Own) were given the duty of clearing these caves, or 'ovens' as they were known. Fifty men under Lieutenant Henry Tryon formed the storming column, with fifty supports under

Lieutenant Claud Bourchier and a hundred reserves under Lieutenant William Montgomery-Cuninghame. The advance was made in a most spirited and determined manner, as they crept stealthily across broken ground and climbed up an incline to launch a surprise attack and highly distinguished themselves as they drove the enemy riflemen from their positions. The Russians poured grape and canister on them, and as they had little cover, Lieutenant Tryon was shot through the head in the moment of capturing the caverns, and nine other 'valuable soldiers' suffered the same fate during the operation. Lieutenant Bourchier succeeded to the command of the leading party, and Lieutenant Cuninghame brought forward the reserves and worked with great energy to hold back a flank attack by the enemy. Under the leadership of these two officers they entrenched themselves and maintained their position, despite three attempts by strong Russian columns to try to dislodge the gallant band of men. They bravely withstood them until they were relieved next day by another party of the regiment.

Lieutenant Wilbraham Lennox of the Royal Sappers and Miners showed cool and gallant conduct in helping to establish the lodgement. Under extreme exposure they managed to repulse the assaults of the enemy as they tried to regain the position throughout the night, until they were relieved next morning. Lieutenants Lennox and Bourchier were the sons of veterans of the Battle of Waterloo, and Lieutenant Cuninghame was the son of a baron.

This brilliant operation drew forth a special order from General Canrobert, and the gallant conduct of these men was recorded in French General Orders. Lieutenant Tryon did not receive official recognition for his bravery because he was killed, but the position was thereafter named by his comrades as 'Tryon's Rifle Pits'.

As the thermometer dropped below freezing point, undernourished and bedraggled soldiers suffered harsh freezing nights on picket duty. On 19 December 1854, Private William Norman of the 7th (Royal) Fusiliers, volunteered for single sentry duty some distance in front of the advance sentries of an outlying picket in the White Horse Ravine before Sebastopol. It was a dangerous post, requiring great vigilance, only 300yd from an advance Russian picket. Three Russian soldiers moved forward under cover of brushwood to reconnoitre, but Private Norman spotted them. He fired his rifle to raise the alarm, and at once pounced almost on top of them as they sneaked along the trench. One of the Russians fled, but Private Norman single-handedly captured the other two and marched them back to the British lines. He did this without alarming the Russian pickets. Later he was wounded by a musket ball through his left leg.

On 14 February 1855, the eight-gun number 9 battery of the Left Attack had been so constantly bombarded by Russian artillery that it finally collapsed. Corporal William Lendrim of the 7th Company, Royal Sappers and Miners, showed courage and praiseworthy example in superintending 150 French Chasseurs in repairing and replacing the whole of the capsized gabions. On several occasions he left himself exposed to heavy enemy fire as he directed the work until it was completed.

On 11 April 1855, he saw some burning sandbags which were close to causing the collapse of a parapet, and was perilously close to a twenty-one-gun battery and its magazine. With great intrepidity he climbed on top of the magazine, where he immediately came under heavy enemy fire, but regardless of this danger he succeeded in extinguishing the sacking and hastily repaired the breach, therefore almost certainly saving the battery from complete destruction.

He showed great bravery and presence of mind on a third occasion, when he was one of four volunteers who went forward on 20 April to destroy a pit that was some distance away from the British lines and very close to the enemy. He had thus continuously proved himself to be a determined and hard-working soldier in building and repairing the defences throughout the harsh winter.

Wilbraham Oates Lennox

Wilbraham Oates Lennox was born on 4 August 1830, at Molecomb House on the Goodwood Estate in Sussex, one of three sons in a family of four children to Colonel, Lord John George Lennox, the Member of Parliament for Chichester from 1819–31, and Louisa Frederica, the daughter of Captain, the Honourable John Rodney MP, who was a son of Admiral Lord Rodney, who was best known for his commands during the American War of Independence. Wilbraham was a grandson of the 4th Duke of Richmond, and his father served as aide-de-camp to the Duke of Wellington at Waterloo.

He was privately educated, and entered the Royal Military Academy at Woolwich in 1846, from where he received a commission as 2nd lieutenant on 27 June 1847. He served at Ceylon (Sri Lanka) from 20 November 1850, and, having been promoted lieutenant on 7 February 1854, he was posted for active service in the Crimea directly from Ceylon in August 1854, where he arrived one month later.

101

He was appointed adjutant to the Royal Sappers and Miners of the left attack on 9 December 1854, He acted as aide-de-camp to Chapman with Eyre's brigade at the attack on the Redan on 18 June 1855, and was present on 8 September at the fall of Sebastopol, after which he was adjutant of all the Royal Engineers in the Crimea, being Mentioned in Despatches on 21 December 1855. He arrived home on 5 August 1856.

For their distinguished service during the Crimean War it was announced in the *London Gazette* of 17 October 1856 that the regiment would be re-titled the Corps of Royal Engineers.

His award of the Victoria Cross was announced in the *London Gazette* of 24 February 1857, and he received the medal in 1857, from Lieutenant G. Ashburnham, the General Officer Commanding the Hong Kong station. He also received the Crimean War Medal with *Inkerman* and *Sebastopol* clasps, the Turkish Order of the Medjidie (5th Class), the Turkish Crimea Medal and the Sardinian Medal of Military Valour.

He was promoted captain on 25 November 1857, and became adjutant of the Royal Engineers at Aldershot, until he sailed to the Far East with the 23rd Company on 25 April 1857, for active service in the Second China War. On arriving at the Singapore station they learned that the Indian Mutiny had broken out and they were diverted to Calcutta, where they arrived on 10 August 1857. British citizens, including women and children, had been victims of an act of merciless brutality at Cawnpore and their bodies thrown down a well, some being still alive. British troops marched to the relief of Cawnpore, and due to a number of officers getting wounded at various engagements on the way he became chief engineer on the staff of Sir Colin Campbell on 14 November. He submitted a plan of action for the second relief of Lucknow in November 1857, which Sir Colin accepted. He took a conspicuous part in the operation, which gained twenty-four Victoria Crosses on 16 and 17 November, the most ever awarded in a 24-hour period.

He continued in his responsible capacity during the engagement at Cawnpore on 6 December, and he was an assistant to the commanding royal engineer during the operation for the final relief of Lucknow, from 2–21 March, being promoted brevet major on 24 March 1858. He commanded the engineers during the operation for the subjugation of Rowhilkhand, and the defeat of the Gwalior contingent. He was present at the assault on the forts at Jhansi on 3 April, at Ruiyh on 15 April and at Gwalior on 17 June 1858. He arrived in Allahabad in September 1858, where he was appointed commanding engineer to the column under Colin Campbell for the subjugation of Oude. Major Lennox was included in the list of officers honourably mentioned for the siege of Lucknow by the commander-in-chief in general orders of 16 April 1858, and he was repeatedly Mentioned in Despatches for action throughout the campaign. He left Lucknow on 30 November 1858 as commanding royal engineer sent out to settle the country to the north-east, and in the Trans-Gogra Campaign, taking part in numerous engagements with the enemy. For his service he received the Indian Mutiny Medal with *Lucknow* and *Relief of Lucknow* clasps.

He left India in March 1859, and soon after arriving home he was promoted brevet lieutenant colonel on 26 April 1859, being appointed to the Brighton sub-division of the south-eastern military district. He married Mary Harriet Harrison in Denbigh on 16 July 1861, the daughter of Robert Harrison of Plas Clough in Denbigh, and they had Lilian Emily and Gerald Wilbraham Stuart, who was born in 1862 and became an officer in the Black Watch. Mary died on 22 July 1863, and he married Susan Hay, daughter of Admiral, Sir John Gordon Sinclair, in London on 12 June 1867. They had Charles Gordon in 1872, Louisa Edith, Cecil George Pelham Gordon and two others. From 14 June 1862–31 October 1865, he was deputy assistant quartermaster general at Aldershot. He was promoted captain on 1 April 1863, and was appointed Companion of the Bath (CB) on 30 March 1867.

For five years from November 1866 he held the post of instructor in field fortification at the school of military engineering at Chatham, where he started the Royal Engineers' Charitable Fund, which was of much benefit to the widows and children of soldiers of his corps. He was promoted brevet colonel on 26 April 1867. In 1868 he visited Coblenz and reported on the experimental siege operations carried on there. In the following year he was on a committee on spade drill for infantry, and inspected the Prussian army manoeuvres. In the summer of 1870 he visited Belgium to study the fortifications of Antwerp.

From November 1870 to March 1871 he was attached officially to the German armies in France during the Franco-Prussian War, being present at the siege of Paris from 11–15 December 1870 and from 10 January–4 February 1871, and at the siege of Belfort from 7 February 1871 to the entry of the German troops on 18 February 1871.

On 13 November 1871, he was appointed assistant superintendent of military discipline at Chatham, and was on a committee on pontoon drill in December, being appointed regimental major on 5 July 1872. He was promoted lieutenant colonel on 10 December 1873, and went to Portsmouth as second-in-command of the Royal Engineers, where he remained until his appointment as military attaché at Constantinople on 24 October 1876. In April 1877 he joined the Turkish armies in Bulgaria during the Russo-Turkish war, and was present during the bombardments of several cities, and on 18 December he accompanied Suleiman Pasha's force from Varna to Constantinople. For his services he received the Turkish War Medal.

On his return home in March 1878 he went to the Curragh in Ireland as commanding Royal Engineer, until his promotion to major general on 13 August 1881. From 2 August 1884 he commanded the garrison of Alexandria, and during the Nile Expedition of 1884–5, in the Sudan, he organised the landing and despatch to the front of the troops, the Nile boats and all the military and other stores of the expedition for the relief of his fellow Royal Engineer, General Gordon, at Khartoum. He was transferred to the command of the troops in Ceylon on 1 April 1887, but his promotion to lieutenant general on 12 February 1888 vacated the appointment. He returned home via Australia and America, and he was appointed Knight Commander of the Bath (KCB) on 30 May 1891. He was director general of military education at the war office from 22 January 1893, until his retirement from the active list on 8 May 1895.

'Great energy, unbending resolution, and masterful decision fitted him for high command, while his kindness of heart and Christian character endeared him to many.' Among his writings he contributed to *The Professional Papers of the Royal Engineers*, papers on 'The Demolition of the Fort of Tutteah', 'The Engineering Operations at the Siege of Lucknow, 1858' and 'Description of the Passage of the Wet Ditch at the Siege of Strasburg, 1870', and he compiled *The Engineers' Organisation in the Prussian Army for Operations in the Field, 1870–1*.

Wilbraham was engaged in writing a memoir of Sir Henry Harness' Indian career when he died on 7 February 1907, aged 67, at Chester Square in Belgravia, London, and he was buried in the family plot at Woodvale Cemetery in Lewes Road, Brighton. There is a military locomotive nameplate bearing his name at the Museum of Army Transport in Beverley, North Yorkshire, with a replica displayed at the Royal Engineers Museum in Chatham. Lennox Row in Wood Street, Chatham, is named after him. His medals are with the Royal Engineers Museum in Chatham.

William James Montgomery-Cuninghame

William James Montgomery-Cuninghame was born on 20 May 1834, in the parish of Maybole at Ayr in Scotland. He was eldest of six children to Sir Thomas Montgomery-Cuninghame, 8th Baronet of Corsehill and Kirktonholm, and Charlotte Niven (formerly Hutcheson). He was educated at Harrow School from 1848.

He enlisted into the 1st (Loyal) Regiment, as ensign by purchase on 11 March 1853, before transferring as 2nd Lieutenant in the 1st Battalion, Rifle Brigade (Prince Consort's Own), on 29 April 1853.

His award of the Victoria Cross was announced in the *London Gazette* of 24 February 1857, and he received the medal at the first investiture. He also received the Crimea Medal with *Alma, Balaclava, Inkerman* and *Sebastopol* clasps, the Turkish Order of the Medjidie (5th Class) and the Turkish Crimea Medal.

He was promoted to captain on 22 November 1856, and became the instructor of musketry with the Rifle Brigade, and he was promoted major on 14 August 1867. He was appointed lieutenant colonel of the Inns of Court Rifle Volunteer Corps on 22 May 1868, becoming a major with the Ayr and Wigtown Militia in 1877.

On 22 April 1869, he married Elizabeth (formerly Hartopp) at Little Dalby in Leicestershire, and they resided at Glenmoor House in Maybole. They had two sons and seven daughters, three of whom died in infancy. He attained the rank of colonel, and when he succeeded to the family title of 9th Baronet on the death of his father on 30 August 1870, he retired from the army having served for more than twenty-four years. He renamed his residency as Kirkbride House, and served as Tory Member of Parliament for Ayr from 31 January 1874–31 March 1880. He was Justice of the Peace for Lanark and Wigtown, and was appointed deputy lieutenant of Ayrshire 28 August 1871.

He was granted the honorary rank of lieutenant colonel with the 4th Battalion, Royal Scots Fusiliers, on 9 August 1884. He was appointed colonel with the volunteer force on 17 October 1888, and placed in command of the Clyde Brigade. He also held the rank of brigadier general with the Glasgow Volunteer Brigade, which he had commanded since its inception.

In July 1897, he was expected to accompany the Glasgow Volunteer Brigade to Aldershot, where they were to become the first volunteer force to perform duties akin to regular battalions stationed there. However, he was forced to resign due to ill-health.

William died on 11 November 1897, aged 63, while at Gunton Old Hall near Lowestoft (now a leisure hotel), and he was buried at Kirkmichael churchyard in Ayr, where there is a headstone and a commemorative window in the church. His wife died in 1936 and is buried with him. A commemorative plaque was placed on the flagpole in Maybole in 2007. His name appears on the Rifle Brigade memorial at Winchester Cathedral, and his medals are with the Royal Green Jackets Museum in Winchester.

His eldest son, Colonel Thomas Andrew A.M. Cuninghame, DSO, served in the same regiment as his father whom he succeeded as 10th Baronet.

Claud Thomas Bourchier

Claud Thomas Bourchier was born on 22 April 1831, at Brayford near Barnstaple, the third son and one of six children to James Claud Bourchier of the 3rd (Prince of Wales') Dragoon Guards, of Lavant House, East Lavant in Chichester, who served as a colonel during the Battle of Waterloo in 1815 with the 11th Regiment of Light Dragoons, and his wife, Maria, daughter of George Caswall of Sacomb Park Manor near Hertford. His brothers, Charles John and James Johnes, also followed a military career. Claud was educated at Charterhouse Public School and entered the Rifle Brigade. He served in the Cape Frontier War of 1852–3, for which he received the South Africa Medal, 1834–53. His mother died in 1850.

His award of the Victoria Cross was announced in the *London Gazette* of 24 February 1857, and he was the last in line to receive the medal at the first investiture. He also received the Crimea Medal with *Alma, Balaclava, Inkerman* and *Sebastopol* clasps, the French Legion of Honour, the Turkish Order of the Medjidie (5th Class) and the Turkish Crimea Medal.

He saw active service in India during the siege and capture of Lucknow, and at the Battle of Nawabganj on 12 June 1857, for which he received the Indian Mutiny Medal with *Lucknow* clasp. He also received the Indian General Service Medal with *North West Frontier* clasp.

His father died in 1859. He became colonel and aide-de-camp to Queen Victoria, and a member of Boodle's Gentlemen's Club in Westminster, London.

Claud died from 'softening of the brain' on 19 November 1877, aged 46, while visiting one of his sisters at a lodging house he owned at 38 Brunswick Road in Stayning, Hove, and he was buried at St Andrew's churchyard at Buxton, a village between Norwich and Aylsham in Norfolk, where his sister, Mary Diana, was the wife of the rector of Buxton with Oxnead and Skeyton. There is a headstone, and a memorial chancel window dedicated to his memory by his brother James at St Margaret's Catholic Church in the village of Felthorpe in Norfolk. His name appears on the Rifle Brigade memorial at Winchester Cathedral, and his medals are at the Royal Green Jackets Museum in Winchester.

William Norman

William Norman was born in Warrington, circa 1832/33. He joined the 4th Battalion, Royal Lancashire Militia on 1 February 1853, and entered the 7th (Royal) Fusiliers on 15 May 1854, as 3443 Private Norman, for active service in the Crimea. He was of very small stature, being about 5ft tall, with a fair complexion, hazel eyes and brown hair. He had the initials 'WN' tattooed on his forearm.

His award of the Victoria Cross was announced in the *London Gazette* of 24 February 1857, and an excursion of 415 people went to London to see him receive the medal during the first investiture. He also received the Crimea Medal with *Sebastopol* clasp and the Turkish Crimea Medal.

He was promoted corporal, and served in India during the Ambela (Umbeyla) Expedition of 1863, for which he was the first man to receive the Indian General Service Medal, with clasp for *Umbeyla, 1863*.

He discharged from the army at Ferozopore in India on 15 May 1865, having served for twelve years, and he returned to his home town to live in Church Street. Described as being 'of a fine soldierly bearing, being respected and esteemed', for a number of years he was a member of the 1st Volunteer Battalion, The South Lancashire Regiment (Prince of Wales' Volunteers), reaching the rank of corporal. His wife was named Elizabeth, and they had three children. William was born in 1868, Charlotte was born in 1872 and Sarah was born in 1875.

He moved to Manchester in about 1885, where he was employed as a labourer, and lived at 33 Fearnley Street, off Great Jackson Street in Hulme. The 1891 Manchester directory begins to describe his occupation as a shop keeper, and in the same year the *Strand Magazine* published his account of his deed, to which he concluded: 'My feelings I can hardly describe, as what I did was on the spur of the moment. But it was no doubt the means of saving our position.'

William Norman died of 'brain fever' on 13 March 1896, aged 63, and he was buried in a Church of England common grave at Weaste Cemetery in Salford, with military honours provided by the Salford Volunteers and the Royal Welsh Fusiliers, who were stationed at Cross Lane Barracks. The streets were lined with people as the cortège made its way to the cemetery. Some local newspapers described him as a 'Balaclava Hero' – presuming all the fuss was because he had ridden in the Charge of the Light Brigade – which suggests he never spoke much of his bravery. There was no marked grave and the area was landscaped, until 2004 when a new headstone was dedicated at the grave site. His medals were sold at auction in 1920 and 1926 and they are now at The Royal Fusiliers Museum in the Tower of London.

William James Lendrim

William James Lendrim was born at Carrick-on-Shannon, County Leitrim, Ireland, on 1 January 1830. At the young age of 15 he enlisted as 1078 Bugler Lendrim in the 7th Company, Royal Sappers and Miners in 1845.

His award of the Victoria Cross was announced in the *London Gazette* of 24 February 1857, and he received the medal at the first investiture. He also received the Crimea Medal with *Sebastopol* clasp, the French Legion of Honour, the French Military Medal and the Turkish Crimea Medal.

He was posted to the 23rd Company, and later achieved the rank of sergeant major, serving during the Indian Mutiny of 1857–8, for which he received the India Mutiny Medal with *Lucknow* clasp.

He was employed as a sergeant major of field works at the staff college in Frimley. He married Louisa (formerly Hobbey), which was registered at Greenwich during the third quarter of 1857, and they had eleven children, who were all alive in 1881.

He was initiated into the Masonic Lodge of Freemasons of the 37th Company of Royal Engineers on 8 July 1863, and passed on 12 August of that year. He was raised in the United Chatham Lodge of Benevolence on 12 April 1864, and he became the first junior warden of the Albert Edward Lodge, chartered by the United Grand Lodge of England in the Province of Surrey in 1877. He became its third Worshipful Master in 1879, he was appointed to Provincial Grand Steward in the Province of Surrey in 1878 and Provincial Grand Pursuivant of Surrey in 1881.

William died after forty-six years' service on 28 November 1891, aged 61, at the Royal Military College in Camberley, and he was buried in the Royal Military Academy Cemetery, where there is a headstone which displays his surname as Lendrum. His name is commemorated on the 'For Valour' board at the Royal Engineers Museum in Chatham.

A memorial tablet and wall poster commemorating his actions was displayed in the market square at Lisburn in 2009, and there is a military locomotive nameplate bearing his name at the Museum of Army Transport in Beverley, North Yorkshire, with a replica displayed at the Royal Engineers Museum. Lendrim Close in Chatham is named after him, as is Lendrim Lines in Sandhurst. His Victoria Cross was stolen while out on loan in Yorkshire in 1955. Fortunately, it was recovered and his medals are at the Royal Engineers Museum.

Chapter 9

Spring, 1855

The terrible conditions the troops were suffering was brought to the attention of the British people, and following a public outcry Lord Aberdeen's government fell. The new government under Lord Palmerston sent out fresh supplies of warm clothing, which began to reach the army in January. The soldiers were obviously grateful, but this was tempered with regret by the fact that they 'didn't come before so many fellows were in their graves'.

Some officers were growing concerned about a lack of discipline which was beginning to show among the rank-and-file, and not surprisingly, there was increased misconduct among some of the units. The 18th (Royal Irish) Regiment had only recently returned from India when they received orders for active service in the Crimea, arriving in the war zone in January 1855.

On taking over command of the 18th Regiment in March 1855, even a stern disciplinarian such as Lieutenant Colonel Clement Edwards, stated: 'I am much afraid that it will be a long time before I can see the results for my improvement of the regiment; the malady was too deep and of too long a standing to hope for any great sign of amendment, or any substantial change for the better, till the whole system is restored.'

Perhaps a more important point he could be more confident about was that his Irish men were a tough unit of soldiers who knew how to fight a campaign. Lieutenant Gordon stated:

> They [the Royal Irish] were a favourite regiment with the Royal Engineers for work, both in the trenches and in the destruction of the docks, from the energy and pluck of the officers and men, and it was then that I formed my opinion of Irishmen being of a different nature than other Britishers inasmuch as they required

a certain management and consideration, which if given them would enable you, so to speak, to hold their lives in your hand. The officers liked the men and the men liked the officers; they were a jovial lot altogether, but they would do anything if you spoke and treated them as if you liked them, which I certainly did. You know what great hardships they went through in the docks in working at the shafts which, 30 ft deep, were full of water if left un-pumped out for twelve hours. Poor devils! Wet, bedraggled, in their low ammunition boots, I used to feel much for them, for the Generals used to be down on them because they were troublesome, which they were when people did not know how to manage them.

With the coming of spring the situation for the Allies improved. Reinforcements of experienced troops arrived from Britain and the colonies, and their weaponry was upgraded. The British Army was in the midst of a significant weapons transformation from smooth-bore muskets to the Enfield P53 Minie rifles, which were more accurate at a much longer range. However, it was to be a contributory cause for the outbreak of the Indian Mutiny in 1857.

The re-commencement of serious hostilities began again on the night of 22 March 1855, when the Russians used the advantage of the darkness 'as black as a wolf's mouth' by pretending to be French soldiers, and made a powerful sortie in vast numbers to try to capture some of the French positions along the Dock Ravine at the foot of the Mamelon, and the British forward trenches to the right of Frenchman's Hill. The battle was fought in atrocious weather conditions, as sleet and rain made the men have to advance ankle-deep in mud.

The Russians had hidden in hollows in the ground until nearly midnight, when they launched an attack with 'diabolical yells' and were among the British working parties before they could get their weapons and fight back, and being taken by surprise they were in danger of being driven out of their positions. For an hour or more both sides were forced to grope at each other in the darkness, firing at the gun flashes facing them, thrusting with butt and bayonet, and kicking and punching as they scrambled over dead bodies, comrade and foe, all the time being encouraged by the shouts of their officers. Eventually the British gained the advantage of the desperate struggle, but General Horace Montague of the Royal Engineers and several men were taken prisoner.

At first light many men discovered that their bayonets were twisted and bent, and Sergeant Major Timothy Gowing of the 7th Royal Fusiliers was of the opinion that the actual hand-to-hand fighting was worse than Inkerman. He wondered by what name this great battle would go down in history.

Detachments of both the 57th (West Middlesex) and 77th (East Middlesex) Regiments acquitted themselves nobly during this engagement. Private Alexander Wright of the 77th Regiment highly distinguished himself and showed conspicuous gallantry throughout the campaign, including on the night of 19 April, when he was in the thick of the fighting during the taking of the pits, and he was noted for the great encouragement he gave the men while holding the pits under a terrible fire, during which he was wounded. He was wounded again while highly distinguishing himself before Sebastopol on 30 August 1855. Sergeant George Gardiner of the 57th (West Middlesex) Regiment kept his head and helped to rally the men, and with his fine example they regained the position.

On 29 March 1855, a lighted shell fell into the trench where Private William Coffey of the 34th (Cumberland) Regiment was stationed. All the rest of the men froze with panic, but Private Coffey picked up the missile and threw it back over the parapet and away from his comrades before it exploded.

The second bombardment of Sebastopol began in atrocious weather on 9 April 1855, and was kept up for three days, and the following day was the 25th birthday of Boatswain's Mate John Sullivan of HMS *Rodney*, who was working the guns at the Greenhill Battery as part of the Naval Brigade.

A concealed Russian battery was doing a great deal of damage to some of the advance works and the men who manned them. It was suggested that someone should go forward to place a flagstaff on a mound to act as an aiming point. It was dangerously exposed and whoever took up the task was likely to be killed. However, John volunteered to carry out the perilous work, and did so with great coolness, undeterred by continuous fire from enemy sharpshooters, and taking care to ensure the flag was in perfect line with the target. His gallant action enabled the battery to open a more accurate fire on the previously concealed enemy guns.

After this exploit his unit was moved to number 9 battery, which was the nearest to the French forts, and close to an enemy position known as the Flagstaff Battery. On one occasion the French had fired so much shot and shell at the Russians that they ran out of ammunition. Noticing the lull in firing, the Russians decided to take advantage of the situation and launched an attack against the French positions, and they were being cut to pieces before Sullivan's eyes. However, the battery had been ordered to cease-fire, and as the man with seniority he had to obey or risk sentence of death for mutiny. Nevertheless, he risked this threat and gave the order for the four guns under his command to open up. The Russians fell back under the bombardment and retreated to their lines. The French were so grateful for the timely assistance that hundreds of them came to shake hands with their rescuers.

On 13 April 1855, it was noted that some of the forward embrasures had become seriously damaged, but they were perilously close to and in full view of enemy positions and anyone who took on the task of repairing them would be in grave danger. However, Private Samuel Evans of the 19th (1st Yorkshire, North Riding) Regiment had already taken on several 'duties of a hazardous nature' and he and another private soldier volunteered to go into one of the embrasures, where they came under constant fire from the enemy, but still rendered very great assistance in repairing damage. Later he was seriously wounded during the final attack on the Great Redan.

On the same day Lieutenant Graham was the engineer on duty in the Left Attack, when a round shot landed near him with such force that it knocked him backwards, and the debris which cascaded at him ripped into his greatcoat and he received several cuts and bruises that caused blood to stream down his face. At first he thought: 'I am done for!' but his worst concern was the fact that his watch had got damaged.

At about 2 o'clock in the afternoon of 17 April 1855, an enemy shell smashed through one of the magazines of the eight-gun battery (number 9) on the Right Attack, commanded by Captain Matthew Dixon of the Royal Regiment of Artillery. The missile burst and blew the man in charge of the magazine to pieces, and wounded several others. It destroyed the parapets, disabled seven guns and covered the eighth with earth. The Russians jumped on their parapets and began to cheer at the devastation the direct hit had caused. Angered by this, Captain Dixon ran to the remaining gun and brought it into action against the enemy. He most gallantly reopened fire before the enemy had ceased cheering, and fighting with it until sunset, despite the heavy concentrated fire of the enemy's batteries and the ruined state of his own. While the men were clearing the debris and remaking the parapets they found the magazine man's hands and nothing else of him.

The Russians had erected screens to shield from view their construction of rifle pits – 'wasp's nests', as they were called – on high ground among rocks overhanging the Woronzoff Road, which ran out of Sebastopol between the Third Parallel, Right Attack, and the Quarries, and across the high ground north of Balaclava. The pits consisted of short trenches with loop-holed parapets in front of them. They were only a few hundred paces from the advanced trenches of the British Second Parallel, and sniper fire from these positions was picking off the men and severely hampering the gun batteries and the progress of the trench works being constructed and repaired on the right attack. These positions had to be taken, so on the dark and windy night of 19 April the British attacked the two most forward of these rifle pits to the right front of the British lines at Frenchman's Hill. Towards the morning of the 20 April the Russians made several determined attempts to re-take the position, but the staunch Brits charged them and drove them back.

As the commanding officer, Colonel Thomas Egerton, said to be the tallest man in the British Army, was pointing out the Russian retreat at the moment of victory he was shot through the mouth and killed. Lord Raglan described the action as a 'brilliant achievement', and the position came to be known as 'Egerton's Pit'.

Colour Sergeant Henry MacDonald of the 10th Company, Royal Sappers and Miners, was involved in digging a trench leading towards the Russian rifle pits and showed gallant conduct when engaged in effecting a lodgement in one of the pits. When all the engineer officers had been disabled from wounds the command devolved upon him, and with great valour he carried one officer to get medical assistance. On his return he discovered that all his men were falling back, so he rallied them and led them to charge the enemy back out of the trench, and he determinately persisted in carrying on with the sap despite repeated attacks by the enemy.

Lieutenant Mark Walker, who had already performed a gallant deed at Inkerman which would gain for him the Victoria Cross, was on trench duty when he volunteered for the attack on the rifle pits, for which he was Mentioned in Despatches and transferred as captain in the 3rd (East Kent) Regiment, The Buffs.

Sergeant John Park, already a hero of the Alma, highly distinguished himself during the struggle, where he was severely wounded, and his valour during the attack called forth the approbation of the late Colonel Thomas Egerton.

The Brits retired from the pits without destroying them completely, and eventually a party of Russian riflemen returned to occupy some of them. Their position overlooked a portion of the Left Attack, and impeded the work of the men in a new battery then being constructed on the extreme right of that section.

On 22 April 1855, Rifleman Roderick McGregor was employed as a sharpshooter in one of the advance trenches with the 2nd Battalion, Rifle Brigade (Prince Consort's Own), along with Riflemen Joseph Bradshaw and Robert Humpston. Bandsman Wright was a popular man in the battalion, and he went out to fetch some water from a well in front of the advance trench, where he was killed by a shot from the pits. This enraged the men to such a degree that a number of them rushed out in broad daylight determined to take revenge and drive the enemy from their positions. The three riflemen mentioned showed determined conduct ahead of the men. They ran across vulnerable open ground, and after taking cover beneath a rock they attacked the enemy, killing some, while others ran for their lives. They occupied the trench, and when further support came up later the pits were filled in and levelled and the Brits retired to their own trenches.

George Gardiner

George Gardiner was born in 1821, at Clonallon, Warrenpoint in County Down, Ireland. All four soldiers of the Middlesex regiments who gained the Victoria Cross in the Crimea were from Ireland, and George enlisted into the 57th (West Middlesex) Regiment, being posted to Lifford Barracks in 1846. The regiment had earned the nickname the 'Die Hards' after the bloody Battle of Albuera, fought during the Peninsular War on 16 May 1811, when their colonel having been struck down and wounded, urged his men on by shouting: 'Die Hard, the 57th, Die Hard!'

His award of the Victoria Cross was announced in the *London Gazette* of 4 June 1858, and he received the medal from Brigadier General William Marcus Coghlan, the British representative in Aden, on 5 October 1858. He also received the Crimea Medal with *Inkerman* and *Sebastopol* clasps, the Distinguished Conduct Medal and the Turkish Crimea Medal.

He saw service during the Maori Wars, for which he received the New Zealand Medal, 1860–6. He discharged from the regular army in 1861, and enlisted for the Prince of Wales' Own Donegal Militia. Another double tragedy devastated the family in 1869, when their only daughter, Elizabeth Jane, died on 7 April, aged 12, and their only surviving son, Richard, died a week later, aged 3. They were probably victims of the Irish potato famine, and in consequence of this he retired as sergeant major from the Militia on 17 July 1869. For his service he received a 'railway clock' at Lifford Barracks, with the inscription: 'as a token of appreciation of the zealous and impartial manner in which he performed his military duties, and of his most obliging conduct in civil life . . . '.

His wife died in 1882, and George passed away on 17 November 1891, aged 70, at his home of Lifford House in County Donegal, and he was buried at the Clonleigh churchyard in Lifford, where there is a headstone. His medals are at the Princess of Wales' Royal Regiment and Queen's Regiment RHQ in Canterbury.

Alexander Wright

Alexander Wright was born in 1826, at Ballymena in County Antrim, Ireland, and entered the 77th (East Middlesex) Regiment, as 2239 Private Wright.

His award of the Victoria Cross was announced in the *London Gazette* for 24 February 1857, and he received the medal from the general officer commanding in Sydney, Australia. He also received the Crimea Medal with *Alma, Inkerman* and *Sebastopol* clasps and the Turkish Crimea Medal.

Alexander died while serving in Calcutta, India, on 25 July 1858, aged 32. His place of burial is not known, but his name appears on the Victoria Cross Memorial plaque at Ballymena, and a picture of him taken from the *Illustrated London News* appears on a stamp from Nauru. His medals are with the Princess of Wales' Royal Regiment and Queen's Regiment RHQ in Canterbury.

William Coffey

William Coffey was born in the parish of Emly, in the village hospital, in Knocklong, County Limerick, Ireland. His service papers suggest his date of birth as 25 January 1829, but this is disputed, and other sources give 5 August 1829. He was the son of William Coffey, a farm labourer, and his wife Johanna. His older brother, Timothy, also entered the army.

He originally enlisted for the 82nd Regiment (Prince of Wales' Volunteers), on 24 November 1846, in Fermoy, County Cork, giving his employment as a labourer. He gave his age as 17 years and 10 months (although he was probably younger), being just over 5ft 5in tall. He had dark-brown hair, hazel eyes and a fresh complexion. He had grown 3in by the time he left the army.

It was suggested by the Prince Consort that Queen Victoria should give her name to the medal for valour which was instituted on 29 January 1856, and men who fought in the Crimean War became the first recipients.

The Victoria Cross is arguably the most coveted medal in the world.

The first investiture of the Victoria Cross took place at Hyde Park in London, on 26 June 1857, when sixty-two Crimean veterans received the medal from the Queen herself.

When a live shell landed on the deck of his ship, Mate Charles Lucas ran forward and picked it up with the fuse still burning. Well-aware that it might explode and blow him to pieces at any moment, he carried it across the deck and hurled it over the side of the ship, where it exploded with a tremendous roar before it hit the surface of the water.

Irish-born Charles Davis Lucas was the first man to perform a deed which would be rewarded with the Victoria Cross.

The citation for the award of the Victoria Cross to Lieutenant Cecil William Buckley was the first of eighty-five to appear in the *London Gazette* of 24 February 1857.

At the first investiture Queen Victoria actually pinned the medal to the skin of Commander Henry James Raby, who was first in the queue and therefore became the first man ever to wear the Victoria Cross – literally!

The Scots (Fusilier) Guards were among the units ordered to storm the heights of the Alma with bayonets fixed and colours flying. They came under heavy bombardment and rifle fire as they advanced over rugged ground, crossed the river, passed ruined buildings, burning huts and other obstacles, but they pressed on and up towards their objective.

Captain William Peel was the son of the late Prime Minister. He was awarded the Victoria Cross for three separate acts of valour during the Crimean War, but he died on active service in India before he had the chance to wear the medal.

Edward St John Daniel was also awarded the Victoria Cross for gallantry on three different occasions while serving alongside Captain Peel, to whom he was devoted. However, he began to fall from grace in 1860 and eventually became the first man and the only officer to forfeit the award.

Robert James Lindsay was awarded the Victoria Cross for rallying the troops of his regiment at the passage of the Alma. He once tasked himself: 'I must do something to justify my existence', and Florence Nightingale qualified this after his death when she stated: 'He was a great gain . . . All are better than if he had not lived.'

The Scots Greys fought with fearless gallantry during the Charge of the Heavy Brigade at Balaclava. As they smashed their way through the Russian ranks Sergeants John Grieve and Henry Ramage performed acts of exceptional courage worthy of the award of the Victoria Cross.

Under heavy fire from all directions Sergeant John Berryman assists his mortally wounded officer from his horse, and with the help of Sergeant John Farrell and Corporal Joseph Malone they managed to carry him back to the British lines.

William Hewett's sometimes offending manner and bad temper earned for him the nickname of 'Bully', but he was the kind of no-nonsense soldier you would want to have fighting beside you in a battle.

Florence Nightingale arrived at the theatre of war on 5 November 1854 with thirty nurses, where she re-organised the hospital at Scutari, nursed the worst cases herself and looked after the welfare of the troops. The men came to adore her and named her 'The Lady with the Lamp'.

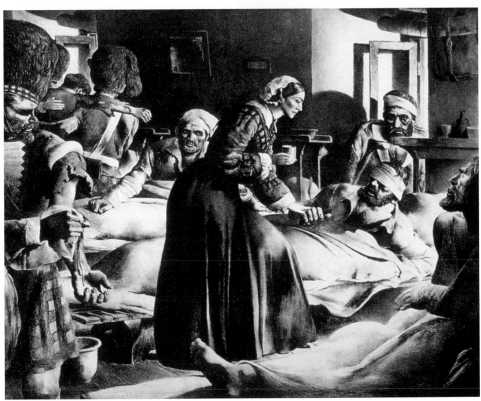

The Battle of Inkerman on 5 November 1854 is considered to be one of the fiercest fought in the history of British arms, and as many officers were rendered ineffective among the thick fog and confusion on the vast battlefield it came to be known as the 'Soldiers' Battle'.

At the height of the Battle of Inkerman Captain Charles Russell aimed his pistol at a Russian and pulled the trigger, but the weapon misfired. The Russian thrust his bayonet forward, but Private Anthony Palmer came to his aid and stunned the Russian with a sharp blow to his head. Captain Russell re-loaded and shot dead the enemy soldier.

During the harsh Crimean winter the soldiers continued to suffer the elements while on sentry duty. One of these was Private William Norman of the 7th Fusiliers, who saw three Russians sneaking along a trench to try to gain some intelligence about the British front line. Private Norman confronted them and single-handedly took two of them prisoner.

George Gardiner was born in Ireland in 1821. He was one of seven men to be awarded the Victoria Cross and the Distinguished Conduct Medal for service in the Crimea, and later saw active service during the Maori Wars in New Zealand. He returned to his native country, where he died in 1891.

During the first attack on the Redan, British troops had to run two hundred yards across an open space under fire and negotiate a ditch and an abattis, before they even got to the heavily-defended Russian fort.

Gerald Graham was the son of a doctor. His tall prominent figure during the first assault on the Great Redan seemed to make him an obvious target to be hit by enemy fire. However, he survived the battle unscathed, and among his many further achievements, including a knighthood, he was one of the 'Sudan celebrities' who became the subjects of waxwork models in the Madame Tussaud Exhibition soon after it moved to its present location in London in 1884.

Captain Thomas Esmonde took part in the only section of the British attack on the Redan which gained some success. His award of the Victoria Cross was the last to be announced for the assault, and he received the medal from Queen Victoria at Southsea Common in Portsmouth on 2 August 1858, along with Edward Bell, Henry Ramage, James Mouat, Henry MacDonald, Matthew Dixon and Howard Elphinstone.

Lieutenant William Hope of the 7th (Royal) Fusiliers was informed that his fellow officer, Lieutenant James Hobson, was lying severely wounded outside the trenches. He went to search for him and on finding him lying in a ditch he organised his rescue with the help of several men, including Private Matthew Hughes.

William Hope was the last survivor of the twenty 18 June Redan Victoria Crosses when he died in 1909. He is one of twelve holders of the Victoria Cross to be buried at Brompton Cemetery in London, including Francis Wheatley, Sam Parkes and Sir Frederick Maude.

William Henry Thomas Sylvester became the first Wiltshire-born man to be awarded the Victoria Cross. He later served in the Indian Mutiny, and he was the last surviving Crimean War Victoria Cross recipient when he died in Devon in 1920.

The section commanded by Henry Raby did not take part in the action at the Redan, but later that day a soldier was heard calling for help, so he, along with Henry Curtis and John Taylor, risked their lives under heavy fire to rescue him.

Howard Elphinstone's impressive array of medals included the Victoria Cross, Commander of the Bath (CB civil division) and (CB military division), Companion of the Order of St Michael and St George (CMG) and Knight Commander of the Order of the Bath (KCB).

Sergeant Alfred Ablett was one of several men awarded the Victoria Cross for picking up live shells and throwing them out of harm's way of his comrades. He became the first Suffolk-born man to receive the medal.

Henry Clifford's sketch of a Rifleman at ease during the Crimea. The Rifle Brigade gained eight Victoria Crosses during the campaign.

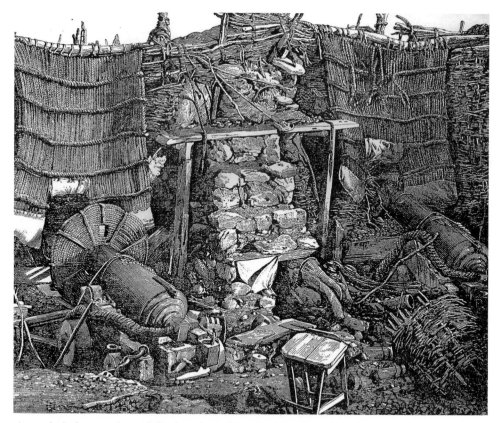

An artist's impression of the interior of the Redan after the city was evacuated on the night of 8 September 1855.

Henry Clifford's sketch of the ditch which formed part of the formidable defences before Sebastopol after the assault on 8 September 1855.

He married a 16-year-old girl named Margaret Lynch (or Linch) in Stirling, in December 1853 or January 1854.

His brother, Timothy, had also joined the 82nd Regiment, and in December 1853, the 82nd Regiment was stationed at Edinburgh Castle under orders for India when they were called upon to provide volunteers for regiments ordered for active service in the Crimea. The 34th (Border) Regiment was among these units, and William joined them as 3837 Private Coffey, on 31 March, along with Timothy. After stopping at Corfu, the unit arrived in the Crimea on 9 December 1854.

He was promoted to corporal on 18 March 1856. He arrived at Portsmouth on 11 July 1856, and six days later the 34th were inspected by Queen Victoria at Aldershot. The Queen mentions that she noticed Corporal Coffey, 'who had received two medals for throwing a live shell out of the trenches', and two days later she spoke to 'the gallant and promising young soldier, Corporal Coffy'. He may have met the queen yet again when she visited Edinburgh on 28 August that year, as Corporal Coffey and his unit formed part of the guard. He was promoted to sergeant on 8 November 1856.

His award of the Victoria Cross was announced in the *London Gazette* of 24 February 1857, and he received the medal at the first investiture. He was one of only three men Queen Victoria mentioned in her diary when she wrote it that night, when she stated: 'I was glad . . . to give the "Victoria Cross" to Corporal Coffey of the 34th; whom I had seen at Aldershot.' He was also awarded the Crimea Medal with *Sebastopol* clasp, the Distinguished Conduct Medal, the French Military Medal and the Turkish Crimea Medal.

He later saw active service during the Indian Mutiny of 1857–8, serving at Cawnpore and during the relief of Lucknow in March 1858, for which he received the Indian Mutiny Medal with *Lucknow* clasp.

Their first child, Mary Joana, was born in Stirling on 6 January 1858, but it is believed she died young. His wife joined him in Calcutta, and William was given a free discharge on 21 December 1860, intending on living as a civilian working on the railways. Their second daughter, Emma Emilie, was born on 20 January 1861. It seems that civilian life was not for him and he re-enlisted as a private in the 75th (Stirlingshire) Regiment on 19 June 1861. The unit was based at Fort William in Calcutta.

He must have lost his original Distinguished Conduct Medal because on 25 October 1861 a replacement was ordered to be cast for him at the Royal Mint. The 75th Regiment was due to return home, so

Private Coffey transferred back to the 82nd Regiment so he could stay in India. His daughter died in 1862, and William John was born in Delhi, but he died on 10 November 1863, having survived for only ten months. Another daughter, Margaret, was born at Mian Meer on 13 January 1865, but his wife died in the following May, and Margaret was adopted.

He was discharged as 'unfit for further service' on 10 October 1867, and he returned to England, being discharged from Netley Military Hospital with chronic bronchitis on 25 August 1868, having served the colours for more than twenty-one years. He was awarded a Long Service Good Conduct Medal on 22 July 1868.

His intended place of residence was given as Pembroke, and he married Margaret Gainey there in 1868. She was the sister of one of his comrades in the army.

William went to live near his wife's family and old army comrade at Stonegravels near Chesterfield in Derbyshire on 1 April 1875, and he lived the last few weeks of his life in a house called Park View. He died of chronic diarrhoea (dysentery) on 13 July 1875, aged 45, and he was buried in a common unmarked grave at the Spital Cemetery in Chesterfield. From a story passed down his family through the years it was believed that William had committed suicide in the drill hall at Hillsborough Barracks in Sheffield but modern research has concluded that this was not true. A song about him was produced in 1969, and following this a headstone was erected by the Commonwealth War Graves Commission. He is named on the Victoria Cross Memorial in Carlisle Cathedral, and on a memorial bench outside Chesterfield Town Hall. His medals are with the Border Regiment Museum housed in Carlisle Castle.

John Sullivan

John Sullivan was born 'in an old house at the foot of Ardnabrahair', at Bantry in County Cork, Ireland, on 10 April 1830. He went to school locally and was remembered for having fist fights with Alexander Sullivan, who later became an Irish Nationalist politician and the MP for Louth.

Having joined the Royal Navy as a Boy 2nd Class in November 1846, he joined the ninety-gun HMS *Rodney*, in March 1852. He sailed for active service in the East as a boatswain's mate, and he volunteered to join the Naval Brigade for shore service in the trenches before Sebastopol.

He was appointed captain of one of the guns at number 5 Greenhill Battery before Sebastopol, and his gun became the first to breach the walls of the Malakoff Tower, one of the strongest points in the Russian defences, destroying one of its magazines. His reputation became such that one day Lord Raglan himself, with other officers, came to witness his firing skills, and Admiral Lyons, the senior naval officer present, called him by name and suggested that one day he would receive a commission.

His award of the Victoria Cross was announced in the *London Gazette* on 24 February 1857, and the medal was sent to him via HMS *Prometheus* in West Africa, and he became the first man to win the Victoria Cross and the Conspicuous Gallantry Medal. He also received the Crimea Medal with *Inkerman* and *Sebastopol* clasps, the French Legion of Honour, the Turkish Crimea Medal and the Sardinian Medal of Military Valour.

On 6 September 1858, HMS *Gorgon* was lying in Halifax Bay, when at about midnight in the pitchy darkness a man fell overboard. Boatswain Sullivan immediately dived into the cold water and guided by the cries for help he swam to the rescue. On reaching him the man was thrashing about in panic and making the task more difficult for his rescuer, so John had to knock him out so he could get him safely back to the boat. On 18 September 1858 it was announced that he had been awarded the Royal Humane Society's Life-Saving Medal in silver.

He spent the last ten of his thirty-seven years of service as chief boatswain of the Royal Dockyard in Portsmouth, and in April 1880 a banquet was held in his honour there. He retired as chief boatswain's mate of HMS *Asia* in April 1884.

Having been granted an allowance of £200 a year, he returned to Ireland and bought a smallholding of 40 acres at Kinsale in County Cork. However, in June 1884 he started to suffer from severe headaches and on 28 April one such attack was too much to bear and he committed suicide by cutting his own throat with a sailor's knife in his garden. He was aged 54, and he is believed to have been buried at Glasnevin Cemetery in Dublin. His wife had died before his retirement and he left two daughters.

His Victoria Cross medal group was presented to HMS *Nelson* in 1967 on behalf of the Royal Naval Barracks at Portsmouth, by the government of Nova Scotia in exchange for the Indian Mutiny VC group which had been awarded to William Hall. His medals are now kept in a display case in the HMS *Nelson* Ward Room in Portsmouth, but the authenticity of the Victoria Cross being the original is unsure.

Samuel Evans

Samuel Evans was born at Paisley in 1821, to James and Anne Evens. He was apprenticed in the shawl-weaving trade until 30 September 1839, when he entered the 26th (Cameronian) Regiment, at Gallowgate Barracks in Glasgow, as 1535 Private Evens.

He joined the regiment in India on 24 October 1840, and moved to China on 5 August 1841 for active service in the First China War, for which he was awarded the China War Medal, 1841–2. The unit returned to Edinburgh Castle in August 1843, and were on duty there for the next eight years, during which time he was promoted corporal on 20 July 1848, but he reverted back to private soon afterwards.

He answered a request for volunteers to join the 19th (1st Yorkshire, North Riding) Regiment, for service in the 8th Cape Frontier War, and when he arrived at Devonport in February 1852 he was given the new regimental number of 2721 Private Evans (not Evens). He was promoted to corporal in September 1853, but was reduced to the ranks and spent three days in confinement. On the declaration of war with Russia, the regiment sailed for the Crimea instead of the Cape.

His award of the Victoria Cross was announced in the *London Gazette* of 23 June 1857, and he received the medal at the first investiture three days later. He also received the Crimea Medal with *Alma, Inkerman* and *Sebastopol* clasps, the French Military Medal and the Turkish Crimea Medal.

After receiving a serious wound during the final assault on the Redan he was sent to Scutari Hospital, where one of Florence Nightingale's young nurses named Margaret McNicholl seems to have caught his eye. He was sent back to England and discharged from the army at Chatham on 13 May 1856, and they married in Edinburgh before the end of the year. He got a job as a time-keeper in the city, before taking employment as a lodge-keeper at Holyrood Palace. He ran a general dealers business at Dumfries for a short time, but ill-health forced him to give it up and he returned to Edinburgh, where he lived the last thirteen years of his life at 332 Lawnmarket. He and his wife were invited to the Curragh Camp in Ireland in 1896, to stay with his old regiment, and after his wife died in 1899 he was invited to stay with the regiment at Bradford Moor Barracks.

Samuel died in Edinburgh on 4 October 1901, aged 80, and he was buried with his wife at Portobello Cemetery at Piershill in Edinburgh, where a headstone was erected by officers of his old regiment. An obituary appeared in the *Illustrated London News* on 2 November 1901, which stated that he was the 'oldest holder of the Victoria Cross in Scotland, and the "father" of the 26th Cameronians and the 19th Regiment'. He is named on the VC memorial stone at Hawkhead Cemetery in Paisley, and there is a Victoria Cross Memorial in Glasgow Cathedral. His Victoria Cross is at the Green Howards Museum in Richmond, Yorkshire.

Matthew Charles Dixon

Matthew Charles Dixon was born on 5 February 1821, at Avranches in Brittany, France. He was the eldest son of Matthew Charles Dixon of the Royal Engineers, and his second wife, Emma (formerly Dalton), and grandson of Sir Manley Dixon KCB, Admiral of the Fleet.

He passed through the Royal Military Academy at Woolwich and entered the Royal Regiment of Artillery on 19 March 1839. He served nine years in Ceylon and six years in Jamaica, being promoted lieutenant on 11 April 1841 and captain on 30 June 1848. He was promoted to major and lieutenant colonel 2 November 1855, and proceeded to the Channel Islands in June 1856.

His award of the Victoria Cross was announced in the *London Gazette* of 23 June 1857, and he received the medal from Queen Victoria at Southsea Common in Portsmouth on 2 August 1858, along with Edward Bell, Henry Ramage, James Mouat, Henry MacDonald, Thomas Esmonde and Howard Elphinstone. He was also awarded the Crimea Medal with *Sebastopol* clasp, the French Legion of Honour, the Turkish Order of the Medjidieh (5th Class) and the Turkish Crimea Medal.

On 13 May 1862 at Enfield parish church, he married Henrietta Letitia Eliza, the daughter of Admiral Charles Bosanquet of Wildwood. They lived at a house called 'Woodgate' in Pembury near Tonbridge.

He was promoted colonel on 8 June 1862, and served in Jamaica from 1862–6. He retired from the army on 19 March 1869 as a lieutenant colonel. He was appointed Commander of the Bath (CB).

Matthew died at Woodgate on 8 January 1905, aged 83, and he was buried in Kensal Green Cemetery in London, where there is a headstone. There is a plaque dedicated to him at St Peter Upper Church in Pembury. He is named on the memorial at the Royal Artillery Chapel in Woolwich. He and Charles Lucas are the Crimean War Victoria Cross recipients commemorated in the Victoria Cross Grove at Dunorlan Park, who had connections to the borough of Royal

Tunbridge Wells. His wife died in 1926, and his medals were in the possession of descendants of his sister, Frances, until being purchased by Lord Ashcroft in 2014 and they are displayed on rotation at the Lord Ashcroft Gallery, as part of the 'Extraordinary Heroes' exhibition at the Imperial War Museum in London.

Henry MacDonald

Henry MacDonald was born on 28 May 1823, at Inverness. It is believed that his original intention before joining the 10th Company, Royal Sappers and Miners was to be a monk.

His award of the Victoria Cross was announced in the *London Gazette* for 4 June 1858, and he received the medal from Queen Victoria on Southsea Common in Portsmouth, on 2 August 1858, along with Edward Bell, Henry Ramage, James Mouat, Matthew Dixon, Thomas Esmonde and Howard Elphinstone. He also received the Distinguished Conduct Medal, the Crimea Medal with *Alma, Inkerman* and *Sebastopol* clasps, the French Legion of Honour and the Turkish Crimea Medal.

Henry rose to the rank of honorary captain, and died on 15 February 1893, aged 69, in Glasgow, and he was buried with military honours at the Eastern Necropolis Cemetery at Cadder in Glasgow, where there is a headstone. His name appears on the 'For Valour' memorial board at the Royal Engineers Museum in Chatham. There is an army locomotive nameplate commemorating his name at the Museum of Army Transport in Beverley, North Yorkshire, and there is a duplicate at the Royal Engineers Museum in Chatham.

His medals were part of the Scottish Exhibition held at the Palace of History in Glasgow in 1911. They were shown to Lord Kitchener by his son, W.H. MacDonald, who was the secretary of Hutcheson's Educational Trust. They are now in the care of the Glasgow City Art Gallery and Museum at Kelvingrove. The Victoria Cross is in storage at the Glasgow Museums' Resource Centre, which is open to the public and the medal can be viewed on request.

Joseph Bradshaw

Joseph Bradshaw was born in 1835 at Pettigreen, (Kilteely-) Dromkeen near Limerick in Ireland. He entered the 2nd Battalion, Rifle Brigade (Prince Consort's Own) as 3471 Rifleman Bradshaw.

His award of the Victoria Cross was announced in the *London Gazette* of 24 February 1857, and he received the medal at the first investiture. He also received the Crimea Medal with *Alma, Inkerman* and *Sebastopol* clasps, the French Military Medal and the Turkish Crimea Medal.

He later served in the Indian Mutiny of 1857–8, for which he received the Indian Mutiny Medal with *Lucknow* and *Central India* clasps. On leaving the army as a corporal, he was awarded the Long Service and Good Conduct Medal.

Joseph died at St John's in Limerick on 29 August 1893, aged 58, and he was probably buried at St John's, although the exact location is not known. His name appears on the Rifle Brigade Memorial at Winchester Cathedral, and his medals are with the Royal Green Jackets Museum in Winchester.

Robert Humpston

Robert Humpston was born at Derby in 1832. He entered the 2nd Battalion, Rifle Brigade (Prince Consort's Own) as 2638 Rifleman Humpston.

He became the first Derbyshire-born man to be awarded the Victoria Cross when it was announced in the *London Gazette* of 24 February 1857, and he received the medal at the first investiture. He also received the Crimea Medal with *Alma* and *Sebastopol* clasps and the Turkish Crimea Medal.

He later served in the Indian Mutiny of 1857–8, for which he received the Indian Mutiny Medal with *Lucknow* and *Central India* clasps.

On leaving the army he gained employment working as a labourer on the railway. He was married and had one son. His grandson, Arthur, was killed at the Battle of Passchendaele Ridge in 1917.

Robert died of gastroenteritis in his home at 45 Duncombe Street in St Ann's, Nottingham, on 22 December 1884, aged 52, and he was buried in a common grave at Nottingham General Cemetery. His name is given as Hempston in the burial register. A headstone was erected at his grave in 2007, and two direct descendants attended the televised ceremony. His name appears on the Nottingham VC memorial at Nottingham Castle, on the Rifle Brigade Memorial at Winchester Cathedral, and his medals are held by the Derby Museum and Art Gallery.

Roderick McGregor

Roderick McGregor was born in 1822 at Dunain near Inverness. He joined the 2nd Battalion, Rifle Brigade (Prince Consort's Own) as 2074 Rifleman McGregor.

His award of the Victoria Cross was announced in the *London Gazette* of 24 February 1857, and he received the medal during the first investiture. He also received the Crimea Medal with *Alma, Inkerman* and *Sebastopol* clasps, the French Military Medal and the Turkish Crimea Medal.

He later served in the Indian Mutiny of 1857–8, for which he received the Indian Mutiny Medal with *Lucknow* and *Central India* clasps. Although he was the type of man anyone would want to have by his side in a fight, his service career was somewhat chequered, in that he was court-martialed seven times and his name appears in the defaulters book on twelve occasions.

Roderick died of bronchitis on 9 August 1888, aged 66, in his home of 'The Pensioner's Croft' at Bunloit, Urquhart in the Highland Region of Scotland (his death certificate records that he died on 10 August). He was buried in St Mary's churchyard at Drumnadrochit (also known as Old Kilmore churchyard), where a headstone was erected by the officers of his regiment. His name appears on the Rifle Brigade Memorial at Winchester Cathedral. His Victoria Cross was sold at auction in 1910, and his medals are at the Royal Green Jackets Museum in Winchester.

Chapter 10

Summer, 1855

On 5 November 1854, at Inkerman, the 68th (Durham) Light Infantry had charged down a hill and driven back three battalions of Russian infantry. During the action they had used all their ammunition, and when they came under attack from the enemy they were forced to retire and leave all their wounded behind. Private John Byrne could not accept this and risked his own life as he went back towards the enemy and brought in Private Anthony Harman under close perilous Russian fire.

Private Byrne performed a second act of valour on the night of 11 May 1855, near the Woronzoff Road. He and Captain Thomas Hamilton, also of the 68th (Durham) Light Infantry, were defending an earthwork which was protecting a battery of guns. Under cover of darkness and driving wind and rain, the Russians launched a most determined attack to try to take it. Private Byrne met the onslaught head-on and bravely engaged in hand-to-hand combat with one of the enemy on the parapet and prevented him from entering the work. After a ferocious bayonet duel he killed his antagonist and captured his arms.

Despite the determination of the defenders some of the enemy eventually gained possession of one of the guns. Captain Hamilton realised the peril of the situation that they might spike the gun, and without hesitation he got together a small force and showed conspicuous gallantry and daring conduct as he boldly rushed forward with his sword flashing in the air, and with his men following close behind with bayonets at the ready he charged at the enemy, and in a sharp and determined fight he and his men forced them from the battery within 2 minutes, and chased them off towards Sebastopol. Their actions saved the enemy from spiking the guns, or prevented the entire works from falling into the hands of the Russians.

On 6 June 1855, Sergeant George Symons of the Royal Regiment of Artillery volunteered to unmask the embrasures of a five-gun battery on the Right Attack, and when so employed, under a terrific fire, which the enemy commenced immediately on the opening of the first embrasure and increased on the unmasking of each additional one; in having overcome the great difficulty of uncovering the last, by boldly mounting the parapet and throwing down the sandbags, when a shell from the enemy burst and severely wounded him.

By mid-May the Russians were observed concentrating their efforts on fortifying an area of diggings known as The Quarries, three irregular shaped rifle pits constructed on low ground about 200 paces in front of the Redan, and a section in front of the French known as the Mamelon Vert. The foreground of these positions was further protected by land mines known as fouglasses. The Allied high command agreed that it was vital to take these positions as a first step towards a grand assault on Sebastopol. They had decided that the most successful form of operation was a full day of intense bombardment, with about an hour's bombardment on the following morning. A third bombardment began on 7 June, and on the following night the British attacked the Quarries.

At 5 o'clock the whole of the Light Division was ordered to parade with arms and accoutrements, and an hour later they occupied the forward trenches preparing to attack. When the signal came that the French had taken the Mamelon, the British launched an attack made mainly by the 7th and 88th Regiments, which took the Russians by surprise and British bayonets and bullets drove them back yet again. The firing was fierce, and among the confusion, uproar and smoke some men in the rear noticed their comrades had started to pelt the enemy with stones because they were running out of ammunition.

The fighting all night was deadly, and there was terrible slaughter as the Brits were driven back three times before they finally took control of the pits and held on, and with picks and shovels they made parapets and embrasures which faced the enemy on the other side and protected them from bombardment by grape and shell. The Russians tried no less than fourteen times during the night to try to win back the position, but the Brits established themselves and by morning they were under good cover. One of the engineers who helped to dig-in was Captain Wolseley, who later became Viscount Wolseley, and led the British Army on numerous expeditions in defence of the British Empire. Lord Raglan visited the trenches and thanked them for their conduct, and the Quarries became known as the Shambles.

126

Once again many men considered the battle to be equal in significance to anything that had been fought previously and thought 'The Battle of the Quarries' would become just as well known, and a man spoke of the assault on the Redan on 18 June as being 'a second great attack'.

Gunner Thomas Arthur of the Royal Artillery suddenly became ill while his battery was in action, so he left it without leave, returning to find that the guns were gone. Noticing that the 7th Regiment was running short of ammunition, he ran to a magazine and carrying a barrel of ammunition on his head he brought it to them under a tremendous fire, and throwing it at their feet he exclaimed, 'Here you are, my lads, fire away!' He then ran back and brought another, continuing to bring as many cartridges as he could to the front. He was marched away under custody for having been absent from his gun, and there was talk of a court martial, but Colonel Yea of the 7th Fusiliers had been watching his gallant actions through his field glasses, and intervened in time for his dereliction to be turned into an act of heroism (*see 18 June 1855*).

The Royal Marine Artillery were providing supporting fire from the advance batteries before Sebastopol, and the return fire from the Russians was destroying much of the embrasures and parapets around the British guns, leaving them vulnerable to shrapnel and exploding bombs. Under this heavy bombardment and galling fire from the enemy fortifications, Bombardier Thomas Wilkinson sprang to the top of the earthworks and called to his comrades to bring sandbags to initiate urgent repairs. By his exertions cover was restored.

He was specially recommended for gallant conduct, and his name having been sent up on the occasion as worthy of special notice by the commanding officer of the Right Attack.

Captain Henry Jones was carrying the Queen's colour of the 7th (Royal) Fusiliers at the passage of the Alma when he was seriously wounded when a slug hit him in the lower jaw. He had recovered enough to distinguish himself while serving with the party that took the Quarries, by repeatedly leading on his men to repel the continuing assaults of the enemy during the night. Although wounded early in the evening, he remained unflinchingly at his post until after daylight the following morning.

The diminutive Private Matthew Hughes of the 7th Royal Fusiliers, 'smoking his clay pipe all the time', twice went for ammunition across open ground. He continually encouraged the men, shouting: 'Keep it up, lads', and even told a young officer to: 'Lend a hand, sir, to distribute these pills.' Later he saw Private John Hampton of his regiment lying wounded so he ran out and brought him in from the front, during which time he was hit in the knee by a shell. His brave actions were noted by Colin Campbell of the 90th Light Infantry (*see 18 June 1855*).

On 29 March, Major Frederick Elton of the 55th (Westmoreland) Regiment, the son of a vicar, who had taken part in the Battle of Inkerman, had set an example to his men by volunteering with a small party to drive off a body of Russians who were destroying one of the new detached works, and succeeded in doing so, taking one of the enemy prisoner with his own hands.

At the Quarries on the night of 7 June 1855, Major Elton was the first of his party to leave the trenches. Leading his men when in the Quarries, he was an excellent role model and several times rallied his men around him. On 4 August 1855, when in command of a working party in the advance trenches in front of the Quarries, Major Elton encouraged and incited his men, by his example, to work under a heavy fire, and, when there was some hesitation shown, in consequence of the fire, he would go into the open and work with pick and shovel – thus showing the best possible example to the men. In the words of one of them: 'There was not another officer in the British army who would have done what Major Elton did that night.'

On 10 June 1855 at Sebastopol, Private John Lyons of the 19th (1st Yorkshire, North Riding) Regiment, who had taken part in the battles of the Alma and Inkerman, picked up a large shell which had landed among the guard in a trench and threw it over the parapet; therefore saving many lives.

Private Joseph Prosser of the 1st (Royal Scots) Regiment had only been at the front for a month when he was on duty in the trenches before Sebastopol on 16 June 1855. He saw a British soldier in the act of deserting, so he pursued him and in spite of coming under fire from Russian positions he caught the man and brought him back to the British lines. This was a valuable act as the man may well have told the enemy of plans to attack the Redan.

On 11 August 1855, Private Prosser ran out of the most advanced trench under very heavy fire from the Russians, and assisted in bringing to safety a severely wounded soldier of the 95th Regiment, who was lying in an exposed position unable to move.

George Symons

George Symons was born on 18 March 1826, at Soutill (now known as South Hill), Callington in Cornwall. A George Symons was baptised at

'Jericho', Soutill, on 2 April 1826, the son of William and Ann Symons, his father being a labourer. The 1841 census shows a George Symons, aged 15, living at Lodge 1 in Manaton Mill, in the civil parish of Soutill, with a blacksmith named Sampson Widger, and his wife and infant daughter. In 1856 a William Symons and Sampson Widger were living at Golberdon.

George was serving with the Royal Artillery when he gained the Victoria Cross, and he later transferred to the 5th Battalion, Military Train. Lieutenant Symons' original citation stated that he performed the deed on 18 October 1854, but this was later amended to 6 June 1855. This caused confusion, and some sources say that he was also awarded the Distinguished Conduct Medal but there is no DCM at Camberley.

His award of the Victoria Cross was announced in the *London Gazette* of 25 September 1857, and he was presented with the medal by Queen Victoria at a ceremony held in the Quadrangle of Windsor Castle on 28 November 1857, with the whole of the Windsor garrison attending. Joseph Malone, James Craig and Sir Christopher Teesdale received their awards at the same ceremony. He also received the Crimea Medal with *Inkerman* and *Sebastopol* clasps, the Turkish Crimea Medal and the Sardinian Medal of Military Valour.

He returned to the Royal Artillery in 1862, and reached the rank of captain in the Yorkshire Volunteer Artillery.

George died on 18 November 1871, aged 45, at Bridlington in Yorkshire, and he was buried at St Mary the Virgin, Burlington Priory churchyard. Most of the headstones were cleared in the 1950s and 1960s, possibly his too, but there is a memorial inside St Mary the Virgin Church, and a new headstone was erected in 2013. He is named on the memorial plaque at the Royal Artillery Chapel in Woolwich. His medals are held by the Royal Logistic Corps Officers' Mess at Camberley.

Thomas Arthur

Thomas Arthur was born on 28 August 1836, at Abbotsham, near Bideford in Devon, and he was baptised at St Helen's Church in the same year. He was the only son and second child of four to Thomas Arthur, a labourer, and his wife Jane. It seems that local parish records show the family name as 'Arthurs', and his father may have died before Thomas was born because parish records show the funeral of a Thomas Arthurs in 1836, and he is not named on the 1841 census. There were older twin sisters named Kitty and Fanny. He is believed to have worked as a labourer on the farm of John Becklick at Parkham, before he ran away from home and enlisted into the Royal Artillery at Devonport in March 1853. He was 5ft 6in tall, with a fresh complexion, hazel eyes and brown hair. He sailed from Liverpool on the troopship *Niagara*, for active service in the Crimea, with the 1st company, 5th Battalion, on 1 December 1854.

His award of the Victoria Cross was announced in the *London Gazette* of 24 February 1857, and he received the medal at the first investiture. He also received the Crimean Medal with *Sebastopol* clasp and the Turkish Crimea Medal.

On his return to Woolwich in March 1857, he took two days off absent without leave, and found himself being court-martialled and serving a twenty-eight-day sentence at Weedon Military Prison in Northamptonshire. He was released only nine days before he attended the first investiture.

In the following year he served in the second Anglo-China (Opium) War of 1860, taking part in another dangerous assault at the Taku Forts on 21 August 1860. On this occasion the assault was successful. The attacking force had to cross a series of ditches and bamboo-stake palisades under heavy fire from the ramparts. Assault parties eventually breached the defences and forced entry into the fort. For his service he received the China Medal with *Taku Forts* clasp.

He married Ann Goddard at Aldershot on 6 July 1859, and they went on to have eight children. He sailed to India in 1866, where his wife gave birth to several more girls. He changed his surname to McArthur and his wife changed her name to Britannia while they were in India.

Sergeant Major Gower states in his memoirs: 'I had the pleasure of meeting him [Arthur] afterwards in India, with the cross upon his noble breast – "Gunner Arthur".'

The 1881 census states that he was living with his wife and five daughters with the surname McArthur, at 7 Cadley Square in South Savernake, Wiltshire. The 1891 census describes him as a Chelsea Pensioner, and by 1901 he was back in Wiltshire, living at 28 Cadley in Savernake, with his wife, a daughter and a granddaughter.

Thomas died at Savernake, on 2 March 1902, aged 67, and he was buried at Christ Church in Cadley near Savernake, where there was a headstone bearing the surname MacArthur. However, the church has been deconsecrated and is now a private house. His wife died in 1915. There is a stone plaque dedicated to him at the foot of the cross commemorating the war dead in St Helen's churchyard, and his name is on the memorial at the Royal Artillery Chapel in Woolwich. His Victoria Cross was sold for £42 in 1902, and his medals are at the Royal Artillery Regiment Museum in Woolwich.

Thomas Wilkinson

Thomas Wilkinson was born at Marygate in York in 1831. Marygate runs along the eastern wall of St Mary's Abbey which now encloses the grounds of the Yorkshire Museum, and includes St Olave's Church. A Mrs Maria Wilkinson is recorded as living in Marygate in 1840, also Charles Wilkinson, a tanner, and John Wilkinson of 23 Marygate.

His award of the Victoria Cross was announced in the *London Gazette* of 24 February 1857, and he received the medal during the first investiture. He also received the Crimea Medal with *Balaclava, Inkerman* and *Sebastopol* clasps, the French Legion of Honour and the Turkish Crimea Medal.

He went on to become a sergeant instructor for the Auxiliary Forces, being invalided from service on 12 October 1859. He returned to York, and lived with his wife, Mary Ann, at 33 North Street, where he managed Rymer's Sand Yard.

Thomas died of exhaustion and diarrhoea in York, on 22 September 1887, aged 55, and he was buried with full military honours in York Cemetery. A commemorative headstone was erected to his memory by his fellow officers to: 'Honour the Brave', and a memorial bench with a commemorative plaque was placed near his grave in 1992. Wilkinson House at the Royal Marines Barracks in Eastney was named after him, as was Wilkinson Drive at the Royal Marines Depot in Deal. His medals were purchased by officers of the Royal Marine Artillery in 1918, and they are with the Royal Marines Museum in Eastney. The Royal Marines Association conduct a service of remembrance each year around the grave.

Henry Mitchell Jones

Henry Mitchell (or Michael) Jones was born at Crumlin in Dublin on 11 February 1831. He was commissioned into the 60th Rifles as ensign in 1849, and exchanged into the 18th (Royal Irish) Regiment in April 1849. He was commissioned as lieutenant in the 7th Royal Fusiliers for service in the Crimea. He carried the bullet he received at the Alma in his jaw for thirty years, until he complained of toothache and a doctor removed the bullet which he been lodged in his jawbone. He was promoted captain in 1855. Several officers who served with him supported his claim to have been wounded eight times and broke out of hospital twice to get back into action.

He is said to have threatened to resign his commission if he was not awarded the Victoria Cross, which he did three months before the announcement in the *London Gazette* of 25 September 1857, and he received the medal in June 1863, from Lieutenant Colonel T. Pattle at Canterbury. He also received the Crimea Medal with *Inkerman* and *Sebastopol* clasps, the French Legion of Honour and the Turkish Crimea Medal.

He entered the diplomatic service in 1858, to become acting vice consul at Bosna Seraj (Sarajevo) and Scutari. He was appointed to the Pacific as consul to the Fiji and Tonga Islands in 1863, consul general at Tabreez (now in Azerbaijan) in 1868, at Christiania in 1875 and at Philippopolis in Eastern Rumelia (now Plovdiv, Bulgaria) in 1880. In 1889 he was appointed resident at Bangkok, and in 1895 he was transferred to be resident minister and consul general at Lima and Quito in South America. He retired from the diplomatic service in 1898.

About thirty years after being shot at the Alma he complained of toothache and a doctor removed the bullet which had been lodged in his jawbone. He claimed that his recipe for long life was 'eighteen holes of golf before lunch, eighteen holes after lunch, and a couple of glasses of whiskey'.

Henry died on 18 October 1916, aged 85, in his home at 25 Gildredge Road in Eastbourne, and he was buried at Ocklynge Old Cemetery in Eastbourne. The headstone gives his middle name as Michael. His medals are held by the Army Museum of New South Wales at Victoria Barracks in Sydney, Australia. The only Crimean War holder of the Victoria Cross to survive him was Surgeon William Sylvester.

His son, Lieutenant Oliver St Michael Jones of the Nottinghamshire and Derbyshire Regiment, was killed in action at the Third Battle of Ypres on 4 October 1917.

Matthew Hughes

Matthew Hughes was born in Bradford in 1822, the son of Samuel and Alice Hughes. Standing only 5ft tall, he joined the 7th Royal Fusiliers at Leeds, aged 18, as 1879 Private Hughes. He discharged by purchase in January 1844, only to re-enlist in June of the same year. He spent a month 'in custody of the Civil Powers' in 1845. He sailed for active service in the Crimea, where he was promoted corporal before his Victoria Cross achievements.

His award of the Victoria Cross was announced in the *London Gazette* of 24 February 1857, and he received at the first investiture. He also received the Crimea Medal with *Alma, Inkerman* and *Sebastopol* clasps and the Turkish Crimea Medal.

His wife was named Ellen, and they had a daughter named Mary Ann born in Staffordshire in 1860. He became a beer-house keeper at 147 Wapping Road in Bradford, and he was believed to be in his 59th year when he died of cirrhosis and exhaustion on 9 January 1882, at the house where he was lodging in Wapping Road. He was buried at Undercliffe Cemetery in Bradford, where a headstone was erected in 1997. His medals are in the Royal Fusiliers Museum at the Tower of London

Frederick Cockayne Elton

Frederick Cockayne Elton was born on 23 April 1832, at the Manor House in Whitestaunton, Chard, Somerset. The house features roman walls nearly two centuries old, and was the subject of a *Time Team* investigation in 2003.

Frederick was the oldest of four sons in a family of eight children to the Revd William Tierney Elton, who was rector of St Andrew's Church in Whitestaunton in Somerset for forty-eight years until his death in 1874, and Lucy Caroline, the daughter of Sir Charles Abraham, 6th Baronet Elton of Bristol. There is a stained-glass window dedicated to them in the church. Frederick was descended from the Bayard family who served as prominent lawyers and politicians throughout American history, and provided six senators from Delaware in the United States government serving from 1789–1929.

Frederick wanted to seek adventure, and when the Crimean War broke out he entered the 55th (Westmoreland) Regiment. In a letter he wrote to his father he expressed his anger of the lack of recognition given to his regiment by Lord Raglan and others.

> We are awfully disgusted at Lord Raglan's despatch about the Quarries. Our party was not only there but was so desperately engaged that we lost one officer and 27 men killed and 28 wounded and yet the number of the regiment is not even mentioned while in every other instance or nearly so, every single officer is mentioned

as having greatly distinguished themselves while they were most of them not nearly so forward as we were nor were they in nearly so much danger. It is enough to disgust one of ever going to the front again if it can be avoided and I should not be surprised if it had that effect on the men for of course they look out for being mentioned as a body in the papers just as much as we do.

His award of the Victoria Cross was announced in the *London Gazette* of 24 February 1857, and he received the medal on 20 July 1857 from Lieutenant General J. Fergusson, the officer commanding in Gibraltar. He also received the Crimea Medal with *Inkerman* and *Sebastopol* clasps, the French Legion of Honour, the Turkish Order of the Medjidie (5th Class) and the Turkish Crimea Medal.

He later served as captain in the 21st (Royal Scots) Regiment and the 67th (South Hampshire) Regiment. He married Mary Jane Rynd on 10 June 1863, at St Ann's Church, Dawson Street in Dublin, his wife being of Irish descent.

Frederick died in London on 24 March 1888, aged 55. He died in the same year as his mother and they were buried in the family plot in the chancel at St Andrew's churchyard in Whitestaunton. There is a headstone, and a bronze plaque inside St Andrew's Church. He is named on the VC memorial plaque at Carlisle Cathedral. His Victoria Cross is held at the Border Regiment Museum housed in Carlisle Castle.

Thomas de Courcy Hamilton

Thomas de Courcy Hamilton was born on 20 July 1825, at Stranraer, Wigtownshire (now Dunfries and Galloway), Scotland, the second son of James John Hamilton of Ballymacoll, County Meath, and Anne Geraldine de Courcy of Kinsale in County Cork. He was the grandson of John de Courcy, 26th Baron Kingsale.

He was commissioned as ensign in the 90th (Perthshire) Light Infantry, on 30 September 1842, and served at the Cape of Good Hope during the seventh Frontier War of 1846–7, where he was promoted lieutenant on 10 April 1847. For his service he received the South Africa Medal, 1835–53. In 1848 he exchanged into the 1st Battalion, 68th (Durham) Light Infantry, becoming adjutant in 1850, and captain on 1 December 1854.

His award of the Victoria Cross was announced in the *London Gazette* of 24 February 1857, and he received the medal alongside Private Byrne from Major General Sir George Butler, the officer commanding at the Ionian Islands station on Corfu, on 22 July 1857. He also received the Crimea Medal with *Alma, Balaclava, Inkerman and Sebastopol* clasps, the French Legion of Honour and the Turkish Crimea Medal.

On 8 September 1857, at Trinity Church, Marylebone, London, he married Mary Anne Louisa, daughter of Sir William Baynes, 2nd Baronet. She travelled to Corfu with him and they made their home on the island for five years. Their first two children were born there, and according to the 1881 census other children were born in India and Gibraltar, two in Malta and another in Hampshire.

He was appointed brevet major at Colchester, and then he accepted a staff appointment at Corfu station of the Ionian Islands. He was appointed brevet major in the 8th (King's) Regiment in 1862, and lieutenant colonel commanding the 64th (2nd Staffordshire) Regiment. He was appointed brevet colonel in 1873, and had gained the honorary rank of major general on his retirement from the army on 24 February 1874.

He settled with his family in the fashionable Pittville area of Cheltenham, where they lived at a house called Dunboyne, at 3 Beaufort Villas (now West Approach Drive). He was a parishioner of St Stephen's Church at Tivoli, where he served as a churchwarden, 1893–4, and of All Saints' Church. He served as a Cheltenham Magistrate from 1881–93, and was a founder of the Gordon Boys Brigade.

Thomas died at Cheltenham on 3 March 1908, aged 82, and after a service at All Saints' Church he was buried in Cheltenham Cemetery, where there is a headstone. He is named on the memorial and the regimental colour in the garrison church of St George at Whittington Barracks in Lichfield, and on the 'For Valour' stone at the Durham Light Infantry Museum in Durham.

John Byrne

John Byrne was born on 27 September 1832, at Castlecomer in County Limerick, Ireland. He enlisted into the 68th (Durham) Light Infantry at Coventry on 27 July 1850, as 2832 Private John Byrne. It seems he was not an ideal soldier as he was sent to military prison for a second time in November 1853, and had to be released from his cell to join his regiment for active service in the Crimea.

His award of the Victoria Cross was announced in the *London Gazette* of 24 February 1857, and he received the medal alongside

Captain Hamilton, from Major General Sir George Butler, the officer commanding at the Ionian Islands station on Corfu, on 22 July 1857. He also received the Crimea Medal with *Alma, Balaclava, Inkerman* and *Sebastopol* clasps and the Turkish Crimea Medal.

Having been made a corporal in 1861, in late 1863 he sailed with his regiment for active service in New Zealand, where Maori warriors had risen up against the expansion of British settlements on the North Island. The Maoris built wooden stockades protected by trenches called pahs and during the campaign British troops had to find the stockades and assault them. On 21 April 1864, British forces came upon 600 warriors building a new pah at Te Ranga. The British attacked, and Corporal Byrne was the first man of his company to jump into the rifle pit, where he bayoneted a warrior. Despite this, the warrior grabbed Byrne's rifle and in a ferocious hand-to-hand fight he tried to disarm him. The warrior then raised his battle axe to bring it down on Byrne, but Sergeant John Murray came to his aid and killed the warrior. For their gallantry during this action John Murray was awarded the Victoria Cross, and Corporal John Byrne received the Distinguished Conduct Medal. For his service he also received the New Zealand Medal, 1860–6.

John was promoted to sergeant in 1866, and took his discharge from the army at Cork on 14 May 1872. He was 5ft 7in tall, with a fresh complexion, grey eyes and brown hair. He settled in Durham, where he and John Murray joined the 2nd North Durham Militia, as a colour sergeant. However, he was discharged within a few months for: 'insubordination and highly improper conduct'. It seems he then went to Cork in Ireland.

His landlady said at the inquest after his death that he had arrived in Bristol in October 1878, claiming that he had lost all his possessions in a fire at Cork. He then went to live in lodgings at 7 Crown Street, Maindee, Caerleon in Monmouthshire, and began working for the new Ordnance Survey at Caerleon. On 10 July 1879, he got into an argument with a fellow workman named John Watts, who had apparently insulted the Victoria Cross. He pulled out a revolver and shot Watts in the right shoulder, which fortunately turned out to be just a flesh wound. John was not aware of how seriously he had injured the man, and when police arrived at his lodgings later that day they heard a bang and found him on the floor of his room having shot himself in the mouth. He was aged 46. An inquest found that he had committed suicide while of unsound mind. He was buried in an unmarked grave at St Woolas Cemetery in

Newport, where a headstone was erected in 1985. He is named on the 'For Valour' stone at the Durham Light Infantry Museum in Durham. The whereabouts of his Victoria Cross and Distinguished Conduct Medal are not known (possible lost in the fire in Cork), and his New Zealand campaign medal is at the Durham Light Infantry Museum.

John Lyons

John Lyons was born in 1823, at Carlow in Ireland. His colleague, Samuel Evans, stated in a newspaper article that he was born in Paisley.

He was employed as a painter before he joined the 19th (1st Yorkshire, North Riding) Regiment as 1651 Private Lyons, on 11 July 1842; his younger brother, Edward, also joined the regiment. He served on the Mediterranean islands of Malta and Corfu, the Caribbean islands of Barbados and St Vincent, and at Montreal and Ottawa in Canada, before returning to England in 1851. He served at various Home stations, and with the Grenadier Company at the Tower of London, before sailing with 8 companies of the regiment totalling 900 hundred men from Portsmouth in May 1854, for active service in the Crimea.

His award of the Victoria Cross was announced in the *London Gazette* for 24 February 1857, and he received the medal at the first investiture. He also received the Crimea Medal with *Alma, Inkerman* and *Sebastopol* clasps, the French Legion of Honour (5th Class) and the Turkish Crimea Medal.

He achieved the rank of corporal, and was returned sick to England in 1861 and discharged from the army on medical grounds on 6 December 1862. He was allowed to remain at the Royal Hospital in Chelsea to convalesce for six months and was released as an out-pensioner on 14 July 1863. He returned to Carlow, and then on to Naas in County Kildare.

John died at Naas on 20 April 1867, aged 44. It is believed that on his death his relatives dressed him in his uniform, attached his medals and prepared him for burial. They then decided to prop his body up in a chair for the local photographer to take his picture. There is no known memorial.

His Victoria Cross and medals were sold at auction in London in 1897 and were purchased by Lieutenant Colonel Andrew Munro, late of the 19th Regiment, who presented them to the Green Howards Museum in Richmond. Lyons Road in Richmond is named after him.

Joseph Prosser

Joseph Prosser was born in 1828, in the village of Moneygall, King's County (now Offaly) in Ireland, which was also home to some of the ancestors of the 44th United States President, Barack Obama, who visited the village in 2011.

Joseph is believed to have enlisted as a drummer boy in 1842, at Kinsale, County Cork, when he would have been aged 14, joining the 2nd Battalion, 1st (Royal Scots) Regiment, as 1672 Private Prosser. He was described as being 5ft 5in tall, with a fresh complexion, blue eyes and brown hair.

His first station was Canada, and he was on board the troopship HMS *Premier* sailing from Quebec to a new station at Barbados when the vessel ran into a bad storm during the dark hours of 4 November 1843. As she tried to keep as close to the coast as she could, she struck a reef and lost her rudder, was holed in her bow and became stranded on a sandbank. All 350 lives on board, including women and children, were in great peril, but they managed to evacuate the ship without loss of life, and survived the harsh North American winter for 3 weeks until being rescued. For their discipline and courage the men received the compliments of Queen Victoria and the Duke of Wellington.

He had apparently built up a reputation for being handy with his fists and prepared to use them, and the first years of his military career were somewhat chequered. In 1846 he was sentenced to twenty-eight days' confinement in cells at Aldershot. He served in Ireland from 1847–52, during which time he witnessed his fellow countrymen suffer the 'Great Hunger' caused by the failure of the potato crop. Having been refused permission to visit his family he went absent without leave, but he was returned to the barracks before he could reach his home town and served twenty-eight days' confinement in cells. He went absent without leave again on 26 April 1848, and this time he managed to reach Moneygall, where he found the village was deserted, and the only information he learned was that his brother John had gone to live in Liverpool.

He returned to his battalion voluntarily, where he was charged with desertion, and a court martial sentenced him to eighty-four days' confinement in cells, and he forfeited all his time in the army from the age of 18. He spent the next two years at the Cephalonia station in the Ionian Islands, before receiving orders for active service as part of the reinforcements destined for the Crimea, reaching Sebastopol in May 1855.

His award of the Victoria Cross was announced in the *London Gazette* of 24 February 1857, and he received the medal from Colonel, Sir Edward Blakeney, the general officer in command at Gibraltar. He also received the Crimea Medal with *Sebastopol* clasp and the Turkish Crimea Medal, and his service record was restored.

From Malta the regiment went to Gibraltar, and then to the Hong Kong station for active service during the Second China War of 1857–60. However, on his arrival he was found to be suffering from hepatitis and was confined to military hospital. He was brought back to health by an Irish nurse named Katherine Riddle. They became a couple, and in 1860 a child named Ellen was born to them.

On their return to England they lived in married quarters at Aldershot, but Joseph's illness continued and he was admitted to the Royal Victoria Hospital in Netley. A medical board at Aldershot found that he was unfit for further service and he left the army on 30 June 1863. His service record was not good, but he did have two good conduct badges, and he was granted a pension.

He decided to go to be near his brother, and set up home at 8 Lancaster Street in Kirkdale, Liverpool, where he became an outdoor customs officer on the docks. Katherine Victoria was born in August 1863, and after a move to 96 Gordon Street off Great Homer Street, Joseph William was born on 4 June 1865. A final move was to 26b Birchfield Street in the Islington district, where Mary was born on 10 March 1867.

By that time Joseph was becoming very ill, and he died of pulmonary phthisis at his home on 10 June 1867, aged 39. He was buried in a public grave at Anfield Cemetery, Liverpool, where a new headstone was erected in 1995. His medals were purchased in 1954 by the Royal Scots Regimental Museum at Edinburgh Castle.

Chapter 11

The First Assault on the Great Redan

Nothing much happened for the next week or so. Some men became frustrated by the stalemate, and some even complained of boredom, but it was literally the quiet before the storm.

A council meeting between Lord Raglan and Marshall Pelissier was held on 10 June, during which it was decided that an assault should be made on the morning of 18 June 1855. The French would try to take control of the Malakoff Tower and the British would battle for the Great Redan, and consequently end the siege. The date was of great significance in that it was the fortieth anniversary of the British victory over the French at the Battle of Waterloo. It was considered to be a good omen for the British – but not so much for the French?

The Great Redan had been constructed by throwing up thick walls of earth stretching 70ft wide and about 15ft high on each side of a middle section that jutted out like the front of a ship known as the salient, which was slightly higher than the rest. This was protected by an enormous ditch that was about 11ft deep and 15ft wide, and beyond that was a rampart of brush and bushes which had been tied together and placed with their branches outward as a kind of barbed-wire entanglement known as *abattis* as an obstacle to impede the advance of attacking troops. It was very high and many feet deep. Fougasses (rudimentary landmines) were buried all around. The fortification bristled with guns, some in two tiers, which could enfilade all the approaches. The cannon were placed behind embrasures protected by rope mantlets to shield the gunners from musket fire. Looking out from the British trenches the men saw that they had to advance across a large expanse of rising open ground and negotiate a steep slope, or glacis, before they even got to the defences. The Great Redan was virtually impregnable to attacking infantry.

The bombardment on 8 June had been instrumental in the success of the attack on the Quarries, so it was decided that a similar bombardment throughout 17 June, and for a few hours before the attack on the following morning, would demoralise the enemy by destroying the defences they had struggled to repair overnight, put most of their guns out of action and force a gap through the *abattis* by blasting it away or setting it on fire.

The plan of action was that the assault would be in three sections. Each section consisted of about a hundred men acting as skirmishers, who were to go forward and use rapid fire to try to pin down the enemy at the walls, followed by men carrying woolsacks and ladders to fill in and bridge the ditches, ready for the storming parties of about 400 men to follow, and the first men over were to use the same ladders to scale the walls. Spiking parties were to disable the enemy guns. In reserve were 800 men made up of 2 infantry regiments, including a working party of 400. Lieutenant Charles Gordon of the Royal Engineers, who would later find fame as Gordon of Khartoum, was with these reserves.

On the morning of the attack Lord Raglan was in the trench at the rear of the Quarries, and Marshal Pelissier was in a battery to the rear of the Mamelon; a considerable distance apart. The British troops had already moved down to the forward trenches preparing for the attack, when Pelissier made the extraordinary decision to cancel the preliminary bombardment, and to bring the French attack forward to when the first light began to dawn. It may have been that he thought his men would get forward quickly in a surprise attack and take the Malakoff by storm, and any bombardment could have put them in danger. He announced his new intentions to the English Engineer-in-Chief who, after some delay, relayed the message to Lord Raglan.

The troops assembling in the trenches preparing for the assault included four teenagers and another man who had only recently turned 20, who were among twenty men about to perform deeds which would help to earn them the Victoria Cross; the most ever awarded for a single action. One cannot imagine how such young men must have felt when they realised the task set before them. An assistant surgeon had to accompany each regiment and the medical men drew lots to see who would have to go. One of those chosen stated: 'I did not esteem the privilege very highly.' What they did not know was that the Russians had worked strenuously to rebuild the defences, and they too had realised the significance of the date. They anticipated an assault, and when they saw the British moving down to their forward trenches they were ready.

The signal to commence the assault on the Mamelon was the firing of three 'Whistling Dicks' (rocket mortars), which cascaded up in what was described as 'a spectacular sight'. The French advanced, only to be met by bullets and grape-shot, which smashed into them and broke their nerve, and the attack quickly faltered. Lord Raglan was able to witness the French failure. He was in the habit of referring to the French as 'the enemy' – as he had done at Waterloo, and a captain of the 38th (1st Staffordshire) Regiment said: 'Lord Raglan, they say, cannot make up his mind to do anything, and is undecided in everything'.

Instead of delaying the British assault, or cancelling it completely, he thought that his army would come under criticism for not supporting the French, and that British pride was at stake. Times differ on exactly when the attack began, but the flag to commence the assault was hoisted, the order was given: 'and away we went'.

For a third time Captain Peel displayed his bravery by volunteering to lead the first ladder party, and Gunner Arthur, who had already shown his desire to act without orders for the chance to go into action, ran out of his battery and formed up with one of the spiking party. Lieutenant Gerald Graham of the Royal Engineers had been wounded for a second time on 5 July 1855, and had to go to Therapia, but he was back on duty in time for the assault on the Redan. He led a section which consisted of over 200 men, including 10 men of the Royal Sappers and Miners leading 2 sections of sailors totalling 90 tars, carrying ladders and wool-bags. Among these were Colour Sergeant Peter Leitch, who had seen service with the Baltic Fleet, and Sapper John Perie.

The men scrambled out of their trenches and advanced towards the Redan. As they were doing so, many senior officers clambered onto the parapets of front trenches and waved their swords in the air, shouting words of encouragement. Captain Peel used unit rivalry to spur his men on, by calling out: 'Come on sailors, don't let the soldiers beat you.'

The Russians allowed the front ranks to get well out into the open where there was no cover before they opened fire with rifles and grapeshot, and other iron missiles of all descriptions ploughed up the ground. The assault columns were swept away in all directions by the thunderous fire, and as they went forward they bent down as they rushed into the storm of bullets in a futile attempt to make a more difficult target, but it was impossible for them to make much progress under such an horrific barrage.

142

Captain Peel was about half-way up the glacis when he came under a hail of withering rifle bullets which tore up his tunic and sliced open the pistol case he had recently received from home. One shot went right through his left arm. As usual, Midshipman Daniel was close by and immediately came to his aid. In full view of the enemy, he tied a tourniquet around the limb to try to stop the bleeding. During the action Daniel's pistol case was twice shot through and his clothes were cut to pieces, but he managed to get his leader to a place of comparative safety without himself being wounded.

Soon after Lieutenant Knox left the trench he came upon Captain Edward William Blackett of his battalion, dragging himself back to the British lines dangerously wounded, and the command fell upon him. On seeing many men carrying the ladders being shot down he realised that there was no point in reaching the parapet if they could not scale it, so he left the skirmishers of the Rifle Brigade and volunteered to assist the ladder party. He and Captain Edward Roland Foreman reached the *abattis*, where they took the chance to fire some rounds in the direction of the enemy positions and discussed what they should do next. Lieutenant Knox had his rifle trained on a Russian when he was shot in the left arm. Captain Foreman remarked: 'You are wounded.' To which Lieutenant Knox replied: 'I fancy I am.' The captain was in the process of binding up the wound with a handkerchief when he was struck by grapeshot and fell dead at his stricken comrade's feet. Lieutenant Knox decided he could do no more and made his way back. As he did so a grape shot struck him in his already injured arm and lodged there. He remained on his feet until he got into the British trenches where he collapsed from loss of blood and shock. Four soldiers of the 23rd Fusiliers put him on a stretcher, and as they rushed him to the nearest casualty station Lord Raglan enquired about him. Lieutenant Knox was twice offered some brandy but refused.

Lieutenant Graham's unit had advanced about 50yd when they halted and came under intense enemy fire and many of them were hit, but it was observed that despite his vast stature, which made him strangely conspicuous in the field, he seemed to lead a charmed life as he directed his men and he was not hit. Colonel Richard Tylden came up waving his sword above his head and shouted for them to go on. Lieutenant Graham pointed out that it was better to assault the salient instead of the right flank, and the colonel agreed: 'Anywhere, as long as you get on!' He was then struck down, and throwing his sword to the ground Lieutenant Graham, helped by Sergeant Coppin and Sapper

Ewen, carried the mortally wounded officer the 50yd or so back towards the British lines, where they found a more sheltered spot for him.

With cool courage Lieutenant Graham returned to collect his sword and re-joined his men, where he directed the woolpack and ladder parties towards the salient. With men being hit by all kinds of metal and falling or being blasted out of existence all around them, some men got beyond the *abbatis* and reached the ditch. Lieutenant Graham halted them there and waited for the Riflemen to cover them before he gave the order to advance further. However, most of the attacking force seemed to be moving westward under the command of Colonel Lord West of the 21st Regiment, where he had decided to lead another storming party made up of men from the Reserves. Many of the soldiers in the ladder parties had been cut down by the furious fire of the enemy, but the sailors were eager for another try. Lieutenant Graham could only muster four men for each ladder instead of six, but on Lord West's request he moved his gallant party of men out under a murderous fire. They got as far as some open ground and lay down on the grass and waited for the skirmishers to arrive. However, when no skirmishers or stormers appeared Lieutenant Graham had no option but to order his surviving men to fall back to the British lines.

Colour Sergeant Leitch immediately began to tear down the gabions from the parapet, and on hastily refilling them he threw some down into the ditch and placed others across the gap to form a ramp, and built up a caponier to try to provide some protection for the stormers. However, as he did so he was disabled by enemy fire. As Sapper Perie was attempting the same difficult work he was wounded in his side, but still found the strength to rescue an injured man.

During the retreat, Sergeant Park and Colour Sergeant Gardiner showed unflinching and devoted courage as they encouraged others to find shelter in the craters made by the explosion of the shells, and by making parapets of the dead bodies of their comrades, they kept up a continuous fire and managed to keep the enemy back from the parapet of the Redan until their ammunition was exhausted. This was done under a fire in which nearly half the officers and a third of the rank-and-file were killed or wounded. Their actions were noted and remarked for determined resolution.

After being engaged in the assault and returning to the relative safety of the trenches when the column had retired, many men repeatedly went out across the open ground in front of the advance trenches under a very heavy fire of musketry and grape and assisted in rescuing wounded comrades from exposed situations, at great personal risk to themselves. Those most noted for this were Corporal Philip Smith of the 17th (Leicestershire) Regiment, Private John Sims of the 34th (Cumberland) Regiment and Private John Alexander of the 90th (Perthshire) Light Infantry.

Lieutenant William Hope of the 7th (Royal) Fusiliers was informed by Sergeant Major William Bacon, who was wounded, that his fellow officer, Lieutenant James Hobson, was lying severely wounded outside the trenches. He went to search for him and found him lying in the agricultural ditch leading towards the left flank of the Redan and tried to assist him. Seeing that he could not be moved without a stretcher, he went back to Egerton's Pit to collect a stretcher and returned to him with four others, including Private Hughes, and this time succeeded in bringing the officer to shelter. All the time they were under continuous fire, and Private Hughes was severely wounded. Unfortunately, Lieutenant Hobson later died of his wounds, and it seems the three other men in the stretcher party were killed.

Lieutenant Henry Raby of HMS *Wasp*, Naval Brigade, acted as second-in-command to Lieutenant Edward D'Aeth of the 4th Ladder Party. This ladder party did not actually take part in the assault on the Redan fortifications, but later that day a soldier of the 57th Regiment, who had been wounded in both legs, was observed sitting up and calling for help. Climbing over the breastwork of the advance sap, Lieutenants Raby and D'Aeth, and two sailors of the Naval Brigade named Henry Curtis of HMS *Rodney* and John Taylor of HMS *London* at once left the shelter of their battery works and, as hundreds of men were running away from the Redan, at the imminent risk of their own lives they ran through heavy gunfire across the open ground towards the danger for a distance of 70yd as far as the salient angle of the Redan. The heavy gunfire persisted throughout the rescue attempt, and they were continuously dodging bullets, but they succeeded in carrying the wounded man to safety.

The three sappers already mentioned showed devoted heroism in sallying out of the trenches on numerous occasions and bringing in wounded officers and men. Sapper Perie did so despite his wound. That night, another Engineer, Captain Howard Elphinstone, requested to command a party of volunteers, who proceeded to search for and bring back the scaling ladders left behind after the repulse; and while successfully performing this task, and of rescuing trophies from the Russians, Captain Elphinstone conducted a long search for wounded men who had fallen close to the enemy, twenty of whom he rescued and brought back to the trenches.

General William Eyre's 3rd Brigade assaulted from the extreme left of the left attack, about ¾ mile west of the Redan. His men included Sergeant McWheeney with the 44th Regiment and Captain Thomas Esmonde of the 18th (Royal Irish) Regiment. General Eyre's section of the line of attack was comparatively successful, and captured a number of positions. Sergeant McWheeney volunteered for the advance guard of his regiment during this assault.

All three section commanders led from the front and lost their lives. Colonel John Campbell displayed: 'a courage amounting to rashness' when he rushed out of the trenches and was shot through the head in the act of cheering on his men. His body, and that of Colonel Yea, were found close to the *abattis*, and there was evidence that an attempt had been made by means of grapnels to drag them into the Redan, presumably to obtain their clothing and anything valuable they had on them. Most of the slain officers had their epaulettes and boots taken from their bodies.

The British casualty list totalled over 1,500 men, and Lieutenant Graham wrote to his father on the day after the battle, saying: 'Sad work we have had today. The attack on the Redan failed . . . I was through it all, but not hurt, only very exhausted and depressed by our failure.' Lord West wrote: 'I wish I could do justice to the daring and intrepid conduct of the sailors. Lieutenant Graham of the Engineers evinced coolness and a readiness to expose himself to any personal risk, which does him the greatest credit.'

The day's events had such a bad effect on the men that one soldier remarked to some of them as they returned: 'All you fellows who have been in action today look about ten years older.'

Two days later, Captain Esmonde was in command of a working party when an enemy fire-ball fell close by intending to light up the area and exposed the position of the party of men. He called out to his men to take cover, then with the most prompt and daring gallantry he rushed out to the spot where the fire-ball lodged, and as he had anticipated, a hail of fire was directed at him, but he effectively extinguished the fire-ball before it had betrayed the position of the working party under his protection – thus saving it from a murderous fire of shell and grape.

Lieutenant Knox's arm had to be amputated from the socket during an operation performed without chloroform, and according to Knox himself he felt no pain. Apparently, only a week later this intrepid man was back on his feet a: 'none the worse man . . . although only one arm left'.

Henry James Raby

Henry James Raby was born on 26 September 1827, at Boulogne in France. He was one of six children of the well-known influential Llanelli industrialist Arthur Tournour Raby and his wife, Henrietta Jane, of Llanelli in south Wales. A street in the town bears the family name. His grandfather, Alexander Raby, had invested his entire wealth in the local iron and coal industries, which failed during the depression after the Napoleonic Wars, and Henry's father had to travel to France after the family home 'Plas Uchaf' (Upper Hall) in the village of Furnace was destroyed by fire. Henry was educated at Sherborne School in Dorset, where he was a member of Abbey House. He left Sherborne in 1838, and finished his education at Greenwich.

He entered the Royal Navy on 8 March 1842, as a volunteer first class on HMS *Monarch*. He was one of the men put ashore at Xanthus and helped with the removal and embarking of the Xanthian Marbles for the British Museum in 1842.

He served as a mate from 7 March 1848–14 January 1850, at various times with HMS *Rodney*, HMS *Trafalgar*, HMS *Victory*, HMS *Ocean* and HMS *Terrible*. He was promoted to lieutenant on 15 January 1850, and from 2 October of that year he served aboard HMS *Wasp* carrying out anti-slavery operations on the West Coast of Africa. He was then sent on active service in the East.

His award of the Victoria Cross was announced in the *London Gazette* on 24 February 1857, and he was the first man to receive the medal at the first investiture. He also received the Crimea Medal with *Inkerman* and *Sebastopol* clasps, the French Legion of Honour, the Turkish Order of the Medjidieh (5th Class), the Turkish Crimea Medal and the Sardinian Medal of Military Valour. Lieutenant D'Aeth, the son of an admiral, died of cholera at the Cossack Bay Hospital on 7 August 1855, and therefore did not receive the Victoria Cross for his part in the action.

He was promoted to commander two days after the action at the Redan in recognition of his bravery. Being described as: 'A very active officer, with considerable knowledge of affairs on the coast of Africa', Henry took command of HMS *Medusa* on 1 August 1856, and then HMS *Weber* on 12 October 1859. He commanded HMS *Alecto* from

27 January 1860, playing a prominent part in the suppression of the slave trade on the west coast of Africa, where he was present at the attack on and destruction of Porto Novo in Dahomey. He was wounded during these operations, on 23 April 1861, and he was frequently Mentioned in Despatches. He received the thanks of the Foreign Office for the conclusion of a treaty with the African chiefs of the Old Calabar River, which had been one of the main centres for the slave trade. He was promoted captain for his services, on 24 November 1862. He commanded HMS *Adventure* on the China station from 22 June 1868– 18 January 1871, when he retired from active service.

Henry married Judith, daughter of Colonel Watkin Forster, of Holt Manor, Trowbridge in Wiltshire, on 9 December 1863, at Bradford in Wiltshire. A son named Montague was born on 1 November 1865, followed by a daughter in 1867, Arthur in 1869 and a son named Henry who died at the age of 9 at Honfleur in France. Montague became a captain in the Royal Artillery, and died in Bath on 21 September 1897. He is buried with his father.

In 1875 he was reported to be living at Crembourne House on Nightingale Road in Southsea, Hampshire. Four years later he moved briefly to Bath, and then back to Southsea, where he lived at 6 Clarendon Parade. The 1881 census records him as having settled at 8 Clarence Parade. He was appointed Companion to the Order of the Bath (CB) on 29 May 1875, and he was appointed rear admiral on 21 March 1878. In July 1878 he returned for a nostalgic trip to Llanelli, where he visited Raby Street and Forge Row, and received a warm welcome from the residents. He also visited the burnt out ruins of the old family home.

He and his wife were involved in various charitable duties in Southsea, and they were listed for various appointments concerning the Royal Seamen and Marines Orphanage in Queen Street, and the Home for Sick Children at 2 Ryde View. Henry was also chairman of the Portsmouth and Hayling Lifeboat Committee from 1885 until his death.

When his wife died she was buried in St Mary's Cemetery in Bath, where his name appears on her headstone. He died of senile decay at his home on 13 February 1907, aged 79, and he was buried at Highland Road Cemetery in Portsmouth. There is a headstone at his grave, a memorial plaque at Holt parish church and a brass tablet dedicated to him at the entrance to Llanelli Town Hall. Having become a club member in 1871, he is one of four Crimean VCs named on the memorial in the corridor of the Royal Naval and Royal Albert Yacht Club in Portsmouth, which was unveiled by the Duke of Edinburgh in 2007. His medals were once displayed at the Royal Naval Museum, until being acquired by Lord Ashcroft in 2011, and they are now displayed on rotation at the Lord Ashcroft Gallery, as part of the 'Extraordinary Heroes' exhibition at the Imperial War Museum in London.

John (T.N.) Taylor

John Taylor was born in February 1822, in the parish of St Philip and St Jacob, Bristol, and later made his home in London. He entered the Royal Navy at the age of 19 as an ordinary seaman, being described as 5ft 9in tall, with a fresh complexion, grey eyes and brown hair. He had a crucifix and the initials JTNT tattooed on his right arm and a tree on his left.

His first ship was HMS *Cornwallis*, which he joined in October 1841, and like Captain Peel he saw active service during the First China War of 1840–2. He served on HMS *Eagle* from 1845–8, before he transferred to the flagship HMS *Hastings*, and like Edward Daniel he saw active service in the Second Anglo-Burmese War of 1852. He left the ship as Captain of the Forecastle in May 1853, and joined HMS *London*. It seems he was marked as a deserter from 17 August–18 October 1853. Having seen active service in China and Burma, he was perhaps the most experienced of all the twenty 18 June Redan Victoria Cross recipients, when he sailed for active service in the East.

John Taylor was later drafted to work with Florence Nightingale in the hospital at Scutari. However, his service in the Crimea had an adverse effect on his health. On his return to England he went to live in Woolwich, where he was a supernumerary boatswain with the Fishguard flagship. He was admitted into the Royal Marine Infirmary in Woolwich, with difficulty breathing and coughing up blood. He died of bronchitis and pulmonary congestion on 25 February 1857, aged 35, which was the day after his award of the Victoria Cross had been announced, and he had only just been informed of it a few hours before he died. A notice in the *Army and Navy Gazette* stated: 'The deceased was much esteemed by the officers in the Dockyard, and by those who knew him, and although covered with honours so unassuming was his character that he could scarcely be prevailed upon to wear them . . . unfortunately, this brave man has left a wife and family unprovided for'.

His widow, Elizabeth, wrote to the Admiralty in March 1857, informing them of his death and asking if she could represent him at the first investiture. A letter was sent back to her on 25 June stating: 'It would not be necessary for you to come to London . . .' – and the Victoria Cross was sent to her from the Admiralty by registered post on 7 July 1857. John was buried in an unmarked grave at Woolwich Cemetery, and a new headstone was erected at the grave in February 1996.

His medals are at the Sheesh Mahal Museum in Patiala, Punjab, India. The group formed part of the Maharaja Bhupendra Singh's collection which was bequeathed to the museum on the death of the Maharajah's son in 1947, and consists of the Victoria Cross, the Conspicuous Gallantry Medal (1st type), the China War Medal, 1842, India General Service Medal, 1835–54, with *Pegu* clasp, the Crimea Medal with *Inkerman* and *Sebastopol* clasps, the French Legion of Honour and the Turkish Crimea Medal. The collection also includes the medals of Thomas Beach and George Fiott Day.

Henry Curtis

Henry Curtis was born on 21 December 1823, and although he gave Romsey in Hampshire as his place of birth on censuses and his naval record, it seems that he was born in the village of Awbridge, in the parish of Michelmersh, near Romsey. The evidence for this is unclear as his place of birth on the 1861 census looks like 'Awbury'. However, his father is recorded as living in Awbridge in 1841, where he worked as a carpenter, and there is a baptism of a Henry Curtis in the neighbouring parish of Lockerley dated 15 February 1824, the son of Robert and Sarah Curtis. Henry is recorded on the 1841 census in Embley, aged 18 and employed as a servant.

Apparently, he was a big man, and he joined HMS *Victory* as a boy second class in June 1841, and after ten years' service he became a coast guard in August 1851. He stated that he was 'picked up' – usually meaning conscripted – to the ninety-gun, two-deck ship HMS *Rodney* in the following November. Midshipman (later Admiral) Kennedy, who joined the ship in the following month, described how crews were 'picked-up anyhow – long-shore loafers, jailbirds and such like, with a sprinkling of good seamen among them'. Henry Curtis was one such 'good seaman', who sailed for active service with the Black Sea Fleet as a boatswain's mate with HMS *Rodney*.

The award of the Victoria Cross to recently married Mate Curtis was announced in the *London Gazette* of 24 February 1857, and he received the medal at the first investiture. He also received the Crimea Medal with *Inkerman* and *Sebastopol* clasps and the Turkish Crimea Medal.

Henry left *Rodney* when she paid off in January 1856, and served aboard HMS *Ringdove* before joining the Coast Guard Service in November 1856. From March 1858 until his final discharge from the navy in November 1864, he served as Boatswain's Mate on the flagship HMS *Marlborough*, known as 'the smartest ship in the Service'. Lord Charles Beresford (later Admiral) joined the ship in 1861, and he remembered Curtis as: 'The great big Botswain's Mate', who remarked to another sailor on seeing the young Beresford: 'Mate, 'er's another orficer kim aboard jist in toime; but pore little beggar! – he aint long fur this world'. After four years' service in the Mediterranean, Henry was paid off with a medal and a gratuity of 10 guineas. His next employment was as chief quartermaster on a cross-Channel steamer sailing out of Southampton. Lord Charles came onboard one day and on recognising him he shook his hand.

Henry married Maria Morley, a brewer's daughter who was fifteen years younger than him, on 7 February 1856, at St Mary's Parish Church in Alverstoke, Gosport, and they made their home at 19 Bailey's Buildings, St Paul's Parish in Portsea. They had a son named Henry William on 17 June 1857, and a daughter named Maria in 1859, both born in Alverstoke, Gosport, and Victoria, born at Landport in Portsmouth in 1862. By 1871 they had moved to 123 Church Street, St Mary's Parish at Sholing in Southampton, where Charlotte was born in 1872 and Mabel was born in 1877. Henry was probably working on the cross-Channel ferry, and the three oldest children had moved away by 1881, leaving Maria and the two youngest girls living at 185 Botany Bay, Weston Common, South Stoneham, Southampton. Henry had retired by 1891, and they had moved to Portsmouth, where they settled at 82 Stirling Street, Buckland, Portsea.

The *Portsmouth News* of 7 April reported that on 1 April 1892, Henry had collected nearly £12 of his pension money, and on his returning home drunk, Maria asked him for some of it to buy food for the family. Henry refused, and set about punching her twice across her nose and threatening her with a 'loaded stick'. She was forced to seek the protection of her neighbours, who stated that he repeatedly shouted: 'I'm a gentleman' as he attacked her. Maria said that her life was 'a perfect misery' because he came home drunk every night. A police officer was called and Henry was issued with a summons to appear in court, to which he failed to comply. He had to be arrested and brought before the court, where he was sentenced to fourteen days' imprisonment with hard labour, and the bench advised him to behave better towards his wife when he came out of prison. There is no mention of him being a holder of the Victoria Cross.

Henry's drinking habits seemed to have had an adverse effect on his constitution, and he died of 'podagra [gout], and chronic Bright's uraemia [kidney failure]' on 23 November 1896, aged 74, and he was buried at Kingston Cemetery in Portsea. Maria was buried with him. The grave had been re-used by a lady whose family agreed to have her name put on a new stone which was erected in his honour at the grave in 1997.

His Victoria Cross was held at the British Steel Headquarters in Sheffield. Ironically, Mrs Freda McKay was working in the offices there when she was informed that her son Ian had been killed during the Falklands War, performing a gallant action for which he would be awarded the Victoria Cross. It was purchased by Lord Ashcroft in 1999, being the last Crimean War Victoria Cross to be sold at auction prior to going to publication. It is now displayed on rotation at the Lord Ashcroft Gallery, as part of the 'Extraordinary Heroes' exhibition at the Imperial War Museum in London.

Howard Crawfurd Elphinstone

Howard Elphinstone was born of a distinguished Scottish military and diplomatic family, at his family's country seat of 'Kumenhoff' at Wattram in Livonia, on 12 December 1829. He was the youngest of four sons to Captain Alexander Francis Elphinstone of the Royal Navy, a noble in Livonia, and his wife, Amelia Anne (formerly Lobach). His great-grandfather was Captain John Elphinstone of the Royal Navy, who became an admiral attached to the Russian Navy, and commanded the Russian Fleet in the victory over the Turks at the sea battle of Tchesme Bay in 1770. He was named after his uncle, Major General Sir Howard Elphinstone, who commanded the Royal Engineers during the Peninsular War.

Howard was educated abroad, and passed out of the Royal Military Academy at Woolwich as the head of his batch. He was commissioned as second lieutenant in the Royal Engineers on 18 December 1848, and became lieutenant on 11 November 1851. He attended military reviews in Prussia in an official capacity in 1853, after which he worked in the Ordnance Survey in Scotland until March 1854, when he received orders for active service in the Crimea.

His award of the Victoria Cross was announced in the *London Gazette* of 4 June 1858, and he received the medal from Queen Victoria on Southsea Common in Portsmouth on 2 August 1858, along with Edward Bell, Henry Ramage, James Mouat, Henry MacDonald, Matthew Dixon and Thomas Esmonde. He also received the Crimea Medal with *Alma, Inkerman* and *Sebastopol* clasps, the French Legion of Honour and the Turkish Order of the Medjidie (5th Class).

In March 1856 he went on an official mission to The Hague in the Netherlands, and reported on a public hospital in Rotterdam, and in September reported on the Koblenz siege operations. He was highly commended for these reports, and he received a promotion to brevet major on 26 December 1856. From 5 September 1857, he was employed in the topographical department of the War Office working on an official history of the Royal Engineers in the Crimea. In 1858, he was involved in the administration concerning the establishment of the 'The Prince Consort's Library' at Aldershot, which was a gift to the army from Prince Albert. He served in the North British Military District, and was promoted captain on 1 April 1862, brevet lieutenant-colonel on 9 April 1968 and he was appointed major on 5 July 1872.

He became a great friend of Albert, who appointed him as governor to his seventh child, the young Prince Arthur, Duke of Connaught, on 24 January 1859. Howard gave a comforting hand to the Queen on the death of her beloved husband in 1861. He became a close confidant to her, and he was appointed treasurer and comptroller of Prince Arthur's household in May 1871.

Bagshot Park in Surrey was a residence of the Duke of Connaught, and as most of his military service now centred around nearby Aldershot, Howard had a house built in Bagshot, which was off College Ride and was named 'Pinewood'.

On 5 December 1876, he married Annie Frances (formerly Cole), who was twenty-six years younger than him, at the Church of St Anne in Bagshot. Annie was the daughter of William Cole of Woodhay House in Newbury, and one of her relations was the famous eccentric prankster Horace de Vere Cole. They had four daughters: Victoria Alexandrina (1877–1952), Irene Francis (1878–1957), Olive Margaret (1882–1968) and Mary Howard (1888–1965). Queen Victoria stood sponsor for Victoria, and they all married army officers.

Howard was made Commander of the Bath (CB civil division) on 23 August 1865, (CB military division) on 20 May 1871, a Companion of the Order of St Michael and St George (CMG) on 28 July 1870 and

Knight Commander of the Order of the Bath (KCB) on 3 July 1871. He was appointed aide-de-camp to Queen Victoria on 1 October 1877.

He commanded the Royal Engineers units at Aldershot from August 1873–30 December 1881, and was colonel commanding Royal Engineer at Aldershot from 31 December 1881–30 December 1886. He became a colonel on 3 May 1884, and during 1884–5 he acted as temporary military attaché at Berlin. He was promoted major general on 29 January 1887, and on 1 April 1889, he was appointed to command the western military district. He was awarded the Queen Victoria Jubilee Medal in 1887, and he was also appointed Grand Officer of the Order of the Red Eagle (Prussia).

On 8 March 1890, he and his wife left Plymouth bound for Tenerife in the steamer *Tongariro* on leave for his health. He was walking on the deck near Ushant in the Bay of Biscay, when he slipped, hit his head and fell overboard. He was aged 60. His body was never recovered, so Queen Victoria, who was said to have been 'Much upset, and cried at the news' of his death, demanded that a memorial service was held at Exeter Cathedral.

His wife died in 1938, and there are brass plaques and a memorial window dedicated to them by their daughters at St Anne's Church in Bagshot, and at St Lawrence's Church in Newbury. There is a memorial at Exeter Cathedral; a memorial plaque at Devonport Chapel; a memorial at St George's Garrison Church in Aldershot; and he is named on the 'For Valour' commemoration board at the Royal Engineers Museum in Chatham. A locomotive nameplate bears his name at the Museum of Army Transport in Beverley, Yorkshire. His Victoria Cross is now displayed on rotation at the Lord Ashcroft Gallery, as part of the 'Extraordinary Heroes' exhibition at the Imperial War Museum in London. It is the only one of the four 18 June Redan Royal Engineers Victoria Crosses not in the regimental museum.

Gerald Graham

Gerald Graham was born at East Acton in West London, on 27 June 1831, the only surviving son of Dr Robert Hay Graham, who practised in London, but his main residence was Eden Brows at Armathwaite near Carlisle, and his wife, Frances, who was a daughter of Richard Banner Oakley of Oswaldkirk in Yorkshire. Gerald had an older sister named Joanna to whom he was devoted. His father was a director of various railway companies, who suffered from gout, and in 1844 he prepared a paper entitled *'Graeffenberg: or a True Report of the Water Cure'*, in which he devalues the claims of Vincent Priessnitz that the use of a water compress is a cure for the disease.

Gerald grew to be 6ft 4in tall and was stockily built. He and his sister were ardent readers of the classics, and he read and later befriended Charles Kingsley. However, he showed his prowess early in life when he is said to have jumped onto the back of a colt that was being difficult in a field at Eden Brows and stayed there despite the horse's wild efforts to throw him off. It had raced into the farmyard and smashed into a gatepost and nearly broke his leg; while several local farm lads looked on in astonishment at his 'fearless audacity'. He was educated in Wimbledon, at Dresden in Germany and at the Royal Military Academy in Woolwich. After completing his training at the School of Military Engineering in Chatham, he was commissioned as a 2nd lieutenant in the 11th Company, Royal Sappers and Miners, on 19 June 1850, becoming lieutenant on 17 February 1854.

He embarked for active service in the East with his company at Southampton, on 24 February 1854, on the steamship *Himalaya*. He was employed on constructing fortifications of Boulair in Gallipoli before moving on to Varna. After the fall of Sebastopol, he was engaged in the destruction of the docks, when he and Major Nicholson made a gallant attempt to rescue a man who was poisoned by the toxic air at the bottom of a shaft.

His award of the Victoria Cross was announced in the *London Gazette* on 24 February 1857, and he became the first member of the Corps of Royal Engineers to wear the medal when he received it at the first investiture. It is a known fact that Victoria pierced the skin of Commander Raby, but she must have done this more than once, as Gerald wrote to his father: 'We were formed in a line and then advanced singly to the Queen, who remained on horseback. She pinned the medal (cross) with her own hand to our coats. She stuck the pin fairly into me, so that I keenly realised my momentary interview with Royalty.' He also received the Crimea Medal with *Alma, Inkerman* and *Sebastopol* clasps, the French Legion of Honour, the Order of the Medjidieh (5th Class) and the Turkish Crimea Medal.

Dr Graham died at Eden Brows on 12 December 1859, and Gerald took over his estate. After being employed in Scotland and at Aldershot he was posted to India in August 1858 to take command of the 23rd Company, Royal Engineers, but the mutiny there was almost over. He was promoted captain on 8 October 1858, and his next tour of active duty was in China in 1859–60, where he served in the Second Anglo-China (Opium) War, taking part in another dangerous assault at the Taku Forts on 21 August 1860. On this occasion the assault was successful. The attacking force had to cross a series of ditches and bamboo-stake palisades under heavy fire from the defences. Assault parties eventually breached the defences and forced entry into the fort. He was seriously wounded when he was hit by a ball from a jingal fired from the ramparts. He received the China Medal with *Taku Forts* and *Pekin* clasps.

For the next sixteen years he was commanding engineer at various stations throughout England and Montreal, and he was appointed captain on 4 August 1864, major on 5 July 1872, lieutenant colonel on 27 September 1876 and he was appointed Commander of the Bath (CB) on 6 April 1867.

He served as brigadier general in Egypt in 1882 with his old friend Garnet Wolseley, commanding the second brigade of the first division throughout the campaign. He was in the thick of the action as usual, in the victories at El Magfar, Kassassin and Tel-el-Kebir. He commanded the Saukin Field Force in the Sudan, 1884–5, where he was in charge of the troops trying to relieve his friend, Charles Gordon, at Khartoum. For his service in north Africa he received the Egypt Medal with *Tel-el-Kebir, Saukin, 1884, El Teb-Tamaii* and *Saukin, 1885* clasps, the Order of the Medjidie (2nd Class) and the Khedive's Bronze Star. He wore on his breast a total of ten medals with nine clasps.

Lord Wolseley, who had known and witnessed the deeds of many gallant soldiers, described him as 'perhaps the bravest man I have ever met'. He also stated that he was 'a man with the heart of a lion, and the modesty of a young girl'. On his return to England he was one of the 'Sudan celebrities' who became the subjects of waxwork models in the Madame Tussaud Exhibition soon after it moved to its present location in London in 1884. He rose to the rank of lieutenant general on 21 May 1884, and received the thanks of both Houses of Parliament on three occasions.

On a short summer tour of the north-east he was presented with a sword of honour by the 1st Newcastle and Durham Engineer Volunteers of Jarrow, on 22 July 1884. In January 1887 he contributed an article to the magazine *Fortnightly Review* entitled 'Last Words with General Gordon', in which he recalled his service and friendship with the Gordon of Khartoum. He was offered the position of Governor of Bermuda in

1888 but he turned it down. He retired on 14 June 1890, being appointed Knight Commander of the Grand Cross (GCB) on 20 May 1896, and Knight Commander of St Michael and St George (GCMG).

For the last six years of his life he lived at a house called 'Springfield' in Northam near Bideford in Devon. He was suffering with a cold when he went out to read telegrams about the Boer War and caught a chill which developed into inflammation of the lungs. He died on 17 December 1899, aged 68, and he was buried at East-the-Water Cemetery in Bideford, where there is a headstone. The mayor and corporation of Bideford were present at his funeral. Graham Close at Chatham in Kent is named after him; there is a painting of him in the Royal Engineers Officers' Mess in Chatham, he is named on the 'For Valour' commemoration board at the Royal Engineers Museum in Chatham and he had an army locomotive named after him. His medals are at the Royal Engineers Museum.

Peter Leitch

Peter Leitch was born in August 1820, at Milnathort, Orwell, Kinross, Scotland. He enlisted into the 2nd Company, Royal Sappers and Miners at Glasgow on 28 August 1843, which was the same company as John Ross. In February 1844 he was posted from the Hospital Company to the 3rd Company at Chatham. At an unknown date he was charged for breaking his spitting cup when in the House of Correction at Cold Bath Fields in Southampton. He returned to the 2nd Company for active service in the Crimean War.

He and John Ross were with the 2nd Company sent to the Baltic theatre of war, taking part in the capture of the Åland Islands and the demolition of the fort at Bomarsund. They returned to England on HMS *Cumberland*, arriving at Woolwich on 16 October 1854, only to be sent back on active service in the Crimea theatre of war before the end of the year.

His award of the Victoria Cross was announced in the *London Gazette* of 4 June 1858, and he received the medal from Sir James Outram at Natal in South Africa, on 2 November 1858, being the last of the 18 June Redan Victoria Cross men to receive it. At the age of 35, Colour-Sergeant Leitch was the oldest of all the 18 June Redan Victoria Cross recipients. He also received the Baltic Medal, 1854–5, the Crimea Medal with *Sebastopol* clasp, the French Legion of Honour (5th Class) and the Turkish Crimea Medal.

He was promoted to sergeant major, and he was injured in the back by a fall of earth at Chatham on 14 January 1858. He sailed for service at the Cape of Good Hope in 1858, where he remained for nine years, and later served in Gibraltar for six years prior to his discharge at Gravesend on 14 March 1872, having served over twenty-eight years. He had two good conduct badges, he had never been in the defaulters' book and his conduct was described as very good. He was awarded the Long Service Good Conduct Medal.

He died at Durville Road in Fulham, West London, on 6 December 1892, aged 72, and he was buried at the Margravine Road Cemetery in Hammersmith. His grave was not marked and the cemetery has now been partially levelled. Leitch Row in Chatham is named after him, he is named on the 'For Valour' commemoration board at the Royal Engineers Museum in Chatham and an army locomotive was named after him. His medals are in the Royal Engineers Museum.

John Pirie

John Perie was born in about June 1829, at Huntly in Aberdeenshire, Scotland. His father was a farm servant living at Gartly in 1821. Apparently, all local pupils were guided to go to the sixth-form comprehensive Gordon Schools in Huntly, founded in 1839. John was a mason by trade, and joined the Royal Artillery at Aberdeen on 8 January 1848, aged 18 years and 6 months. He transferred to the 8th Company, Royal Sappers and Miners, on 1 March 1848, and it seems that he pronounced his name in the local dialect – Peerie, and the English clerk wrote his name on the roll as Perie. He thus sailed for active service in the Crimea as 854 Sapper Pirie.

His award of the Victoria Cross was announced in the *London Gazette* on 24 February 1857, and he received the medal at the first investiture. He also received the Crimea Medal with *Alma, Balaclava, Inkerman* and *Sebastopol* clasps, the French Military Medal and the Turkish Crimea Medal.

Regarded as 'an unlettered man, but a first class sapper and leader', Sapper Pirie was tried by a regimental court martial at Sebastopol on 31 January 1856, for habitual drunkenness, and he was sentenced to twenty-eight days in prison with hard labour.

He served at Gibraltar for five-and-a-half years, before sailing for active service in the second Anglo-China (Opium) War of 1860, taking part in another dangerous assault at the Taku Forts on 21 August 1860. On this occasion the assault was successful. The attacking force had to cross a series of ditches and bamboo-stake palisades under heavy fire from the ramparts. Assault parties eventually breached the defences and forced entry into the fort. For his service he received the China Medal with *Taku Forts* clasp. On his return from the East he discharged at Chatham on 3 September 1860, and returned to Scotland.

It would seem that his excessive drinking habits continued and eventually had a bad effect on his constitution, because he was aged only 53 when he died of liver disease and general debility, in his home at 69 East North Street in Aberdeen, on 17 September 1874. He was considered a pauper and he was buried in the 'Strangers Ground' at St Peter's Cemetery in Aberdeen. The grave was not marked and the burial register records his name as 'Pirie'. A new headstone bearing the surname 'Perie'was erected against a wall at the cemetery in 2001 near to where he is believed to be buried, which gives his date and place of birth as '7 April 1821 in Gartly'. He is named on the 'For Valour' commemoration board at the Royal Engineers Museum in Chatham, Perie Row in Chatham is named after him, as is an army locomotive, and a new Territorial Army centre in Huntly was named after him. His medals are at the Royal Engineers Museum.

William Hope

William Hope was born at 20 Moray Place in Edinburgh, on 12 April 1834, the only surviving son of The Right Honourable John Hope, the Lord Chief Justice Clerk of Scotland, and his wife, Jesse Scott (formerly Irving). William was educated by private tutors, and matriculated at Trinity Hall in Cambridge before he entered the 7th Royal Fusiliers on 12 April 1855, for active service in the Crimea.

His award of the Victoria Cross was announced in the *London Gazette* of 5 May 1857, and he received the medal at the first investiture. He also received the Crimea Medal with *Sebastopol* clasp, the Turkish Crimea Medal and the Sardinian Medal of Military Valour. In 1893 a submission was made to the War Office that he should receive a bar to his Victoria Cross for this action, but it was rejected.

The 7th Fusiliers landed at Portsmouth on 26 July 1856, and Lieutenant Hope retired from the regular army on 3 March 1857. However, he was a supporter of the Volunteer movement and became colonel of the 1st (City of London) Artillery Volunteer Corps, when it was formed in 1863. He married Margaret Jane Cunningham, the daughter of Robert Graham of Cartmore in Fife, and they lived at Parsloes Manor in Dagenham, Essex (now Greater London) from 1867–78. A painting of the manor commissioned by him is now in the Valence House Museum collection in Dagenham. The house was demolished in 1925.

He eventually became military attaché to the celebrated diplomat Lord Napier, who visited several times at Parsloes. He was involved in various business ventures, being the inventor of the shrapnel shell for rifled guns. In 1862 he was described as general manager of the International Financial Society, and he was also director of the Lands Improvement Company, through which he had been involved in reclamation and irrigation work in Spain and Majorca, and reclaiming marshland in Essex. With William Napier he proposed a scheme to convey sewage from the northern outfall of Joseph Bazelgette's London sewer system some 44 miles across Essex to reclaim 20,000 acres of land from Dengie Flats and a similar area from Maplin Sands, off the shore of Foulness Island. The estimated cost of the project was over £2 million, and although work started in 1865, a crisis in the banking system, when the Overend Gurney bank failed, made it difficult to obtain finance, and the scheme foundered.

He was the last survivor of the 18 June Redan Victoria Crosses when he died at a nursing home in Chelsea, London, on 17 December 1909, aged 75, and he was buried in the family plot at Brompton Cemetery in London. He is one of twelve holders of the Victoria Cross buried at Brompton, including Francis Wheatley, Sam Parkes and Sir Frederick Maude. His medals are at the Royal Fusiliers Museum in the Tower of London. A blue plaque was placed at the Bowling Pavilion at Parsloes Park in Dagenham. He is the subject of a painting by Louis Desanges which is in the Royal Fusiliers Museum.

(Felix) Philip Smith

Philip Smith was born on 5 October 1825, at Lurgan, Virginia, County Cavan, Ireland. His father was named Thomas. He enlisted into the 17th (Leicestershire) Regiment, on 17 May 1847, in Dublin. After seven years of Home service, the regiment was posted to Gibraltar before receiving orders for active service in the Crimea.

The award of the Victoria Cross to Corporal Smith was announced in the *London Gazette* on 24 February 1857, and he received the medal from Brigadier General Sir Charles Trollope at the Citadel in Quebec, Canada, on 1 August 1857. He also received the Crimea Medal with *Sebastopol* clasp, the French Military Medal and the Turkish Crimea Medal.

He was an in-pensioner at the Royal Hospital in Kilmainan from 1 October 1871–1 June 1876; from 1 December 1881–1 February 1883; and in 1903.

He died of bronchitis and pneumonia, at Our Lady's Hospice, Harold's Cross in Dublin, on 16 January 1906, aged 80. He was buried in St Bridget's section at Glasnevin Cemetery in Dublin, in a burial plot which was later purchased by his son-in-law, John Scully, who was High Sheriff of Dublin in 1913. His name was not included on the memorial stone, but in 2003 five generations of the Smith family joined veterans from the Royal Leicestershire Regimental Association in a service to place a footstone at the graveside. His name appears on the Lurgan War Memorial.

His medals were the first complete Victoria Cross group to appear at auction, and were sold in 1886 as part of the Captain E. Hyde Greg collection. The sale was considered exceptional, and it was the first time a catalogue included details about the recipient. It was bought by 'regular dealer' Mr Partridge. They are now with the Royal Leicestershire Regimental Museum.

Thomas Esmonde

Thomas Esmonde was born on 25 May 1829, at Pembrokestown House in County Waterford, Ireland, the son of Sir Thomas Esmonde, 9th Baronet, and his first wife Mary (formerly Payne). His father represented Wexford in the British Parliament. The Esmonde family home was at Ballynastragh House at Killinierin in County Wexford, which was burnt down by the Irish Republican Army in 1923.

He entered the 18th (Royal Irish) Regiment, and served in India. The Royal Irish played a major part in the operations during the Second Anglo-Burmese War of 1852–3, being in the forefront of the troops which captured the Golden Pagoda in Rangoon. Disease and heatstroke took a terrible toll on the troops, and the Royal Irish lost 365 men, mainly to disease. For his service he received the Indian General Service Medal (1854–95) with *Pegu* clasp. Therefore he was the only soldier of the 18 June Redan Victoria Crosses who had seen previous active service.

The award of the Victoria Cross to Captain Esmonde was announced in the *London Gazette* of 25 September 1857, the last to be announced for the assault on the Redan, and he received the medal from Queen Victoria at Southsea Common in Portsmouth on 2 August 1858, along with Edward Bell, Henry Ramage, James Mouat, Henry MacDonald,

Matthew Dixon and Howard Elphinstone. He also received the Crimea Medal with *Sebastopol* clasp and the Turkish Crimea Medal.

His mother had died in 1840, and on his return from the Crimea in 1856 his father had married again. He reached the rank of lieutenant colonel.

While following the 'Kildares' – a local hunt at Bruges in Belgium, late in 1872, he was trying to jump a thorn fence when he was struck in the eye by a branch. The eye became badly inflamed and the other eye also became infected, and the injury got worse. He died from his injuries on 14 January 1873, aged 43, at Bruges, and he was buried in the Bruges Town Cemetery, where there is a headstone. His medals are at the Imperial War Museum in London, but they are not part of the Lord Ashcroft Collection.

John Joseph Sims

John Joseph Sims was born in February 1836, at Bloomsbury in London. Little is known of his early life except that his father died when he was about 14 years old, and he worked as a labourer trying to help his destitute family, before he entered the 34th (Cumberland) Regiment as 3482 Private Sims, at Westminster on 4 January 1854. He was aged only 18 when the regiment was serving in the Mediterranean, and received orders for active service in the Crimea.

His award of the Victoria Cross was announced in the *London Gazette* of 24 February 1857, and he received the medal at the first investiture. He also received the Crimea Medal with *Sebastopol* clasp and the Turkish Crimea Medal.

On his discharge from the army in 1857 it was stated that: 'his character has been good'. He died of phthisis (tuberculosis) on 6 December 1881, aged 46, in the Union Workhouse at Thavies Inn, in the City of London, and he was buried in a common grave at the City of London Cemetery at Manor Park. There is no headstone, but a plaque was erected in the memorial garden at the cemetery in 2003, and he is named on the Victoria Cross memorial at Carlisle Cathedral. The location of his Victoria Cross is not known, but he may have lost or pawned it as a replacement medal which had been awarded to him was auctioned in 2015.

John Alexander

John Alexander was born at Mullingar in County Westmeath, Ireland, and he entered the 90th (Perthshire) Light Infantry as 2932 Private

Alexander. He had married prior to receiving orders for active service in the East.

The award of the Victoria Cross to Private Alexander was announced in the *London Gazette* of 24 February 1857. He was also entitled to receive the Crimea Medal with *Alma, Inkerman* and *Sebastopol* clasps, the French Military Medal, the Turkish Crimea Medal and the Bentinck Medal, which was normally presented only to men of the Guards Brigade, but he received it for helping to save the life of the Scots Guards officer on 6 September 1855. On the same day as the first investiture in Hyde Park, a letter was sent out authorising him to be presented with his medal at an investiture in Hong Kong. However, the 90th were diverted from the China station to India, where a mutiny among local forces had broken out in May 1857.

On 24 September 1857, during the British Expeditionary Force's advance towards the relief of the Lucknow garrison, he was at the Alum Bagh on the outskirts of the city and in rear of the main force with an escort of the 90th Light Infantry, which was protecting the baggage being transported to the front, when it was treacherously attacked by rebel cavalry. The officer in command was hacked to pieces, three other soldiers were killed and many more wounded, before the enemy were driven away. Private Alexander was killed during the fight. His remains are believed to have been buried where he fell. For his service he received the Indian Mutiny Medal with *Relief of Lucknow* clasp.

His medals were sent by registered post to his widow, and they are now displayed at the National War Museum of Scotland housed in Edinburgh Castle.

Chapter 12

The Final Phase

On 23 June 1855, a live shell was thrown from one of the enemy's batteries, which flew through the air and landed in a British trench, menacing a number of men of the 57th (West Middlesex) Regiment. As was the usual case, most of the men did not quite know what to do in such a dangerous situation. However, Private Charles McCorrie kept his nerve, ran to the missile and on picking it up he threw it back out of the trench. After it exploded Private McCorrie received the thanks of his comrades, who suggested to their superiors that the action was worthy of the greatest reward.

It was not long before the British had their revenge on the Russians for the repulse at the Redan. British intelligence discovered that the Russians planned to launch an overwhelming attack from Sebastopol to push the Allies back into the sea, presuming that the recent losses would have considerably depleted the Allied forces and morale would be at its lowest. The attack materialised on 26 June. However, as Sergeant Gowling put it: 'Although they had just thrashed us, we were not going to give up the game for one black eye.'

A strong force of British troops advanced to the front trenches and as soon as darkness fell, sentries were sent out, and just before midnight they returned to report that massive columns of the enemy were advancing towards them. The British lay in wait and allowed them to come on. The British sent up a number of fire balls which lit up the area and exposed the Russians, who came under a barrage of shot, shell, grape, canister and rockets. At a given signal all but the mortars stopped firing. The Russians were about fifty paces away when the British, six-deep in the trenches, opened up a withering fire, which broke the enemy's will and they began to retreat in disorder. The British stormed out of the trenches and rushed at them with bayonets.

A flag of truce was raised next morning so the Russians could collect their dead and bury their wounded, and this revealed a ghastly sight, as the enemy had been dreadfully cut to pieces and their bodies were piled up in heaps, in some places level with the top of the trenches. There were 4,000 killed or wounded, and the 2-hour cease fire had to be extended. Some Russian officers shouted sarcastic taunts at the British, asking when were they going to take the town, to which the Brits asked when they were going to push the Allies into the sea, and warned that one day soon they will take them by surprise. As soon as the white flag was taken down the bombardments resumed.

Lord Raglan died on 28 June 1855, and three days later General Sir James Simpson was appointed to the command of the British forces in the Crimea.

On 15 July 1855, in Sebastopol harbour, Boatswain's Mate John Sheppard, of HMS *St Jean D'Acre*, proceeded in a canvas punt which he had constructed for the purpose, with an exploding apparatus which he intended to fix to the side of a Russian warship in an endeavour to blow it up. He got past the enemy's steamboats but was prevented from going beyond the entrance to Careening Bay by a line of vessels carrying enemy troops to the north. However, he managed to bring back useful information concerning the enemy. He made a second attempt on 16 August, but although both these actions were unsuccessful they were conceived and carried out in the face of great danger.

On 21 July at Sebastopol, Corporal John Ross of the Royal Corps of Sappers and Miners, showed distinguished conduct when he was placed in charge of a working party of 200 men, each carrying an entrenching tool and a gabion, which went out into the darkness, and by the following morning had built a long line of covering parapets to link the 4th Parallel, Right Attack, with an old Russian rifle pit.

On 23 August 1855, Corporal Ross showed extremely creditable conduct in charge of the advance from the 5th Parallel, Right Attack on the Redan, in placing and filling twenty-five gabions, under a very heavy fire, while being annoyed by the presence of light balls. A gabion was a round wicker basket for filling with earth and stones for building and repairing fortifications.

Sergeant John Coleman of the 97th (The Earl of Ulster's) Regiment showed great coolness and bravery on the night of 30 August 1855, at Sebastopol, when the enemy attacked a new sap and drove the working party in. He remained in the open, perfectly exposed to the enemy's rifle pits, until all around him had been killed or wounded. He finally carried one of his mortally wounded officers to the rear.

On 2 September 1855 at Sebastopol, Sergeant Alfred Ablett of the 3rd Battalion, Grenadier Guards, was working in the trenches when a sentry cried: 'Look out, there!', and he saw a shell fall in the centre of a number of ammunition cases and powder. Any hesitation could be fatal, so he rolled the ball between his legs away from the ammunition, and instantly seized it up and threw outside the trench. It burst as it touched the ground, and the force from it blew Sergeant Ablett off his feet and to the ground and covered him with gravel and dirt, but there was a great number of men in the trench at the time, but because of his gallantry and quick thinking no one was hurt. He was visibly shaken as Sergeant Baker and others picked him up, and the sergeant reported the circumstances to the officer in charge. On coming off duty he was taken before the commanding officer and promoted to the rank of corporal, and then sergeant.

On the night of 6 September 1855, at Sebastopol, Captain Ducombe Buckley of the Scots (Fusilier) Guards went out of the trenches in front of the Redan to check on Privates Allen and Sankey on sentry duty, when they came under fire. He and two sentries were hit. The officer was dangerously wounded and was believed to be lying out in the open. Sergeant James Craig of his regiment, who had fought at the passage of the Alma, got together a number of volunteers to go out with him under a heavy fire of grape and small arms, including Sergeant Thomas McBeath, who was in charge of the section that night, Drummer Thomas Smith and Private John Alexander of the 90th Light Infantry, who was with a working party in the most advanced trench. They found the officer was dead, and together Craig, Smith and Alexander brought the officer's body in, while McBeath brought in Sankey on his back. During the endeavour Sergeant Craig was wounded. Captain Buckley was buried on Cathcart's Hill two days later.

While on duty in the trenches in the month of September 1855, an enemy shell fell into the crowded trench where Private George Strong of the Coldstream Guards was stationed. He was well aware of the danger involved but disregarding his own safety he picked it up from the place where it had landed and threw it over the parapet, thus saving many lives. There is no exact date for the incident, but the citation states that the incident occurred 'during operations', which suggests that it may have been as the troops were preparing for the second assault on the Redan. The Coldstream Guards took a major part in the attack as part of the Second Division, and their commanding officer, Major General Charles Windham, was the only officer to penetrate the Redan battery.

Charles McCorrie

Charles McCorrie was born in 1830, at Killead near Aldergrove in County Antrim, Ireland (his name is shown as McCurry on some records). He enlisted into the 57th (West Middlesex) Regiment, as 1971 Private McCorrie.

His award of the Victoria Cross was announced in the *London Gazette* of 24 February 1857. The medal was sent to Malta to be presented to him by the officer commanding, Lieutenant General J.L. Pennefather, but Charles died on 8 April 1857, aged 27, and he is believed to have been buried in an unmarked grave at Msida Bastion Cemetery at Valetta in Malta. His Victoria Cross was returned to the War Office, and it was reported to have been placed in an auction on 21 February 1879, and remained unsold. Its present location is not known. He was also entitled to the Crimea Medal with *Inkerman* and *Sebastopol* clasps and the Turkish Crimea Medal. A memorial headstone was unveiled at the cemetery by the Duke of Gloucester in 2012, and a memorial plaque was placed at the entrance to the village of Killead.

John Sheppard

John Sheppard was born at Kingston-upon-Hull on 22 September 1817. At the time of the Crimea he was Boatswain's Mate with the *St Jean D'Acre*. His deed might be compared to a modern commando raid or a mission carried out by a Special Services unit. His service, which he attempted on two occasions, was described by Lord Lyons as 'a bold one, and gallantly executed'.

His award was announced in the *London Gazette* of 24 February 1857. The medal was sent to him care of HMS *Highflier*. He was also awarded the Baltic Medal, the Crimea Medal with *Sebastopol* clasp, the French Legion of Honour, the Turkish Crimea Medal and the Sardinian Medal of Military Valour.

He later served in the Second China War, for which he received the China War Medal with *Canton* clasp.

He died at the home of Mr John Harris at Padstow in Cornwall on 17 December 1884, aged 67, and he was buried in Padstow parish churchyard. The headstone gives his age as 68. His medals are at the

National Maritime Museum in Greenwich. His name appears on the Victoria Cross memorial at Paragon Square in Hull.

John Ross

John Ross was born in 1822 at Inch near Stranraer, Wigtownshire (now Dumfries and Galloway), Scotland. He entered the 2nd Company, Royal Sappers and Miners, as 997 Corporal Ross. It was the same company as Peter Leitch, and they were sent to the Baltic theatre of war, taking part in the capture of the Åland Islands and the demolition of the fort at Bomarsund. They returned to England on HMS *Cumberland*, arriving at Woolwich on 16 October 1854, only to be sent back on active service in the Crimea theatre of war before the end of the year.

His award of the Victoria Cross was announced in the *London Gazette* of 24 February 1857, and he received the medal at the first investiture. He also received the Baltic Medal, 1854–5, the Crimea Medal with *Sebastopol* clasp, the French Military Medal and the Turkish Crimea Medal.

His wife was named Lydia. They had a daughter named Ann Jane, who was born in 1857, and a son named Harry James, who died on 12 June 1879, aged 14. John died peacefully in London a few months later, on 23 October 1879, aged 57, and he was buried in an unmarked common grave in Islington Cemetery at East Finchley, London. He is named on the family headstone in Islington Cemetery, which was renovated in the 2000s. His wife died in 1900 and is buried with him, as is his daughter, Ann Jane, who died in 1957 in her 100th year. He is named on the 'For Valour' board at the Royal Engineers Museum in Chatham, and he had an army locomotive named after him. His medals are with the Royal Engineers Museum.

John Coleman

John Coleman was born in Norwich in about 1821. Some sources say he was born on 12 July 1798, at St Mary-in-the-Marsh, Romney Marsh, Kent. But if he had been born in 1798 he would have been nearly 60 when he went on active service during the Indian Mutiny, and death notices in Norwich newspapers reported that he was in his 38th year when he died in 1858, making his year of birth about 1821, and they also state: 'He was a native of this city.'

He entered the 97th (The Earl of Ulster's) Regiment, in about 1838. From 1836–41 the regiment alternated service between England

and Ireland. It was then in the Mediterranean for most of the 1840s, garrisoning Corfu and then Malta. It moved to Nova Scotia for five years in 1848. The regiment was in Greece in 1854, when it received orders for active service as part of the reinforcements sent to the Crimea. They arrived at Sebastopol on 20 November 1854.

His award of the Victoria Cross was announced in the *London Gazette* of 24 February 1857, and he received the medal at the first investiture. He also received the Crimea Medal with *Sebastopol* clasp and the Turkish Crimea Medal.

He received orders for active service during the Indian Mutiny. He was with the British forces which relieved Lucknow in March 1858, where he died of fever on 22 May 1858, in his 38th year. Some sources say 4 June 1882, but this is mistaken for the man who was born in 1798. The exact location of his burial place is not known. For his service in India he was awarded the Indian Mutiny Medal with *Lucknow* clasp.

His medals are held at the Queen's Own Royal West Kent Regiment Museum in Maidstone. There is also a display consisting of a daguerreotype photograph, a prayer book and silver cross, a captured Russian musket, a model of Russian cannon and a Russian Orthodox altar front.

Alfred Ablett

Alfred Ablett was born at Weybread in Suffolk, on 3 August 1830, the fifth son in the family of eight children to a bricklayer named Samuel Ablett and his wife, Elizabeth (formerly Cockfort). He entered the 3rd Battalion, Grenadier Guards, as 5872 Guardsman Ablett, on 20 February 1850.

He became the first Suffolk-born man to be awarded the Victoria Cross when it was announced in the *London Gazette* of 24 February 1857, and he received the medal during the first investiture. He also received the Crimea Medal with *Alma, Balaclava, Inkerman* and *Sebastopol* clasps, the Turkish Crimea Medal and the Bentinck Medal. He also received the Long Service Good Conduct Medal. He was also presented with a silk necktie apparently made by Queen Victoria.

He was invalided out of the army in 1862. In 1868 he was accused of the serious offence of attempting to kill himself with a rifle but he was found not guilty by a court in Norwich. Like fellow ex-Guardsman Anthony Palmer, he lived in Poplar and gained employment with the Millwall Docks Police. He served the force for twenty-six years and reached the rank of sergeant.

Alfred suffered a heart attack and died on 12 March 1897, aged 66, at his home in East India Dock Road, Poplar, London. On the centenary of his death in 1997, a marble plaque dedicated to him was placed in St Andrew's Parish Church in Weybread, by the Grenadier Guards Association; Ablett Close in Weybread is named after him, and the Weybread village sign displays a Victoria Cross in recognition of their gallant son. He is number one of the subjects of a series of cigarette cards entitled 'Victoria Cross Heroes', and features on a souvenir tin depicting Victoria Cross heroes. His Victoria Cross is with the Grenadier Guards Museum at Wellington Barracks in London, where there is also a painting of him in the Officers' Mess.

James Craig

James Craig was born on 10 September 1824, at Balbeggie, in the parish of St Martin's, Kinnoul, Perth, in Scotland, the son of James and Ann (formerly Guthrie).

He had worked as a labourer, before he enlisted into the 1st Battalion, Scots (Fusilier) Guards on 25 August 1843, as 3075 Private Craig. He was aged 18 years and 3 months, with a fresh complexion, blue eyes and fair hair. He took to soldiering well and promotions came quickly. He became corporal on 11 June 1846, sergeant on 22 July 1851 and he was awarded good conduct badges.

He married Elizabeth Ann Scruse (or Scruze) at St Dunstan's Church in Stepney, on 17 March 1849, and a daughter named Annie was born on 13 May 1850.

The regiment received orders for active service in the Crimea, where he took part in the passage of the Alma. He was promoted to colour sergeant on 27 June 1855, and he transferred to the 3rd Battalion, Military Train, on 26 January 1856.

His award of the Victoria Cross was announced in the *London Gazette* of 20 November 1857, and he was presented with the medal by Queen Victoria at a ceremony held in the Quadrangle of Windsor Castle on 28 November 1857, with the whole of the Windsor garrison attending. Joseph Malone, George Symons and Sir Christopher Teesdale received their awards at the same ceremony. He also received the Crimea Medal with *Balaclava, Inkerman* and *Sebastopol* clasps, and the Turkish Crimea Medal.

He was promoted to lieutenant in January 1858, and presumably having by then sufficiently recovered from his wounds he transferred into the 2nd Battalion, 10th (Lincolnshire) Regiment, on 12 February 1858. His unit was ordered to South Africa in 1860 for service in various stations in the colony.

His first wife having died, he married Harriet Mary, the daughter of the late Captain Rowley, RN, at the Presbyterian (Scottish) Church of St Andrew's in Cape Town, on 15 February 1861. They had probably met in Ireland, and she had travelled to the Cape for the ceremony. After the wedding the couple sailed in the coaster *Sir George Grey*, and then set off overland to join his regiment in Grahamstown. On 18 March 1861, while passing a creek at the Swartkops River, he suddenly ran from the wagon, plunged into the river and attempted to take his own life by cutting his throat. During this dreadful situation he plunged forward into the water and drowned. An inquest returned a verdict of suicide. He was aged 36, and it was stated: 'He was an active and accomplished officer, and respected by all who knew him.' He was buried at St Mary's Cemetery in Port Elizabeth, South Africa. The headstone which had been placed there slid down an embankment during a storm and is not believed to be in its original place. His medals are at the Scots Guards Museum at Wellington Barracks in London.

George Strong

George Strong was born at Ham Hill, Odcombe near Yeovil in Somerset, in April 1833, and he was baptised on the 7th of that month. He was the oldest of four children to Job and Mary Strong, Job being a mason by trade. He was employed as an agricultural labourer before he entered the 1st Battalion, Coldstream Guards as 4787 Private Strong in 1854, for active service in the Crimea.

His award of the Victoria Cross was announced in the *London Gazette* on 24 February 1857, and he received the medal during the first investiture. He was the last member of the British Army to perform an act that gained the medal during the Crimean campaign. He also received the Crimea Medal with *Sebastopol* clasp and the Turkish Crimea Medal.

In 1861 he was living at the Five Ales Inn at Chippenham in Wiltshire. On 4 April 1863, he married Eliza, the only daughter in the family of seven children of John and Mary Ann Dickenson, who lived in High Street, Sherston Magna in Wiltshire. George left the army as a corporal in 1864 and they settled in the town. The 1881 census records that they had three sons and a daughter, all born in Sherston Magna.

George died at Sherston Magna on 25 August 1888, aged 55 (the death certificate states his age as 52), and he was buried at the Church of the Holy Cross in Sherston. The exact location of his remains is uncertain but he is believed to have been buried close to his son, Thomas, who died in 1936, and a memorial was placed next to his son's grave in 1986. His name also appears on his brother's headstone in the same churchyard. A framed display case honouring the man and his deed has been on permanent display in the church since 2015. His medals are at the Coldstream Guards Museum in London.

Chapter 13

The Fall of Sebastopol

On 16 August the Russians launched an attack from the Mackenzie Heights to the north-east, across the Tchernaya River against French and Sardinian troops on the Fediukhine Heights. Even the Russian commander, Prince Gorchakov, had little faith in the likely success of the attack, and his forces were defeated with heavy casualties within hours. Russian morale began to waver, and a pontoon bridge linking the south side and north side of Sebastopol was completed on 26 August, in preparation for an emergency evacuation.

The Allied command made plans for what they believed would be the final assault on Sebastopol, and gave orders to recommence a massive bombardment of the city by over a thousand field pieces on 5 September, which lasted for three days. The assault was to commence at about midday on 8 September. The French would assault the Malakoff Tower, and if or when successful they were to raise the tricolour on the bastion which was the signal for the British to attack the Redan.

The morning of 8 September 1855 broke cold and wintry. The troops of the Second and Light Divisions fell in at 9 o'clock, with two days' rations in their packs, and each man was issued with a dram of rum. There were a lot of very young men in the ranks who had not much idea of the terrible struggle they were about to endure, and others who knew too well how difficult and dangerous their task would be. From about 9.30 they waited under arms for the outcome of the French attack on the Malakoff, and for the order to advance.

The wait was long and the trenches soon became congested and units became mixed up, but one lesson learned from the assault on 18 June was that no British attack was to begin unless the French were successful. The Tricolour to signify a French victory was raised at about midday and the order to advance was given.

Men will go into situations with great vigour when they have not yet realised what they are letting themselves in for, as they did during the First World War, but for many of the men who were ordered to assault the Great Redan for a second time it was a case of once bitten twice shy. Some men were of the opinion that if the Malakoff was taken the Allies would command Sebastopol, and therefore the British attack would be a waste of lives; which indeed it was!

The pattern of events was similar to the first assault. Men were cut down by showers of grape and canister as they ran across the open ground. This time many got over the defences, planted the ladders and scaled the parapet of the Redan, but there were always signs that most of them had not much stomach for the fight. In defiance of their officers' exertions to get them to advance they held back, preferring to retain some cover, and they would not charge forward and take the Redan. At first the Russians faltered and fell back from the parapet, but when they saw that the British were reluctant to advance they rallied, and with reinforcements arriving they ran forward and with bayonets, bullets and even stones they beat the Brits back down into the ditch and forced them to retire to the advance trenches. Even so, there were some men who performed gallant deeds against all the odds that day.

Captain Gronow Davis of the Royal Regiment of Artillery showed great coolness and gallantry while in command of a spiking party. Lieutenant Gilbert Howard Saunders of the 30th Regiment had received several severe wounds, the worst of which was a broken leg, which prevented him from getting back to the British lines. On seeing Lieutenant Saunders in distress, Captain Davis leaped over the parapet of a sap and twice proceeded some distance across the open under a murderous fire to assist in rescuing the officer and placing him under cover. He repeated the act in the conveyance of other wounded soldiers from the same exposed position.

Bombardier Daniel Cambridge, of the Royal Regiment of Artillery, was severely wounded in the leg early in the day, and was asked to leave the assaulting party to get his wound attended to. However, he volunteered for the spiking party to go out of the advance trenches in front of the Quarries. Later, he went out in front of the advanced trench, under a heavy fire, to bring in a wounded man, and during the rescue attempt he was shot for a second time. However, finding that he still had the strength to stand up, he went forward again with the 3rd Buffs, and it was only when he received a bullet in his right jaw that he was finally put out of action.

174

Lieutenant Colonel Frederick Maude of the 3rd (East Kent) Regiment (The Buffs) showed conspicuous and most devoted gallantry when in command of the ladder and covering party of the 2nd Division, and gallantly led his men to the Redan. Having entered the Redan with only nine or ten men with him, they held a position between traverses, and only retired when all hope of support was given up. He was dangerously wounded.

Private John Connors of the 3rd (East Kent) Regiment (The Buffs) distinguished himself most conspicuously in personal combat with the Russians. He rescued an officer of the 30th Regiment, who was surrounded by Russians, by shooting one and bayoneting another, and was observed in personal combat with the Russians inside the Redan for some time.

Captain Henry Jones was hit by a piece of shrapnel during the assault on the 5th Parallel and fell to the ground dangerously wounded. Assistant Surgeon Thomas Hale of the 7th (Royal) Fusiliers remained with the officer when everyone but he and Lieutenant Hope had retreated. Later that day, after the regiment had retired to the trenches, he and Sergeant Charles Fisher of his regiment, cleared the most advanced sap of the wounded and then carried into the sap, under heavy fire, several wounded men from the open ground.

Assistant Surgeon William Sylvester and Corporal Robert Shields of the 23rd (Royal Welsh) Fusiliers, went out under a heavy fire in front of the 5th Parallel, Right Attack, to a spot near the Redan where Lieutenant and Adjutant Douglas Dyneley, 23rd Fusiliers, was lying mortally wounded in a dangerous and exposed position. Under withering fire they dressed his wounds.

Sergeant O'Connor, 23rd Fusiliers, who had already distinguished himself at the Alma, was shot through both thighs as he behaved with great gallantry during this part of the attack.

Sergeant Andrew Moynihan of the 90th (Perthshire) Light Infantry was one of the men who got into the Redan, where he personally encountered and killed five Russians, and rescued Lieutenant Swift and Ensign Maude from certain death. He received twelve wounds during this gallant action.

Captain Charles Lumley of the 97th (The Earl of Ulster's) Regiment had been selected to lead a storming party, and he distinguished himself highly by his bravery, being among the first inside the work, where he fought fiercely. He was immediately engaged with three Russian gunners reloading a field piece, who attacked him. He shot two of them with his revolver, when he was knocked down by a stone, which stunned him for the moment, but, on recovery, he drew his sword, and was in the act of cheering his men on when he received a ball in his mouth, and he was brought back to the British lines wounded severely and in a bad state.

The British assault had failed, and in a desperate attempt to save face, Colonel Simpson ordered that another assault was to be undertaken on the following morning. However, it never took place because the capture of the Malakoff prompted the Russians to form the opinion that further defence was futile and they decided to evacuate the south of Sebastopol. For 6 hours beginning at about 6 o'clock on the night of 8 September 1855 a constant stream of people with their wagons, carts and livestock swarmed across the pontoon bridge, covered by some riflemen and gun crews. As they retreated they spiked their guns, blew up their ammunition magazines, booby-trapped the outer bastions and destroyed anything they thought would have been of use to the Allies. When everyone was across the bridge they blew it up.

In what seems to have been the last act of bravery which would be rewarded with the Victoria Cross during operations around Sebastopol, Corporal John Ross, the engineer who had already performed two deeds worthy of the award, showed intrepid and devoted conduct in creeping to the Redan, where he witnessed the evacuation of Sebastopol. On his return he came upon a wounded man and brought him back to the British lines, and reported what he had seen.

Gronow Davis

Gronow Davis was born on 16 May 1828, at Clifton in Bristol, the son of John Davis and his wife Mary. At the time of the 1841 census the family lived in Wilson Street, St Paul's, Bristol. He entered the Royal Regiment of Artillery on 18 December 1837, becoming lieutenant on 11 April 1841 and captain on 30 March 1848.

His award of the Victoria Cross was announced in the *London Gazette* of 23 June 1857, and he received the medal with Bombardier Cambridge at the first investiture three days later. He also received the Crimea Medal with *Sebastopol* clasp, the Turkish Order of the Medjidie (5th Class) and the Turkish Crimea Medal.

He also received the brevet of major for his gallantry, and was appointed full major on 28 August 1857.

In Bristol on 30 May 1866, he married an Irish girl named Alma Wilhelmina (formerly Reade). They had eight children, the eighth child,

Nora Reade, died at birth in 1889. The 1871 census shows the family as living at 70 Gun House, Nether Hallam in Sheffield.

He was promoted lieutenant colonel on 29 August 1868, colonel on 1 October 1876, becoming major general on 29 October 1881, and he retired from military service soon afterwards.

His son, Major Gronow John Davis, was awarded the DSO while serving with the 22nd Punjabi Regiment, Indian Army, during the First World War.

Gronow died on 18 October 1891, aged 63, at 5 Royal Park at Clifton in Bristol, and he was buried at Arnos Vale Cemetery in Bristol, where there is a headstone. He is named on the memorial at the Royal Artillery Chapel in Woolwich, and he is named on his daughter Gwendoline's headstone at Ryde Cemetery on the Isle of Wight. His medals are at the Royal Artillery Regimental Museum in Woolwich.

Daniel Cambridge

Daniel Cambridge was born at Carrickfergus in County Antrim, Ireland, on 27 June 1820, the son of Archibald Cambridge and his wife Bridget (formerly Murray).

At Lisburn in County Antrim on 24 June 1839, he entered the 2nd Company, 4th Battalion, Royal Regiment of Artillery, as a driver and gunner, being described as 5ft 8in tall, with a fresh complexion, dark-grey eyes and brown hair. He served with the unit in Malta from 1841–7, and then served with the 7th Battalion in Canada from 1848, until returning to Woolwich on 21 December 1853.

On 28 August 1849, in Quebec, he married Ann, the daughter of James Bingham and his wife, Ann. Their first child William was born at Woolwich in 1854.

He received orders for active service in the Crimean War, with the 8th Company, 11th Battalion, arriving at the theatre of war on 19 September 1854, the day before the Passage of the Alma. He was promoted to bombardier on 3 April 1855, sergeant on 21 April 1856 and quartermaster sergeant in April 1857. Later in 1857 he was promoted master gunner with the 8th Coastal Battery at Athlone in County Roscommon, Ireland, and on 21 February 1862, he was posted to Fort Tarbert in County Kerry.

His award of the Victoria Cross was announced in the *London Gazette* of 23 June 1857, and he received the medal with Captain Davis at the first investiture three days later. He also received the Crimea Medal with *Inkerman* and *Sebastopol* clasps, the Turkish Crimea Medal and the Sardinian Medal of Military Valour. On 12 July 1865, Daniel wrote to James Alex Browne, the author of the book *England's Artillerymen*:

> I was three times wounded on 8th September. However, it is very little difference now although I suffer from my wounds and still will from what doctors say until my last. I was twice wounded when asked to retire to the rear but that I did by all means declined to do although hard pressed to do so by several officers. But finding I had the strength to stand another chance I advanced a third time with the 3rd Buffs, when I received a gunshot wound in my right jaw and by the assistance of several doctors I have at present got 185 bits of bone out of my jaw. And I can assure you that I suffer very much from my head. I may say all over.

He was pensioned off as a master gunner on 27 June 1871, and in the same year he was appointed Queen Victoria's Bodyguard with the Yeomen of the Guard. He received the Long Service Good Conduct Medal in 1861 for his thirty-two years with the colours. He is said to have lost his original Victoria Cross and a new one was issued to him. Subsequently both medals came onto the market, and the duplicate was the subject of court proceedings. However, both medals eventually came into the possession of the purchaser of the original cross.

Further children to Daniel and Ann were: Mary (born in Athlone in 1857); Agnes (born in Athlone in 1859); Daniel (born in Athlone in 1861); and twins named Catherine and Elizabeth (born in Tarbert in 1865).

Daniel is said to have died from the effects of the wounds he received in the Crimea at his home of 32 Frederick Place in Plumstead, London, on 12 June 1882, aged 62, and he was buried at St Nicholas' parish churchyard in Plumstead. All the flat headstones were later removed and used as paving or placed around a wall, and his grave site was not marked. His name appears on the memorial at the Royal Artillery Chapel in Woolwich, and his medals are with the Royal Artillery Museum in Woolwich.

Frederick Francis Maude

Frederick Francis Maude was born on 20 December 1821, at Lisnadill in County Armagh, Ireland. He was the son of the Revd, the Honourable John Charles Maude, and his wife, Mary Cely (formerly Trevilian). His grandfather was the 1st Viscount Hawarden and Baron de Montalt of Roscommon.

He entered the 3rd (East Kent) Regiment (The Buffs), and first saw active service during Gwalior Campaign in India, for which he received the Gwalior Campaign Star, 1843, with *Punniar* clasp.

On 22 February 1853, he married Catherine Mary, daughter of the Very Revd, Sir George Bisshopp, 9th Baronet, and Dean of Lismore from 1831–4.

His award of the Victoria Cross was announced in the *London Gazette* of 24 February 1857, and he received the medal on 22 July 1857, from Major General Sir George Butler, the officer commanding at the Corfu station on the Ionian Islands. He also received the Crimea Medal with *Sebastopol* clasp, the French Legion of Honour and the Turkish Crimea Medal.

His cousin, Francis Cornwallis Maude, entered the Royal Artillery, and was awarded the Victoria Cross for action during the first relief of Lucknow, on 25 September 1857, during the Indian Mutiny.

He commanded the 2nd Battalion of the Buffs from 1857–61, he was adjutant general at Gibraltar from 1861–6 and was inspector general of Militia in Ireland from 1867–73. He saw active service guarding lines of communication with the Peshawar Field Force, for which he received the Afghanistan Medal, 1878–80. He was appointed Knight Grand Cross, Order of the Bath (GCB), during Queen Victoria's birthday honours list, on 24 May 1886.

Frederick had five children: Ada Cecil (died in 1886); Alice Emily (1855–1936); Frederick Eustace Cecil (1859–62); Amy Kathleen (1863–1937); and Frederick Stanley, who was born in Gibraltar in 1864. He entered the Coldstream Guards, and rose to the rank of lieutenant general. He died of cholera in 1917, while serving in Mesopotamia (now Iraq) during the First World War.

Frederick died in Torquay, on 20 June 1897, aged 75, and he was buried in Brompton Cemetery, west London, where there is a headstone. There is a memorial plaque at St McNeiss Cathedral in Enniskillen, County Fermanagh. He is one of twelve holders of the Victoria Cross buried at Brompton, including Francis Wheatley, Sam Parkes and William Hope. The National Army Museum in London holds a display related to him: a replica Victoria Cross, an original medal ribbon, a blue patrol jacket, a tunic, a field service forage cap, a framed photograph, a lacquered snuff box, a flask and a metal sandwich case. His Victoria Cross is not publicly held.

John Connors

John Connors was born in October 1830, at Davaugh, Listowel in County Kerry, Ireland. He left his job as a labourer and entered the 3rd (East Kent) Regiment (The Buffs) on 8 January 1849, as 2649 Private Connors.

His award of the Victoria Cross was announced in the *London Gazette* of 24 February 1857, but he had died less than a month earlier, and the medal was sent by registered post to his next-of-kin. It is likely that he would have received the medal at the same investiture as Lieutenant Colonel Maude at Corfu, had he survived. He was also entitled to the Crimea Medal with *Sebastopol* clasp, the Turkish Crimea Medal and he was selected by his company for the award of the French Military Medal.

John fell to his death from the battlements of Port Neuf at the Corfu station, Ionian Islands, on 29 January 1857, aged 26, and he was buried in the British Cemetery at Corfu Town, where there is a headstone. A display and replica Victoria Cross dedicated to him was at the Buffs (Royal East Kent) Regimental Museum and Art Gallery in Maidstone, which is now at the National Army Museum in London. His original Victoria Cross is lost and believed to have been destroyed.

Thomas Egerton Hale

Thomas Egerton Hale was born on 24 September 1832, at Cook's Pit Farm, Faddiley near Nantwich. He was the eldest son of George Peter Hale, a landowner, and his wife, Sarah (formerly Lunt), who came from Hatherton near Nantwich. One of his brothers, Egerton Peter, fought with General Garibaldi in the Italian War of Liberty in 1860, and his other brother, Albert Egerton, died of cholera while serving as assistant surgeon with the 103rd Regiment at Gwalior in India in 1869. There was another son named Leslie.

He was educated at St Andrew's University and at the Royal College of Surgeons in London, before joining military service as assistant surgeon with the 1st Battalion, 7th (Royal) Fusiliers, on 14 December 1854.

His award of the Victoria Cross was announced in the *London Gazette* of 5 May 1857, and he received the medal during the first investiture. He also received the Crimea Medal with *Sebastopol* clasp and the Turkish Crimea Medal.

He served with his regiment during the Indian Mutiny, for which he received the Indian Mutiny Medal with *Central India* clasp. He remained in India when the campaign was over, becoming medical officer in charge at Chitral Fort in 1860, and served with distinction in medical charge of the 2nd Punjab Infantry and other European Detachments in the Peshawar Hills on the Punjab Frontier, 1864–6. He became surgeon lieutenant colonel with the 94th Regiment, and retired from the army on 20 June 1876.

He met Emily Harriett Rowswell while serving at Gibraltar, and they married at St Mary's Church, Bathwick, Bath, on 12 September 1872. His father had died in 1871, and they lived with his mother at Faddiley Lodge at Acton near Nantwich. He was a Fellow of the Royal Geographical Society and the Royal Horticultural Society, and he became a fellow of the Royal Meteorological Society on 18 April 1888. He was appointed Commander of the Bath (CB) for the jubilee of the Crimean War in 1905.

He contracted a chill, which got worse during the following week, and he died at his home on Christmas Day 1909, aged 77. He was buried at St Mary's churchyard in Acton. His wife placed a memorial plaque in the church, and on her death in 1921 his name was inscribed on her memorial at Locksbrook Cemetery in Bath. There is a plaque at the National Memorial Arboretum in Lichfield. His medals were sold at auction in 1955 and they are now at the Army Medical Services Museum in Aldershot, along with other artefacts associated with him.

William Henry Thomas Sylvester

William Henry Thomas Sylvester was born in Long Street, Devizes, Wiltshire, on 16 April 1831, and he was baptised on 17 May that year, at the Church of St John the Baptist. He entered the 23rd (Royal Welsh) Fusiliers.

He became the first Wiltshire-born man to awarded the Victoria Cross when it was announced in the *London Gazette* of 20 November 1857, and he received the medal while serving in India in 1858. He also received the Crimea Medal with *Sebastopol* clasp, the French Legion of Honour and the Turkish Crimea Medal.

He later served in the Indian Mutiny for which he received the Indian Mutiny Medal with *Relief of Lucknow* and *Lucknow* clasps.

He appears on the army lists as being on half-pay on 13 December 1868, and in 1871 he was a doctor at the New Hospital in Swansea, becoming chief medical officer at Millbank Prison in London. By 1881 he was living in Westminster with his wife, Martha, and their daughter, Alice, who was born in Westminster in 1876. The 1911 census states that he was living as 'medical retired' with his wife and daughter at Paignton in Devon.

William was the last surviving Crimean War Victoria Cross recipient when he died on 13 March 1920, aged 88, in his home at 8 Beach Road in Paignton. He was buried in Paignton Cemetery, where his headstone shows his age as 89. His wife was buried in the same grave.

There is a memorial plaque dedicated to him at the National Memorial Arboretum in Staffordshire, and Sylvester Court at Hightown in Wrexham is named after him. His medals are at the Army Medical Services Museum at Mytchett in Surrey.

Robert Shields

Robert Shields was born in 1827, at the *Rope and Anchor Inn* at 41 St Mary Street, Cardiff. In 1841 he was living and working at the Beaufort Iron Works, Shop Row, Bedwelty in Monmouthshire. He entered the 23rd (Royal Welsh) Fusiliers as 2945 Private Shields.

He became the first Welshman to be awarded Victoria Cross when it was announced in the *London Gazette* of 24 February 1857, and the first Welshman to wear the medal when he received it during the first investiture. He also received the Crimea Medal with *Inkerman* and *Sebastopol* clasps and the Turkish Crimea Medal.

At the time he received his medal, Queen Victoria stated that he was a gate keeper, probably at Regent's Park in London. He eventually went to live in Bombay (now Mumbai) where he died of delirium tremens (severe withdrawal from alcohol) on 23 December 1864, aged 37, and he was buried in the Back Bay section of St Thomas' Cathedral in the Kala Ghoda Fort in Bombay. It is believed a possible headstone may have been removed. The *Boy's Own* volume for 1860 carries an illustration of Corporal Shields, with a long bushy beard, finding the body of Adjutant Dyneley. The artist does not seem to have fully researched the subject as Surgeon Sylvester does not feature in the picture. Shields Court at Hightown in Wrexham is named after him. In 1923 a Wellingborough hairdresser is said to have placed the Victoria Cross in a strong-room at the offices of the local urban council, which had been given to him as security for a loan made in 1911. The Royal Welsh Fusiliers made a search for the medal in 1956, but its whereabouts are still not known.

Andrew Moynihan

Andrew Moynihan was born on 1 January 1830, at Saw Yard in Wakefield, and he was baptised on 14 March 1830. Some sources incorrectly give his date of birth as 8 September 1831, which if true would have meant that his Victoria Cross deed was performed on his 24th birthday. He was the son of Malechi Monaghan of Ireland, and his wife, Ann (formerly Scott).

His family moved to live at Crescent Road in Dukinfield when Andrew was a child, and he attended the Wesleyan Methodist school in Ashton-under-Lyne. He began his working life at the Flash Hall Mills in Old Street, before moving to James Ogden's Mill at Hall Green.

The 90th (Perthshire) Light Infantry were stationed in Ashton, where Andrew enlisted in 1848, and he remained stationed in Ashton for six years. With his name now being spelled as Moynihan, he married Ellen Anne, the daughter of Thomas Parkin, a cabinet maker of Hurst near Ashton-under-Lyne, at Ashton parish church on 31 December 1853. In the following year he received orders for active service in the Crimea. He was promoted to sergeant major, and transferred as ensign in the 8th (King's) Regiment.

His award of the Victoria Cross was announced in the *London Gazette* of 24 February 1857, and he received the medal at the first investiture. He also received the Crimea Medal with *Sebastopol* clasp, the French Military Medal and the Turkish Crimea Medal. On his return from the Crimea he received a special reception at the Astley Arms on Chapel Hill in Dukinfield, where he received an inscribed commemorative watch.

He later served as a lieutenant during the India Mutiny, for which he received the Indian Mutiny Medal with *Relief of Lucknow* and *Lucknow* clasps. After service in Ireland and Gibraltar, he was promoted to captain in 1863, and was posted to Malta as musketry instructor. He lived at Moynihan House in St George's Bay.

Andrew drank some unsterilised goat's milk that was contaminated with the brucellosis bacteria and he died of Malta (typhoid) fever at his home in Floriana, Malta, on 19 May 1867, aged 37, and he was buried it Ta Braxia International Cemetery in Floriana. The headstone at his grave was renovated in 2013. He left a widow, a son and two daughters, who returned to Britain to live in Leeds, and when his daughter, Ada, died in 1936, he was named on her gravestone at Lawnswood Cemetery in Leeds. The Moynihan Chirurgical Club mounted a plaque at his house in Floriana in 1969 to commemorate him and his son, Berkeley;

a blue plaque was unveiled at the Astley Arms in 1996, and another at St Austin's Community Centre Theatre in Wakefield in 2013. There is a plaque outside the Museum of the Manchesters at Ashton Town Hall in Ashton-under-Lyne. His medals are with the Cameronians (Scottish Rifles) Regimental Museum in Hamilton, Scotland.

His son, Berkeley George Andrew Moynihan, born in Floriana on 2 October 1865, became a prominent surgeon, and in 1929 he was created the 1st Baron Moynihan of Leeds. Colin, 4th Baron Moynihan, was a prominent sports administrator and politician. He gained an Olympic silver medal for rowing at Moscow in 1980, and served as Minister for Sport from 1987–90, and chairman of the British Olympic Association from 2005–12, during which time he worked on the London bid to stage the Olympic Games in 2012. He was Member of Parliament for Lewisham East from 1983–92.

Charles Henry Lumley

Charles Henry Lumley was born in 1824 at Forres House, Forres, Morayshire, in the Grampian region of Scotland.

He was commissioned by purchase in the 2nd Battalion, 97th (Earl of Ulster's) Regiment, on 30 August 1844. The regiment was in the Mediterranean for most of the 1840s, garrisoning Corfu and then Malta. It moved to Nova Scotia for five years in 1848. The regiment was in Greece in 1854, when it received orders for active service as part of the reinforcements sent to the Crimea, and on being promoted captain, he arrived at Sebastopol on 20 November 1854.

On being seen to by a surgeon it was found that the ball which wounded him had only damaged soft tissue but he was badly disfigured. He was invalided back to Deptford on 29 September 1855, and while he was recuperating at home with his wife, Letitia (formerly Beaulieu), he was promoted brevet major on 2 November 1855.

His award of the Victoria Cross was announced in the *London Gazette* on 24 February 1857, and he received the medal during the first investiture. He also received the Crimea Medal with *Sebastopol* clasp, the French Legion of Honour and the Turkish Crimea Medal.

The 97th Regiment received orders for active service in India in the spring of 1857, but Major Lumley remained behind on the unattached list. He and his wife lived at Shooter's Hill near Woolwich for a while. He received his majority with the 2nd Battalion, 23rd (Welsh) Fusiliers, and was stationed at St Mary's Barracks in Brecon.

During the weekend beginning 15 October 1858, Charles began to act in a preoccupied and agitated way, visibly in very low spirits. On the morning of 17 October he made the unusual step of calling out the guard. Later that day he shot himself in the head. He was aged just 34. An inquest found he had 'destroyed himself while labouring under temporary insanity'.

He was buried in the north-east corner of Brecon Cathedral churchyard, where there is a headstone. His name also appears on his wife's headstone at Locksbrook Cemetery in Bath, where she died in 1890. His medals are at the Queen's Own Royal West Kent Regimental Museum at the Maidstone Museum and Art Gallery.

Chapter 14

The Attack on Sveaborg

When the winter ice had thawed in 1855, a second expedition was sent to the Baltic, under Rear Admiral Sir Richard Dundas. This time the Allied Fleet was to enforce the naval blockade and attack the fortresses along the coast of the Gulf of Finland, including Kronstadt – the gateway to the Tsar's capital at St Petersburg – and thus threaten the security of the heart of the Russian Empire. After a reconnaissance Admiral Dundas was advised not to attack Kronstadt, so all attention was turned to the fortress of Sveaborg, which was heavily fortified, and protected by a thousand mines around the area. As the British ships approached Sveaborg, HMS *Arrogant* and HMS *Magicienne* were engaged in action with the batteries at Hango Head, the destruction of twenty-nine vessels laden with granite blocks in the bay of Werolax, assisted in the burning of the government buildings at Loviss and dislodged a Cossack force encamped in a commanding position near Kounda Bay. Sveaborg was bombarded and partly destroyed on 9 August 1855, which shook the confidence of the Russian command.

During one of these actions, on the evening of 13 July 1855, while the boats of HMS *Arrogant* were engaged with the enemy's gunboats and batteries off the Fort of Sveaborg, her second rocket boat was swamped by the blowing up of her magazine, which killed Midshipman W. Storey, and drifted into a dangerous situation under a battery, in danger of sinking or being captured or destroyed by the enemy. Notwithstanding that he was wounded in the arm, and that the boat was under a very heavy fire, on his own initiative, Captain of the Mast George Ingouville jumped overboard, caught hold of her painter and tried to drag her away from the batteries. In the meantime, Lieutenant George Dowell of the Royal Marine Artillery, of HMS *Magicienne*, with Lieutenant

186

H.V. Haggard, and two other volunteers from the gunship HMS *Ruby*, jumped into a rowing boat and came to his assistance, and the party of gallant men managed to tow the stricken boat and crew out of range of the batteries. All the time during the rescue attempt they were under constant musket fire and bombarded with grapeshot.

George Henry Ingouville

George Henry Ingouville was born on 7 October 1828, at 16 La Motte Street, St Saviour, on the island of Jersey. He was the eldest son of Pierre Ingouville and his wife, Elisabeth Marie (formerly French). He had three brothers, including twins, and two sisters. The family home was La Fregonniere, owned by his Uncle George, which is now a hotel, and he was educated at St Edmund's College on Jersey.

He began his career at sea aged 15, serving on several Jersey-based ships of the Merchant Navy. His first journey on the brig *Three Sisters* was up the east coast of England to the Tyne, but just off the coast at Bridlington it lost its anchor and chain and had to be towed into the Tyne. George seems to have remained in the North-East, because it was from the Tyne that he sailed to places like Algiers, Malta, Italy, Ireland and as far afield as South America. He returned Home in August 1842, to be told that his father had died at Hyères near Toulon in Southern France, on 4 January 1841, aged 41.

He entered the Royal Navy on 6 July 1851. He was 5ft 6½in tall, with a dark complexion, hazel eyes and dark hair. He joined the 120-gun HMS *Trafalgar*, on which he sailed for active service in the Black Sea, and remained with her until joining HMS *Samson* on 16 April 1854, being promoted to Captain of the Mast on 30 September that year. He joined HMS *Arrogant* on 1 February 1855, and was part of the fleet which entered the Baltic in March 1855. George was especially Mentioned in Despatches from Captain Hastings Yelverton on 18 November 1855 and Rear Admiral Richard Dundas on 12 December 1855.

He became the first Channel Islander to be awarded the Victoria Cross when it was announced in the *London Gazette* of 24 February 1857, and he received the medal during the first investiture. He was also awarded the Conspicuous Gallantry Medal, the Baltic Medal, 1854–5, the Crimea Medal, 1854–5 and the Turkish Crimea Medal. A picture of Queen Victoria presenting medals at the first investiture produced by the artist, George Houseman Thomas, depicts her presenting the medal to George Ingouville; but the medal has a crimson ribbon when it should have been blue. The picture is now in the Queen's Collection at Windsor Castle.

On leaving the navy he was appointed boatman with the coastguard on 26 April 1857, but on 20 November that year he was sent to prison for desertion. He returned to the service on 29 December. He was serving with the Coastguard Station at Birling Gap near Beachy Head in East Sussex when he twice deserted again during the summer of 1858.

On 4 April 1861, he married Mary Anne, the daughter of Captain Matthew Le Rossignol, a master mariner, at the Roman Catholic church in Brighton.

George finally left his life on the ocean waves in August 1863, and just under six years later he was lost at sea in unknown circumstances, apparently having 'drowned in a very shallow place when going abroad'. It is believed to have been on 13 January 1869, because that is the date on which his Victoria Cross pension ceased to be paid. His body is believed to have been washed ashore at Hyères. However, this has not been substantiated, and there may have been a mix-up in that his father died there at around the same age. His name appears on his wife's grave at St Andrew's churchyard, First Tower, St Helier, and both Ingouville Lane and Ingouville Place at St Helier are named after him. When his Victoria Cross was purchased by the Jersey Public Works Committee in 1970, it was discovered to have a crimson ribbon, but it is said to have been accompanied by two ribbons. It is held at the Jersey Maritime Museum in St Helier.

George Dare Dowell

George Dare Dowell was born on 15 February 1831, at Fishbourne in Chichester, the son of George Dowell, a Royal Navy paymaster, and his wife, Ann (formerly Tulman). He was educated at the Royal Naval School at New Cross in London, and then he joined the Royal Marines as 2nd lieutenant, on 25 July 1848, transferring to the Royal Marine Artillery on 18 July 1849. He was officially appointed to the Chatham Division, but had studied for the Artillery Companies at Portsmouth. On 26 June 1850, he was appointed to the Plymouth Division to retain his seniority in the Artillery Companies, which at that time were attached to the main divisions. He was appointed 1st lieutenant on 6 October 1851, and on 29 November 1852 he was appointed to HMS *Magicienne*, in which he sailed to the Baltic.

His award of the Victoria Cross was announced in the *London Gazette* of 24 February 1857, and he became the first Royal Marine to wear the medal when he received it at the first investiture. He also received the Baltic Medal, 1854–5.

He left HMS *Magicienne* on its return to England on 3 January 1856, and he was at the Portsmouth headquarters until 28 February, when he attended the Hythe School of Musketry, returning to Portsmouth on 19 May 1856. He was promoted to captain on 22 September 1859, being appointed instructor of musketry to the Artillery Companies on 3 October.

At Alverstoke on 12 April 1860, he married Mary, the daughter of Colonel Robert Mansel. Their first child, George Cecil, was born in 1862, and later became a colonel in the Royal Artillery. They eventually had four more sons and four more daughters.

He was promoted to brevet major on 17 September 1861, and on 11 May 1865, he was placed on half-pay to enable him to accept the appointment of adjutant to the Haddington Militia Artillery, and by 1870 he was adjutant to the Devon Militia Artillery. He was promoted to brevet lieutenant colonel on 23 April 1872, and he was placed on the retired list with the appointment of adjutant to the 3rd Brigade, Western Division of Artillery, on 29 January 1886.

George eventually migrated to New Zealand, where he was a member of the council for the Te Puke Road Board at Tauranga. One of his daughters, Clara Josephine, married Surgeon T.J. MacLoughlin on 4 July 1898, in Auckland. Hampshire newspapers record the marriage of his grandson, George Dare Blakeley Russell, 1st Battalion, Prince of Wales' Volunteers, the son of Mrs Barry Taylor Russell (formerly Dowell), at Andover parish church, on 14 November 1928.

George died on 3 August 1910, aged 79, at 'The Haven' Mountain Road, Remuera, Auckland, and he was buried in the Purewa Public Cemetery at Meadowbank in Auckland, where there is a headstone. The burial register gives his age as 74. His medals are at the Royal Marines Museum at Eastney Barracks in Southsea. Dowell House at the barracks was named after him, as was Dowell Mews at the Royal Marines Depot in Deal. A plaque was placed at his grave in the year of the 150th anniversary of the Victoria Cross in 2004 'Respecting Valour'.

Chapter 15

The Siege of Kars

On the same day as the first attack on the Redan on 18 June 1855, the Russian Caucasus Army under General Nicolay Muraviev began a siege on the Turkish garrison at Kars in the north-east of Turkey: 'The key of the frontiers of Asia', which was led by British officers including General William Fenwick-Williams. Lieutenant Christopher Teesdale of the Royal Regiment of Artillery was acting as his aide-de-camp. On the morning of 23 September 1855 the Russians launched a fierce attack but the defenders repulsed them. However, the enemy simply went back to their positions and continued the siege, while launching sorties to attack the outer defences of the city.

On 29 September 1855, Lieutenant Teesdale volunteered to take command of the force engaged in the defence of the most advanced part of the works – the key of the position – against an enemy attack which had penetrated one of the redoubts. He threw himself into the midst of the Russians and vigorously encouraged the garrison to make an attack to drive out the Russians to prevent its capture.

During the hottest part of the action, when the enemy's fire had driven the Turkish artillerymen from their guns, he rallied them, and by his intrepid example induced them to return to their post.

After having led the final charge which completed the victory of the day, he risked his own life to protect a number of disabled enemy soldiers, who were lying wounded outside the works, and were in great peril from the fury of the revengeful Turks – an action witnessed and gratefully acknowledged by General Muraviev and his staff.

After the garrison had been devastated by disease and cold, and food supplies and ammunition had depleted, the town was forced to surrender on 25 November 1855. General Williams was allowed to lead his men out of the garrison bearing their arms, and they had put up such a determined defence of the city and behaved so honourably that Muraviev stated: 'General Williams, you have made yourself a name in history, and posterity will stand amazed at the endurance, courage and the discipline which the siege has called forth in the remains of the army.'

Lieutenant Teesdale was wounded and taken prisoner, being held in Russia, where he met Tsar Alexander II, until his release in 1856.

Christopher Charles Teesdale

Christopher Charles Teesdale was born on 1 June 1833, at Grahamstown in South Africa, to Lieutenant General Henry George Teesdale of the Royal Horse Artillery and his wife, Rose. The family home was in Bognor Regis, and they moved back to England when Christopher was aged 2. He was educated at the Royal Military College in Sandhurst, and joined the Royal Regiment of Artillery as a cadet on 29 April 1848. His first posting was to the Corfu station in the Ionian Islands. He was promoted to 2nd lieutenant on 22 March 1853, and was appointed aide-de-camp to General Fenwick-Williams. They left Corfu in April 1853 for active service in the East.

He became the first South African-born man to be awarded the Victoria Cross when it was announced in the *London Gazette* of 25 September 1857, and he was presented with the medal by Queen Victoria at a ceremony held in the Quadrangle of Windsor Castle on 28 November 1857, with the whole of the Windsor garrison attending. Joseph Malone, George Symons and James Craig received their awards at the same ceremony. He also received the French Legion of Honour, the Turkish Order of the Medjidie (5th Class) the Turkish Imtiyaz Silver Medal with *Kars* ribbon and clasp and the Turkish Defence of Kars Medal, 1854. He was also made an honorary Commander of the Bath (CB) on 21 June 1856.

Christopher was a talented water colourist, and he was responsible for the illustrations in a book on the siege by Humphry Sandwith, MD, the regiment's doctor at Kars. The illustrations were possibly done while he was in captivity in St Petersburg.

Fenwick-Williams became inspector general of artillery at Woolwich, and Lieutenant Teesdale served two terms of office as his aide-de-camp from 1856–64. On 1 January 1858 he was promoted to second captain, and later that month to brevet major for distinguished service in the field. He was appointed Extra Equerry to the Prince of Wales on

9 November 1858. He was promoted to captain on 3 February 1866, brevet lieutenant colonel on 14 December 1868, major on 5 July 1872 and lieutenant colonel on 23 September 1875. He was appointed aide-de-camp to Queen Victoria, and promoted to colonel on 1 October 1877. He became regimental colonel on 1 October 1882, and major general in March 1887. He was appointed Knight Commander of St Michael and St George (KCMG) in the Queen's jubilee honours list of 8 July 1887, and received the Queen Victoria Golden Jubilee Medal. He was Master of the Ceremonies from 1890–3, during which time he retired from the active service list on 22 April 1892.

In addition to the medals mentioned, for his administrative and civic duties he also received the Knight, Royal Hanoverian Guelphic Order; the Danish Knight Grand Cross, Order of Dannebrog; the Greek Grand Cross, Order of the Redeemer; the Hawaiian Order of Kalakaua; the Russian Order of St Anne, and Commander of the Order of Vladimir; and the Turkish Grand Officer of the Order of Osmanieh, and Commander of the Order of Osmanieh.

Having never married, Sir Christopher lived in a house called 'The Ark' in South Bersted (which no longer exists) and he was a local magistrate and county councillor for the district of Bersted. He suffered a minor seizure while attending to the estate he had on the Rhine in Germany, and on returning home he was attending church when he collapsed from a paralytic stroke, and died at his home on the following day, 1 November 1893, aged 60. He was buried in the parish church of Mary Magdelene in South Bersted, where there is a headstone. The royal family were represented at his funeral. He is named on a commemorative paving stone near the Bognor Regis War Memorial and he is named on the memorial at the Royal Artillery Chapel in Woolwich, and at the Royal Military College at Sandhurst. His impressive array of medals were acquired by Lord Ashcroft in 2011, and they are now displayed on rotation at the Lord Ashcroft Gallery, as part of the 'Extraordinary Heroes' exhibition at the Imperial War Museum in London.

Chapter 16

The Sea of Azov

The Allies decided that if they gained control of the Sea of Azov at Kertch, 'the northern extension of the Black Sea', an important supply line to Sebastopol could be cut. An expedition to Kertch had been aborted as the ships approached their objective because they were needed elsewhere. However, the bombardment of Sebastopol was not as effective as expected and the siege was dragging on, so the Allied commanders decided to try a different tactic and attempt to restrict the Russian supply lines. A second expedition was sent and Allied naval forces entered the Sea of Azov on 22 May 1855. Allied troops landed at Kertch two days later and took the town without much opposition, although the success was soured by rampant looting and pillaging. As the ships moved along the coastline searching for targets, they were repeatedly engaged with the enemy's defences, bombarding forts and batteries, shelling Cossack encampments, and embarking on several Special Forces-type sabotage missions to destroy supplies and equipment.

On 29 May 1855, it was discovered that the large corn stores and transport vessels at Genitchi were in a very favourable position for supplying the Russian army, and their destruction was of the utmost importance. Under a flag of truce the British commander, Captain Edmund Lyons of HMS *Miranda*, offered to spare private property and allow the people to leave the town if they surrendered the stores and vessels before he commenced a bombardment, and when a high-ranking Russian officer refused to accept the terms, stating that any attempt to land or destroy the stores and vessels would be resisted, the bombardment began. However, the British Fleet could not get near enough to the enemy shores and not all the corn stores were destroyed, and there were other ships available to transport what was left to the Russian front.

Lieutenants Cecil Buckley, of HMS *Miranda*, and Hugh Burgoyne, of HMS *Swallow*, the son of a veteran of the Peninsular campaigns, and Gunner John Robarts, of HMS *Ardent*, volunteered to land alone and set fire to the remainder of the stores. They were fully aware of the imminent risk there would be in landing a party in presence of such a superior force, and out of range of any protective cover fire the British ships might be able to provide. However, they most gallantly went ahead and accomplished this very dangerous service. As they were trying to get back to their landing craft a party of Cossacks was seen roaming around the area trying to find and capture them, but they managed to reach their boat and get back to the British Fleet. The British then destroyed the remaining enemy ships.

A second volunteer service was performed by Lieutenant Buckley on 3 June 1855, while the town of Taganrog was being bombarded by the British Fleet, under Captain Lyons. Lieutenant Buckley, in a four-oared gig, accompanied by Boatswain Henry Cooper of HMS *Miranda*, and manned by volunteers, repeatedly landed and fired the different stores of government buildings. This dangerous and desperate service was most effectually performed in a town containing upwards of 3,000 troops constantly endeavouring to prevent it, and only checked by the fire of the guns from the British Fleet. The expedition returned to the Black Sea on 12 June 1855, and Captain Lyons was mortally wounded as HMS *Miranda* provided cover fire from Sebastopol harbour for the troops who assaulted the Great Redan on 18 June 1855.

A large floating pontoon bridge had been built across the Straights of Genitchi, to connect the town with the Spit of Arabat as a main route to supply the troops in Sebastopol. It was therefore a strategic objective for sabotage. Men of the Royal Navy made two unsuccessful attempts to cut the hawsers of the floating bridge, and to add to the problem the Russian garrison was alerted and was prepared for another attempt. Despite this a further attempt was made on 3 July 1855, using the crews of a four-oared gig, and two men in one of the paddle-box steamers from HMS *Beagle*, under William Hewett, and including Seaman Joseph Trewavas.

They could see that the beach, only 80yd away, was completely lined with enemy troops, and the adjacent houses were filled with riflemen, but they did not open fire, and the men on the beach could be seen secreting themselves behind mounds of coal. The steamer's gun misfired and was put out of action, leaving the six men with a cutlass each, one rifle and ten rounds of ammunition between them.

Seaman Trewavas was pulling the bow oar, and as soon as they were near to the bridge he leapt onto it and cut the hawsers as quickly as he could with an axe. He jumped back into the boat again and they shoved off, but made little progress at first because the water was very shallow. They were sitting ducks.

The Russians had believed they were coming to destroy shipping, and therefore had been told to hold their fire with the intention of taking them prisoners. However, when they realised the true objective they opened fire, and the shot came at the Brits like hailstones, wounding Trewavas as he climbed back into the gig, and two other men. When they got back to the ship the boat was full of water and sinking.

A detachment of men consisting of Mate Charles Odevaine, Boatswain Joseph Kellaway and three seamen, all of HMS *Wrangler*, arrived on the shore near Mariupol on 31 August 1855, the eve of Boatswain Kellaway's 31st birthday. Their brief was to burn some boats and hay stacks, and destroy some fishing stations, on the opposite side of a small lake. They had nearly reached the spot, when they were fired upon by a party of fifty Russian soldiers, who suddenly rushed from their ambush, and endeavoured to cut off their retreat. One of the seamen fell into the enemy's hands, but Boatswain Kellaway and the others had contrived to make good their escape, when Mate Odevaine accidentally fell. The two seamen managed to run away, but Boatswain Kellaway, apparently imagining him to be wounded, without a moment's hesitation returned to his rescue, risking his own life to succour his commanding officer. Unfortunately, while lifting up Mate Odevaine, they were surrounded by five of the enemy, four of them grabbing his arms and legs while the other took a firm grip on his beard. Kellaway shook off the men holding his limbs, but the other kept hold of his beard until they recovered, and notwithstanding a gallant and stout, but hopeless resistance by Boatswain Kellaway they were both made prisoners. The three captured men were dragged away by their heels for a long distance, tied to trees expecting to be shot at any time, but they were spared and taken to Taganrog for interrogation. Commander Burgoyne stated: 'I was myself an observer of the zeal, gallantry, and self-devotion that characterised Mr Kellaway's conduct.'

To the north-east of the Crimean peninsula is a low-lying, marshy chain of lakes and inlets known as the Putrid Sea. The Straits of Genitchi forms the only entrance into it from the Sea of Azov. The Russians brought their stores across this swampy tract, mostly across the Bridge of Chingan, which the Naval Expedition intended to destroy at all costs.

Along the Sea of Azov lies a tongue of land, about 70 miles long, called the Spit of Arabat, which varies in width from about ½ to 3 miles, its nose forming one side of the Straight. Behind the Spit were the Russian stores, and opposite the town of Genitchi were anchored four gunboats commanding the channel, and the Spit was garrisoned by a strong force of Cossacks and horse artillery.

On the dark, but fine night of 17 September 1855, Lieutenant George Day, of HMS *Recruit*, who had seen much service all around the world, resolved to cross this tongue of land to carry out a reconnaissance to find out the positioning of the bridge, batteries and gunboats. Getting into an open boat, with only the assistance of a pocket compass, the officer was pulled by two blue-jackets to the shore, and on landing alone, he told them to pull out of gunshot and wait until he hailed them on his return With great enterprise and gallantry he trudged through 4 or 5 miles of low swampy ground, sometimes up to his knees in water, and on sneaking past the Cossack outposts he eventually got to within about 200yd of the vessels. From the perfect silence on board them, it was his conviction that they were without crews, and when he returned 7 hours later it was with the full impression that the expedition was an achievable one. This opinion, however, he was induced to change on the following day, in consequence of the increasing activity which was apparent in the direction of the vessels, and therefore he determined on making a second visit to the spot.

On this occasion the night was a squally one, and the journey longer and more difficult than before. On reaching the spot and finding that the vessels were manned, and their crews apparently on the alert, he decided that any attempt to surprise them was out of the question. However, on this occasion he was ashore for so long that the blue-jackets gave him up for lost and returned without him. Fortunately, a Mr Parker came back to look for him. And finding him lying exhausted from exposure took him back to the ship. It was while attempting a reconnaissance on the same ground that Captain L'Allemand of the French steam vessel *Monette* lost his life.

On 11 October 1855, in the last deed performed during the Crimean campaign to be rewarded with the Victoria Cross, newly married Commander John Commerell, Quartermaster William Rickard, Mate Lillingstone, Seamen George Milestone and Hoskins, all from the six-gun steamer HMS *Weser*, set out in the dead of night to destroy 400 tons of forage and corn bags stacked on the shore of the Sivash (Putrid Sea) in the Sea of Azov. Having hauled their small landing craft over the Spit of Arabat and re-launched it to get across the Putrid Sea, they left Lillingstone and Hoskins to look after the boat, and at 4.30am the other three men made the difficult and dangerous journey of 2½ miles through a region swarming with Cossack patrols. They waded neck-deep across two channels, and on their arrival at first light they discovered that their objective was dangerously close to a guard house and a large red-brick building. Nevertheless, they managed to ignite the stacks, and Commander Commerell was trying to set fire to the red-brick building when the fodder store blazed up and alerted the Cossack guards, who immediately stormed out of their post and opened fire. The three men took to their heels with the Cossacks in hot pursuit. However, after all their exertions they began to tire, and Milestone became so fatigued that he fell into the mud between the two channels and could not get himself free. Commerell and Rickard, although they too were exhausted, went back and assisted him by loosening his boots and pulling him out of them, and with Milestone pleading with them to leave him, they dragged him to the next channel, held him as they swam across it, and got back to the rowing boat. The enemy were almost upon them, so Commander Commerell shot the nearest horseman, and they returned fire to hold back the rest of the Cossacks while they pushed off and sailed into the darkness. The gallant party finally reached their ship, and later the look-outs reported that the fodder store had burned to the ground.

Cecil William Buckley

Cecil William Buckley was born in the Patricroft district of Eccles in Salford near Manchester (which at that time was in Lancashire), on 7 October 1830, and he was baptised at Manchester Cathedral on 9 November that year. He was the son of Joseph Buckley of Manchester, and his wife, Mary Bury Entwistle, who was the second daughter of Richard Entwistle of Rusholme in Manchester. She re-married when Joseph died. A brother named Percy Johnson died young, and there were three sisters.

Cecil entered the Royal Navy in 1845, and first served as a midshipman on the frigate HMS *Tweed*, then on the gunboat HMS *Cormorant*, posted at the American station for intercepting slave ships from West Africa, during which time he was commended for his part in an attack on a Brazilian fort at the mouth of the River Paranagua in July 1850, and the destruction of several slavers. He joined the fourteen-gun steam corvette HMS *Miranda* for a short period in 1850, which was the ship on which he was serving when he found fame. He then served at the Pacific station as mate on HMS *Daedalus* from July 1851–November 1853, before being transferred to the battleship HMS *Royal George* at Devonport. He was promoted lieutenant on 11 January 1854, and rejoined HMS *Miranda* under Captain Lyons.

His award of the Victoria Cross was the first on the list of eighty-five recipients which appeared in the *London Gazette* of 24 February 1857, and therefore Captain Buckley was the first man ever to be gazetted for the medal. His Victoria Cross was sent to be presented to him c/o HMS *Merlin* in West Africa in 1857.

He was appointed lieutenant commander on HMS *Snake* on 15 June 1855, which withdrew from the Crimea to Malta, where, on 28 January 1856, he was inducted into the Freemasons, as were many naval personnel. Being promoted commander on 27 February 1856, he joined HMS *Merlin* on 24 May 1856 for service in suppressing the slave trade in West Africa until April 1858, and during this time he was presented with the Victoria Cross. From 25 January 1860 he served at various times on HMS *Forte*, and HMS *Turnour* at the Cape of Good Hope. He then commanded HMS *Persian* until being paid-off at Sheerness, being promoted to captain on 15 April 1862.

He married Catherine Senhouse Falcon on 30 August 1865, and they had a daughter named Cecile Isabel, and sons named Percy Falcon, born on 9 August 1867, and Frank, born on 20 December 1871.

On 4 December 1867 he was commissioned as captain of HMS *Plyades* at Sheerness, and he was sent to the Pacific station, until being paid off at Gibraltar in July 1870. He joined HMS *Valiant* in December 1871, on the River Shannon, for the Southern Irish Coast Guard.

Captain Buckley fell into ill health (probably cancer), and was admitted to the Stonehouse Hospital in Plymouth. His condition was diagnosed as terminal and he was invalided from service on 18 October 1872. He retired to Funchal on the Portuguese island of Madeira, where he died on 7 December 1872, aged 42. He was buried at the Rua Da Carreira English (British) Cemetery in Funchal. His son, Frank, died as an infant soon after him, on 5 February 1873, Percy died at Funchal on 28 June 1899, and both his sons are buried with him. There is a memorial headstone at the grave, and a plaque in the church which was unveiled by Lance Corporal Johnson Beharry VC on 25 February 2007. Unfortunately, the plaque gives the wrong place and date of birth. When his wife died she was buried in the family tomb at St Peter's churchyard at Leckhampton in Gloucestershire, where Cecil's name also appears. Buckley Point off the coast of British Colombia in Canada was named after him. His medals are in the collection of Her Majesty Queen Elizabeth II at Windsor Castle.

His grandson and Cecile's son, Tom Falcon Hazell, was a fighter pilot awarded the DSO, MC, DFC and bar, serving with the Royal Flying Corps as one of the most successful flying aces during the First World War, and he served with the Royal Air Force during the Second World War.

Hugh Talbot Burgoyne

Hugh Talbot Burgoyne was born on 17 July 1833 in Dublin. He was the only son in the family of eight children of Field Marshall Sir John Fox Burgoyne, and his wife, Charlotte, daughter and co-heiress of Colonel Hugh Rose of Holme. His father had fought in the Peninsular War under Wellington, fought in the war of 1812 and was an official adviser to Lord Raglan at Sebastopol. He was the inspector general of fortifications at the time of the Crimean War, and it was he who had made the decision to put Sebastopol under siege rather than launch an all-out attack. Sir John was also chairman of the Board of Public Works in Dublin.

Hugh Burgoyne entered the Royal Navy aged 14 in 1847. He was serving as mate on the maintop on HMS *Queen* in 1852, and Evelyn Wood, then a midshipman, said of him: 'Many of the young officers were above the average in ability and efficiency, the most striking personality being Hugh "Billy" Burgoyne. Mr Burgoyne was as brave as a lion, as active as a cat, and a very Mark Tapley in difficulties.' (Mark Tapley was a character in the Dickens novel *Martin Chuzzlewitt*, known for his cheerful personality under any circumstances.) During a gale at sea, Mr Wood and Mr Burgoyne were required to send down the top-gallant masts, a particularly difficult operation, during which Mr Burgoyne had two of his fingers crushed, and Mr Burgoyne 'showed a courage and power of bearing pain I have seldom seen equalled'.

Hugh passed his examination on 18 January 1853, served at the Cape of Good Hope as mate on HMS *Peregrine*, and later on HMS *Dolphin*. He was promoted to lieutenant on 11 January 1854, when he received orders for active service in HMS *Boscawen* for service with the Baltic Fleet, transferring to HMS *Swallow* on 16 September 1854, for service in the Mediterranean Sea, before becoming attached to the Fleet in Sebastopol harbour. After his Victoria Cross exploit he transferred to the despatch gunboat HMS *Wrangler* for the rest of the conflict.

He became the first Dubliner to be awarded the Victoria Cross when it was announced in the *London Gazette* of 24 February 1857, and he received the medal at the first investiture. He also received the Baltic Medal, 1854–5, the Crimea Medal with *Azov* and *Sebastopol* clasps, the French Legion of Honour, the Turkish Order of the Medjidie (5th Class) and the Turkish Crimea Medal.

He was appointed commander on 10 July 1856, and on 16 July 1857, he was appointed to HMS *Ganges*, the flagship of the Royal Navy's Pacific station, seeing service in the waters around Vancouver Island and British Columbia. He was appointed captain on 15 May 1861. When the American merchant ship *Northern Eagle* was burned at Esquimalt Harbour, Captain Burgoyne was highly commended for his efforts to save everything possible from the stricken vessel.

The British government unofficially favoured the Confederacy during the American Civil War and secretly aided them, with many of the Royal Navy's most skilled seamen being used to run supply ships through the Union blockades. One of these men was Commander Burgoyne, under the thinly disguised false name of 'Captain Talbot', for which he is said to have been paid $1,500 in gold.

In 1863 he served as second-in-command of HMS *Pekin* in the Anglo-Chinese Squadron. During one of his rare visits to England, he married Evelyn Laura, the daughter of Admiral Sir Baldwin Wake-Walker, on 25 August 1864.

He was given command of HMS *Wivern*, from 27 September 1865–22 October 1867, when he was appointed to the frigate HMS *Constance*, on the North American and West Indian station. In 1868 he was appointed to superintend the building and fitting out of HMS *Captain*, a controversial experimental craft of a full-rigged ship with rotating gun turrets and a low freeboard. Critics considered the design to be top-heavy. She was commissioned on 30 April 1870.

In August 1870, HMS *Captain* accompanied the Channel Fleet to Gibraltar, and shortly after midnight on 7 September 1870, during the return voyage, she ran into rough seas in the Bay of Biscay, off Cape Finisterre, Spain, and a squall hit the craft and she capsized and sank; 483 officers and men went down with her. When the ship rolled a lifeboat launched and some men manned it. Captain Burgoyne and a few men were seen stranded on the keel of the ship, and as the lifeboat approached most of them jumped into the freezing cold water and were picked up. However, Captain Burgoyne was not one of them, and he was lost at sea. He was aged 37. John Commerell sat on the board of inquiry concerning the disaster.

His wife's brother, Charles, also died in the tragedy, and when the ship's signal flags were rescued from the sea by another ship they were sent to Admiral Sir Baldwin at 'Dapperhaugh' – his home in the village of Hoxne in Suffolk. They were given a place of honour above two memorial tablets commemorating the tragedy in his parish church of St Peter and St Paul. After more than a century they had deteriorated and were taken down and burned and the ashes were placed in an urn. The urn was handed over to the crew of the aircraft carrier HMS *Illustrious*, and in 2008 the ashes were scattered with full military honours at the place where the ship went down in the Bay of Biscay.

Captain Burgoyne's name appears on the family grave at Brompton Cemetery in London; he is named on the HMS *Captain* memorial at St Paul's Cathedral, there is a memorial plaque at Westminster Abbey and a window at St Anne's Church in Plymouth Dockyard. There is a memorial plaque at Hoxne parish church in Suffolk. Burgoyne Bay in British Columbia, Canada, was named after him in 1859. His Victoria Cross is believed to have been lost with the ship, and a replica was commissioned by the family but its whereabouts is unknown.

John Robarts

John Robarts was born in about 1816 at Wendron in Cornwall, the second son in a family of eight children to a farmer named Anthony Robarts, and his wife Margaret (formerly Hodge). In 1841 the family lived at 41 Hendra in Wendron, and John worked as a tin miner before joining the Royal Navy in 1842. He served in China with HMS *Welleseley*, for which he received the China War Medal, 1841–2. He took the gunnery course on HMS *Excellent* in 1846–7, before joining HMS *Ardent* in 1851.

He became the first West Country man to be awarded the Victoria Cross when it was announced in the *London Gazette* of 24 February 1857, and he received the medal at the first investiture. He also received the Crimea Medal with *Azov* and *Sebastopol* clasps, the French Legion of Honour and the Turkish Crimea Medal.

At Chelsea in September 1861, he married Annie Emma Victoria (formerly Butts), and they had three sons named John, Thomas and William.

He left *Ardent* in 1856, and went back to *Excellent*. In 1860 he served on HMS *Orion*, and from 1864–6 he served on HMS *Asia*. He saw action on HMS *Revenge* from 1868–9, and from 1869–71 he served on HMS *Royal Alfred*, being promoted chief gunner in 1870. He saw further service on HMS *Pembroke* from 1871–5, before retiring from the sea and taking up several shore posts in Portsmouth, Cornwall and London.

John lived at 4 Park Lane in Southsea in 1881. He died of heart disease on 17 October 1888, aged 70, at his home of Providence House, Castle Road in Southsea, and he was buried in the Highland Road Cemetery at Southsea, where there is a headstone. One of his pall-bearers was Israel Harding, who gained the Victoria Cross while serving with the Royal Navy in Egypt in 1882, and is buried in the same cemetery. There is a memorial dedicated to him in the village hall at Chacewater. His wife and their youngest son, William Cecil, were laid to rest in the same grave.

Henry Cooper

Henry Cooper was born in 1825 at Devonport in Plymouth. He entered the Royal Navy in 1841, serving on HMS *Philomel*, before transferring to HMS *Miranda* for active service during the Crimean War.

He became the first Devonian to be awarded the Victoria Cross when it was announced in the *London Gazette* of 24 February 1857, and he received the medal at the first investiture. He also received the Crimea Medal with *Azov* and *Sebastopol* clasps, the Baltic Medal, 1854–5, the French Legion of Honour and the Turkish Crimea Medal.

He retired from the Royal Navy in 1864, having served as a boatswain for twenty-three years. His wife Margery (formerly Searle) was born in the village of Wilcove near Torpoint in about 1832. They had six daughters and two sons. Margery Elizabeth was born at Sheerness in 1853; Emma Louisa was born at Wilcove in 1858 (she died at the age of 4); Rosa Matilda was born at Sheerness in 1859; William Henry James was born at Torpoint in 1861; Alice Louisa was born at Torpoint in 1864; John Edward was born at Pembroke Dock in July 1867; Emily Frances was born at Torpoint in 1869; and Myra Beatrice was born at Torpoint in 1875.

Henry died on 15 July 1893, aged 68, at his home of 8 Wellington Street, Torpoint, Cornwall, and he was buried in St James' churchyard at Antony near Torpoint, where there is a headstone. His wife, Margery, died in 1915 and is buried with him. There is a memorial dedicated to him at Torpoint, and Cooper Road in Chatham was named after him. The Torpoint branch of the Royal British Legion visit his grave on Armistice Day each year. His medals were acquired by Lord Ashcroft in 1993, and they are now displayed on rotation at the Lord Ashcroft Gallery, as part of the 'Extraordinary Heroes' exhibition at the Imperial War Museum in London.

The Antony Village War Memorial records: 'Corporal Horace Stanley Travers, Royal Army Service Corps. Born in Plymouth in 1886. Son of Edward James and Alice Louisa Travers. In 1901 census he was aged 14, grandson of Margery Cooper, living at 8 Wellington Street, Torpoint, Antony, St Germans. He died in 1918 suffering from the effects of service in the Great War.'

Joseph Trewavas

Joseph Trewavas was born on 14 December 1835 at Mousehole (pronounced Mowsul) in Penzance, Cornwall, and attended the National School in the parish of St Paul. He entered the Royal Navy and joined the battleship HMS *Agamemnon* on 15 December 1853. He landed in the Crimea with the Naval Brigade on 23 October 1854.

His award of the Victoria Cross was announced in the *London Gazette* of 24 February 1857, and he received the medal at the first investiture. He also received the Conspicuous Gallantry Medal, the Crimea Medal with *Inkerman, Azov* and *Sebastopol* clasps, the French Legion of Honour and the Turkish Crimea Medal.

He discharged from service on 10 December 1862, and returned to Mousehole, where he lived at Dumbarton House. He married Margery Harry in 1866 and they had four children – Joseph, Elizabeth, Sara and Annie Margaret, who only lived for a year. Following tradition, he bought a fishing lugger, naming it *Agamemnon* after his first Royal Navy ship. He was a member of the Cornwall County Council for many years, and he was a valued member of the County Fisheries Commission. When the compilers of *Who's Who* asked him about his hobbies he told them he had no time for hobbies because he was too busy earning his living.

Towards the end of his life he suffered a stroke and was struck down with paralysis, which caused him to suffer from severe depression. On 19 July 1905, he cut his own throat with a cheese knife, and although he was attended by two doctors he had severed his windpipe and they could not save his life. He died the next day from shock and haemorrhage. He was aged 69. An inquest recorded suicide while of unsound mind. He was buried in a pauper's grave behind the school building at the Old School Cemetery in Paul Village, Mousehole.

His medals are at the Penlee House Gallery and Museum of Penzance, having been purchased in 1996, and a memorial plaque was unveiled in St Pol de Leon Church, Paul Village, in 2002.

Joseph Kellaway

Joseph Kellaway was born at Stinsford near Dorchester in 1826, where he was baptised on 30 August of that year. He was the third son of five in a family of ten children to John Kellaway and his wife, Phoebe (formerly Fever). His father was a carpenter and dairyman and moved around the towns and villages in the area.

Joseph left the family home at Buckland Newton to join the Royal Navy in 1841. He served in the First China War, for which he received the China War Medal, 1841–2.

On 28 December 1853, he married Hannah Cleverly at Portsea, and they had two daughters born at Portsea. Hannah Phoebe in 1857, and Ada Emma in 1859, but she survived for less than a year.

HMS *Wrangler* was launched on 19 June 1854, and Boatswain Kellaway was with the ship when it sailed for the Black Sea theatre of war on 9 December 1854, where Lieutenant Commander Hugh Talbot Burgoyne took charge on 15 June 1855. It is presumed that Mate Odevaine and Boatswain Kellaway were liberated at the end of hostilities.

He became the first Dorset-born man to be awarded the Victoria Cross when it was announced in the *London Gazette* of 24 February 1857, and he received the medal at the first investiture. He also received the Crimea Medal with *Azov* and *Sebastopol* clasps, the French Legion of Honour, the Turkish Crimea Medal and the Sardinian Medal of Military Valour.

He was serving as a boatswain, 1st class, on HMS *Clio* in 1861, at Guaymas Harbour on the west coast of Mexico. His father died in 1869, and in the following year he was appointed chief boatswain at the Chatham Dockyard on 1 September 1870, a position he held until 1878.

Joseph died at his home in Luton Road, Chatham, on 2 October 1880, aged 56, and he was buried in the Maidstone Road Cemetery in Chatham, where there is a headstone. His death certificate gives his age as 54. His surviving daughter died unmarried at Chatham in 1890, and his wife died in Chatham in 1909. Kellaway Road in Chatham is named after him. His Victoria Cross was advertised for sale in 1971, and is believed to be in a private collection.

George Fiott Day

George Fiott Day was born on 20 June 1820, at Spear Hall in Bobis Hill, Bevoir Mount, Southampton, where his father, Charles, had moved in 1814. He had two brothers and other family members in the Services. Charles Day (1870–1946) founded Day, Summers and Company at Northam in 1834.

He joined the Royal Navy from the Royal Naval College in Greenwich, as a first class volunteer in August 1833. He sailed to the Pacific Ocean on the twenty-eight-gun HMS *Challenger*, which was wrecked off the coast of Patagonia on 19 May 1835. He next served on HMS *Conway* around the coast of Spain during the Carlist Wars.

He served in West Africa from 1835–8 to enforce Britain's anti-slavery policies, during which time in June 1837 he volunteered to join HMS *Childers*, even though he was aware that almost all of its officers and crew had fallen prey to yellow fever. While patrolling the coast in an open boat with 5 other men, he challenged a large schooner with a crew of 30 well-armed men carrying 230 captive slaves, and he forced them to surrender by threatening them with a large 18-pounder gun he had mounted on a makeshift pivot. He returned to Portsmouth in August 1838, where he completed his time on board HMS *Racer* and HMS *Orestes* during their fitments, and he passed his examination on 10 November 1838.

He then served for six-and-a-half years on HMS *Benbow*, HMS *Queen* and HMS *Formidable* in the Mediterranean Sea. While serving on the *Benbow* he commanded the ship's barge, and had four men wounded during the attack on Tortosa on 25 September 1840, and was present during the bombardment of St Jean d'Acre on 3 November. For his service he received the Turkish St Jean de'Acre Medal, 1840 and the Naval General Service Medal, 1793–1840, with *Syria* clasp.

He received a commission as lieutenant on 13 December 1845, and was appointed to HMS *Bittern* on which he returned to the African station. He transferred to HMS *Excellent* on 31 March 1847, and on 3 August 1848, he was appointed gunnery lieutenant on HMS *Southampton* at the Cape of Good Hope. For his service he received the South Africa Medal, 1835–53.

He sailed to South America with *Southampton*, firstly patrolling the coast of Brazil, and then he was appointed commander of the three-gun steamer HMS *Locust* on 12 November 1851, patrolling the Rivers Plate and Paraguaya during the hostilities between the Argentine Confederation and Buenos Aires. For this valuable service he was thanked by both the British ministers stationed there. He was tasked to convey the British Plenipotentiary, Captain Sir Charles Hotham, to the Paraguayan capital of Asuncion, which had never before been visited by a steamer or a man-of-war, and while doing so he did a survey and prepared the first ever running track-chart of the river, for which he received the thanks of Rear Admiral Sir Charles Napier and the Admiralty.

The *Locust* was sent to the Baltic, where it took part in the bombardment of Bomarsund, and seized two large boats full of Russian troops. Lieutenant Day then proceeded to join the Mediterranean Fleet, where he was appointed lieutenant commander of HMS *Recruit*, a paddle steamer with two white funnels, the first iron vessel built for the navy in 1846, and together with HMS *Weser* came under orders for active service in the Black Sea on 4 April 1855. HMS *Weser*, with John Commerell as its commander, got into difficulties on 24 April and *Recruit* had to rescue the stricken ship.

HMS *Recruit* took part in the expedition to Kertch, rendering important service in the disembarkation of troops, being engaged in the attacks on Arabat. Before the attack on Taganrog, Lieutenant Day and *Recruit* discovered during the night a passage that enabled Captain Lyons to successfully reconnoitre the town.

In September 1855, he was entrusted with watching the Straits of Genitchi, and on 15 October 1855, his left foot was severely injured in an accident, but despite this, on 4 November 1855, he landed with two other officers and a party of marines to the west of Glofira in the Sea of Azov to carry out the sabotage of Russian fuel depots and corn stacks. Another party landed in the east to divert the enemy's attention, and the mission was successful. During the winter he was engaged with the Turkish contingent. He was promoted commander on 19 November 1855.

He became the first Hampshire-born man to be awarded the Victoria Cross when it was announced in the *London Gazette* of 24 February 1857, and the medal was sent to him care of HMS *Firefly* in 1857. He also received the Crimea Medal with *Azov* and *Sebastopol* clasps, the Baltic Medal, 1854, the French Legion of Honour (16 June 1856), the Turkish Order of the Medjidie (5th Class) and the Turkish Crimea Medal.

On 26 May 1856 he joined the four-gun steamer HMS *Firefly* and saw further service on the West Coast of Africa, returning Home in August 1858.

On 19 October 1858, he married Mary, third daughter of the late James Ruddell-Todd, who had been the Liberal Member of Parliament for Honiton in Devon from 1832–4.

He then saw active service in charge of two gunboats during the Second China War of 1857–60, for which he received the Second China War Medal, 1857–60, with *Pekin* and *Taku Forts* clasps. He was promoted captain on 20 August 1861, but in consequence of failing health he was obliged to decline active employment, and on 14 February 1867 he was placed on the Captains' Retired List. In further recognition of his service he was appointed Commander of the Bath (CB) on 29 May 1875.

George died after a long illness, on 18 December 1876, aged 56, at the Anchor Head Hotel situated at 8 Claremont Crescent, Weston-super-Mare, and he was buried in a common grave at the Milton Road Cemetery in Weston-super-Mare. The plot was purchase by the Revd Foster for his daughter Caroline, who died in 1908, where there was a marker, until a new headstone was unveiled at the site in 2002. There is a commemorative plaque at the Anchor Head Hotel. His medals are part of the Sheesh Mahal Museum collection at Patiala in India, along with those of Thomas Beach and John Taylor.

John Edmund Commerell

John Edmund Commerell was born on 13 January 1829, at Park Street, Grosvenor Square, London. He was the second son of John William Commerell, of Strood Park in Horsham, and his wife, Sophia (formerly Bosanquet). His father died in 1836.

He was educated at Clifton College in Bristol, and at the Royal Navy School, joining the Royal Navy as volunteer, first class, on 8 March 1842. He served on HMS *Cornwallis* in China, and with the steam frigate HMS *Firebrand* on the Parana River in South America, in November 1845. He passed for mate on 16 May 1848, becoming lieutenant on 13 December of that year. He commanded the six-gun HMS *Vulture* from 15 February 1854, in the Baltic, being appointed commander on 20 February 1855, and taking command of HMS *Weser*, which he sailed to the Black Sea on 4 April, along with Commander Day's HMS *Recruit*. The ship got into difficulty while negotiating the entrance to the Dardanelles, and beached, having to be towed to Constantinople by *Recruit*.

On 13 October 1853 he married Matilda Maria, the fourth daughter of Joseph Bushby of St Croix in the West Indies, and of Belgrave Square in London. They made their home at Alverbank, Stokes Bay Road,

Gosport, where Ella Maud was born on 29 January 1862, and in the next three years Alice and Jessie were born.

He became the first London-born man to be awarded the Victoria Cross when it was announced in the *London Gazette* of 24 February 1857, and it was sent to him care of HMS *Snake* in China. He also received the Crimea Medal with *Azov* and *Sebastopol* clasps, the Baltic Medal, 1854, the French Legion of Honour, the Turkish Order of the Medjidie (5th Class) and the Turkish Crimea Medal. He received the medal from the commanding officer of HMS *Snake* in China in 1857.

He left *Weser* after the surrender of the Kinburn Forts on 17 October 1855, and went on to command HMS *Snake* in the Mediterranean Sea. He served on the six-gun steam vessel HMS *Fury* in the Second China War, 1857–60, during which he again distinguished himself while leading a division of seamen in an unsuccessful assault against the Taku Forts on 25 June 1857. For his service he received the Second China War Medal with *Taku Forts* clasp, received an illuminated address and thanks from both Houses of Parliament, and he was promoted to captain.

He took command of the paddle steamer HMS *Magicienne* at the China station on 18 July 1859. In 1865 he took command of the ironclad vessel HMS *Scorpion*, and in the following year he commanded the twenty-one-gun steam vessel HMS *Terrible*, and assisted in the laying of the first trans-Atlantic cable, for which he was appointed Civil Companion of the Bath (CB). While commanding the ironclad turret ship HMS *Monarch* in December 1869, he transported the body of the philanthropist George Peabody for burial in the United States.

He was appointed military CB in 1870, and was a member of the Board of Inquiry held in Portsmouth in 1870 on the loss of HMS *Captain* and the crew, including the loss of Captain Burgoyne. In 1871 he was commodore and senior officer on the west coast of Africa. He went on active service during the Ashanti Expedition. In August 1873 he was reconnoitring the Prah River when he was hit in the lungs by a musket ball and was sent home dangerously wounded. He recovered, and for his service he received the Ashanti Medal, 1873–4. On St George's Day, 1874, he attended Queen Victoria when she inspected the Naval Brigade at the Royal Clarence Victualling Yard in Gosport.

From 1874–9 he was groom-in-waiting to the Queen, and in the latter year he was appointed county magistrate for the Fareham Division. He was promoted rear admiral on 12 November 1876, and in the following year, when he nearly lost his life in a sailing accident, Admiral Hornby, considered to be one of the finest seamen of his day, commented: 'The country would indeed have suffered a grievous loss if Commerell had been drowned the other day.' He was appointed second-in-command of the Mediterranean Fleet, and he was junior naval lord; commander-in-chief of the North America and West Indies station, from November 1882–5.

He stood as parliamentary candidate for Southampton in 1880, but he was unsuccessful, and he became Conservative Member of Parliament for Southampton from 25 November 1885–23 May 1888. He was re-elected in June 1888, but resigned on being appointed commander-in-chief at Portsmouth on 20 June 1888. He lived at Admiralty House in the Portsmouth Dockyard from 1888–91, where he was a supporter of the Hampshire Volunteer Artillery and the Hampshire Volunteer Engineers. He was a director of the Royal Sailors Home in Portsea.

He was appointed Knight Commander of the Bath (KCB) on 30 March 1874, and Knight Grand Cross, Order of the Bath (GCB) on 21 June 1887. He received the Queen Victoria Golden Jubilee Medal, 1887 with *1897* clasp, and he was also a holder of the Knight of Grace, Order of St John of Jerusalem (KStJ) and the Russian Knight, Order of the Red Eagle. He was promoted to Admiral of the Fleet on 14 February 1892, and retired from this position on 13 February 1899.

Sir John spent the last years of his retirement at 45 Rutland Gate, near Hyde Park in Knightsbridge, London, where he died from acute gout and kidney trouble on 21 May 1901, aged 72, and he was buried in the consecrated section at Cheriton Road Cemetery in Folkestone. A new headstone was placed at his grave during a rededication service in 2011. Dame Commerell died in Knightsbridge in June 1930.

There is a memorial plaque dedicated to him at St John's Church in the Portsmouth Dockyard. Having become a club member in 1869, he is one of four Crimean VCs named on the memorial in the corridor of the Royal Naval and Royal Albert Yacht Club in Portsmouth, which was unveiled by the Duke of Edinburgh in 2007. His medals were purchased in 1994, and they are now displayed on rotation at the Lord Ashcroft Gallery, as part of the 'Extraordinary Heroes' exhibition at the Imperial War Museum in London.

William Thomas Rickard

William Thomas Rickard was born on 10 February 1828, at Stoke Damerel, near Devonport in Plymouth. He joined the Royal Navy at an early age, and was quartermaster on HMS *Weser* when he was posted for active service in the Black Sea, along with Commander Day's ship HMS *Recruit*. On 24 April 1855, the ship caught fire and struck on a rock at the entrance to the Dardanelles and was beached to avoid sinking. After some days of exertion she was got off by *Recruit* and towed to Constantinople badly damaged.

His award of the Victoria Cross was announced in the *London Gazette* on 24 February 1857, and the medal was sent to him care of HMS *Weser*, and he was presented with it by Commander Johnstone. George Milestone was from William's home town of Stoke Damerel.

He was awarded a Long Service Good Conduct badge in July 1857, but he forfeited it on the following 26 December. He regained his rate in July 1858, and he was a quartermaster when he was paid off from HMS *Impregnable* at Devonport in June 1859.

He married Rebecca Whittingham, of Kingsbridge, South Hams in Devon, in June 1860, at St Andrew's Holy Trinity Church in South Huish, South Hams. They had four sons and two daughters, one of whom, Elizabeth, died in 1880 aged only 15. The family home was Arethusa Cottage at Smallbrook in Ryde on the Isle of Wight. He became a member of the Coast Guard, from which he retired as Chief Officer of Coast Guards in the 1870s. In retirement he became boatman to the Ryde Rowing Club.

William died on 21 February 1905, aged 77, in the Royal Infirmary at Ryde, and he was buried with his daughter in Ryde New Cemetery. His wife died in the following year and was buried with them. The grave was refurbished in 2010. His Victoria Cross action was depicted on a biscuit tin produced in 1898. His medals were sold at auction in 1994, and are displayed on rotation at the Lord Ashcroft Gallery, as part of the 'Extraordinary Heroes' exhibition at the Imperial War Museum in London; the museum also hold in their archive some of his private papers relating to his Victoria Cross action.

Chapter 17

The Most Victoria Crosses for a
Single Action

Numerous sources have stated that the most Victoria Crosses awarded for a single action were gained for the defence of Rorke's Drift on 22/23 January 1879, during the Zulu War. However, while the eleven Victoria Crosses for that battle has never been equalled since, and it did produce the record of seven Victoria Crosses awarded to one regiment for a single action (they being the 24th Foot, now amalgamated into the Royal Welsh), my original research from 1992–4 for compiling *The Chronological Roll of the Victoria Cross* first brought to light that there were three prior superlatives.

At that time I carried out a comprehensive study of all the citations for the Victoria Cross which were announced in the *London Gazette* from 24 February 1857 to date, and my findings were published in my 1994 book *Deeds of Valour*, announcing that the superlative award of the Victoria Cross for a single action is the twenty for the first attack on the Great Redan at Sebastopol on 18 June 1855, during the Crimean War. This is followed by the seventeen awarded for the assault on the Sikandar Bagh at Lucknow on 16 November 1857, and the twelve (probably thirteen) for the second attack on the Redan on 8 September 1855.

Some military enthusiasts I have consulted still want to believe that the eleven Victoria Crosses awarded to the defenders of Rorke's Drift should be recognised as the highest, based on the fact that it was an individual fight, while the assault on the Sikandar Bagh was part of a continuing battle (the twenty-four Victoria Crosses gained at Lucknow on 16/17 November 1857 was the most for a single 24-hour period), and the men who were awarded the Victoria Cross for both attacks on

211

the Redan performed other acts of gallantry which were recorded. My theory is that if an action is mentioned in a Victoria Cross citation then it should be included in the total number for that particular action, and should not be devalued because other deeds are quoted in the same citation.

The following are the relevant sections from the citations published in the *London Gazette* on 24 February, 5 May and 25 September 1857, and 2 June 1858, which make reference to the assault on the Great Redan at Sebastopol on 18 June 1855:

Captain William Peel, Naval Brigade: 'on 18 June 1855, for volunteering to lead the ladder party at the assault on the Redan . . .'.

Midshipman Edward St John Daniel, Naval Brigade: 'For devotion to his leader, Captain Peel, on 18 June 1855, in tying a tourniquet on his arm on the Glacis of the Redan . . .'.

Commander Henry Raby, Captain of the Forecastle John Taylor and Boatswain's Mate Henry Curtis, all Naval Brigade: 'On 18 June 1855, immediately after the assault on Sebastopol, a soldier of the 57th Regiment, who had been shot through both legs, was observed sitting up and calling for assistance. Commander Raby and the two seamen proceeded upwards of seventy yards across the open space towards the salient angle of the Redan . . .'.

Gunner and Driver Thomas Arthur, Royal Artillery: 'Volunteered for, and formed one of, the spiking party of Artillery at the assault on the Redan, 18 June 1855.'

Captain Howard Elphinstone, Royal Engineers: 'For fearless conduct, in having, on the night after the unsuccessful attack on the Redan, 18 June 1855, volunteered to command a party of volunteers, who proceeded to search for and bring back the scaling ladders . . .'.

Lieutenant Gerald Graham, Royal Engineers: 'Determined gallantry at the head of a ladder party at the assault on the Redan, 18 June 1855.'

Colour Sergeant Peter Leitch, Royal Engineers: 'For conspicuous gallantry in the assault on the Redan, 18 June 1855.'

Sapper John Perie, Royal Engineers: 'Conspicuous valour in leading the sailors with the ladders to the storming of the Redan, 18 June 1855.'

Lieutenant William Hope, 7th Fusiliers: 'After the troops had retreated on the morning of 18 June 1855, being informed . . . that Lt Hobson was lying outside the trenches badly wounded, went out to look for him . . . towards the left flank of the Redan . . .'.

Private Matthew Hughes, 7th Fusiliers: 'On 18 June 1855, he volunteered to bring in Lt Hobson . . .'.

Corporal Philip Smith, 17th Regiment: 'For repeatedly going out in front of the advance trenches against the Great Redan, on 18 June 1855 . . . and bringing in wounded comrades'.

Captain Thomas Esmonde, 18th Regiment: 'For having, after being engaged in the attack on the Redan, on 18 June 1855, repeatedly assisted . . . in rescuing wounded men from exposed situations'.

Private John Sims, 34th Regiment: 'For having, on 18 June 1855, after the regiment had retired into the trenches from the assault on the Redan, gone out into the open ground . . . and brought in wounded soldiers . . . '.

Sergeant William McWheeney, 44th Regiment: 'Volunteered for the advance guard . . . in the Cemetery, Redan, on 18 June 1855'.

Colour Sergeant George Gardiner, 57th Regiment: 'For unflinching and devoted courage in the attack on the Redan, 18 June 1855'.

Sergeant John Park, 77th Regiment: 'Remarked for determined resolution on both attacks on the Redan'.

Private John Alexander, 90th Light Infantry: 'After the attack on the Redan, on 18 June 1855, went out of the trenches under very heavy fire, and brought in several wounded men'.

Lieutenant John Knox, Rifle Brigade: 'Volunteered for the ladder party in the attack on the Redan, 18 June 1855'.

Chapter 18

The Chronological Roll of Crimean War Victoria Crosses

The first line contains the date and place of the action, and the second line displays the rank and name of the recipient and the unit in which they served at the time of the award. Where more than one action was included in the citation these are depicted in italics below the main text.

1854

21 June at *Bomarsund in the Baltic Sea*
Mate Charles Davis LUCAS, HMS *Hecla*, Royal Navy

8–12 August at *Wardo Island in the Baltic Sea*
Lieutenant John BYTHESEA, HMS *Arrogant*, Royal Navy
Stoker William JOHNSTONE, HMS *Arrogant*, Royal Navy

20 September at *The Battle of the River Alma*
Captain Robert James LINDSAY, Scots (Fusilier) Guards
(also 5 November 1854 at Inkerman)
Sergeant John Simpson KNOX, Scots (Fusilier) Guards
(also 18 June 1855 at the Redan with 2nd Battalion, Rifle Brigade)
Sergeant James McKECHNIE, Scots (Fusilier) Guards
Private William REYNOLDS, Scots (Fusilier) Guards
Captain Edward William Derrington BELL, 23rd (Royal Welsh) Fusiliers
Sergeant Luke O'CONNOR, 23rd (Royal Welsh) Fusiliers
(also 8 September 1855 at the Redan)

Sergeant John PARK, 77th (East Middlesex) Regiment
(also 5 November 1854 at Inkerman; 19 April 1855 at Sebastopol; and 18 June and 8 September 1855 at the Redan)

12 October *at Sebastopol*
Private Francis WHEATLEY, Rifle Brigade (Prince Consort's Own)

17 October *at Sebastopol*
Lieutenant Colonel Collingwood DICKSON, Royal Regiment of Artillery

18 October *at Sebastopol*
Captain William PEEL, HMS *Diamond*, Royal Navy (Naval Brigade)
(also 5 November 1854 at Inkerman and 18 June 1855 at the Redan)
Midshipman Edward St John DANIEL, HMS *Diamond*, Royal Navy (Naval Brigade)
(also 5 November 1854 at Inkerman and 18 June 1855 at the Redan)
Private Thomas GRADY, 4th (King's Own) Regiment
(also 22 November 1854 at Sebastopol)

20 October at *Sebastopol*
Sergeant William McWHEENEY, 44th (East Essex) Regiment
(also 5 December 1854 at Sebastopol, and 18 June 1855 at the Redan)

25 October at *the Battle of Balaclava*
Sergeant Major John GRIEVE, 2nd Dragoons (Royal Scots Greys)
Sergeant Henry RAMAGE, 2nd Dragoons (Royal Scots Greys)
Surgeon James MOUAT, 6th Dragoons (Inniskilling)
Private Samuel PARKES, 4th Light Dragoons
Lieutenant Alexander Roberts DUNN, 11th Hussars (Prince Albert's Own)
Corporal Joseph MALONE, 13th Light Dragoons
Troop Sergeant Major John BERRYMAN, 17th Lancers (The Duke of Cambridge's Own)
Sergeant Major Charles WOODEN, 17th Lancers (The Duke of Cambridge's Own)

Sergeant John FARRELL, 17th Lancers (The Duke of Cambridge's Own)

26 October at *Little Inkerman, Sebastopol*
Acting Mate William Nathan Wright HEWETT, HMS *Beagle*, Royal Navy (Naval Brigade*)*
(also 5 November 1854 at Inkerman as a lieutenant)
Private William STANLAKE, Coldstream Guards
Sergeant Ambrose MADDEN, 41st (Welsh) Regiment
Lieutenant John Augustus CONOLLY, 49th (Hertfordshire) Regiment
Corporal James OWENS, 49th (Hertfordshire) Regiment

28 October at *the Windmill Ravine at Sebastopol*
Brevet Major Gerald Littlehales GOODLAKE, Coldstream Guards

5 November at *the Battle of Inkerman*
Seaman James GORMAN, HMS *Albion*, Royal Navy (Naval Brigade)
Seaman Thomas REEVES, HMS *Albion*, Royal Navy (Naval Brigade)
Seaman Mark SCHOLEFIELD, HMS *Albion*, Royal Navy (Naval Brigade)
Corporal John PRETTYJOHNS, Royal Marine Light Infantry
Lieutenant Frederick MILLER, Royal Regiment of Artillery
Sergeant Major Andrew HENRY, Royal Regiment of Artillery
Colonel Henry Hugh Manvers PERCY, Grenadier Guards
Captain Charles RUSSELL, Grenadier Guards
Private Anthony PALMER, Grenadier Guards
Lieutenant Mark WALKER, 30th (Cambridgeshire) Regiment
Captain Hugh ROWLANDS, 41st (Welsh) Regiment
Private John McDERMOND, 47th (Lancashire) Regiment
Sergeant George WALTERS, 49th (Hertfordshire) Regiment
Private Thomas BEACH, 55th (Westmoreland) Regiment
Lieutenant Henry Hugh CLIFFORD, 1st Battalion, Rifle Brigade (Prince Consort's Own)

20 November at *the Rifle Pits, Sebastopol*
Lieutenant Wilbraham Oates LENNOX, Royal Sappers and Miners
Captain William James Montgomery CUNNINGHAME, Rifle Brigade (Prince Consort's Own)

216

Captain Claude Thomas BOURCHIER, Rifle Brigade (Prince Consort's Own)

19 December at *the White Horse Ravine, Sebastopol*
Private William NORMAN, 7th (Royal) Fusiliers

1855

22 March at *Sebastopol*
Brevet Major Frederick Cockayne ELTON, 55th (Westmoreland) Regiment
(also 7 June 1855 at the Quarries, Sebastopol, and 4 August 1855 at Sebastopol)
Colour Sergeant George GARDINER, 57th (West Middlesex) Regiment
(also 18 June 1855 at the Redan)
Private Alexander WRIGHT, 77th (East Middlesex) Regiment
(also 19 April and 30 August 1855 at Sebastopol)

29 March at *Sebastopol*
Private William COFFEY, 34th (Cumberland) Regiment
10 April at *the Green Hill Battery, Sebastopol*
Boatswain's Mate John SULLIVAN, HMS *Rodney*, Royal Navy (Naval Brigade)

13 April at *Sebastopol*
Private Samuel EVANS, 19th (1st Yorkshire, North Riding) Regiment

17 April at *Sebastopol*
Captain Matthew Charles DIXON, Royal Regiment of Artillery

19 April at *Sebastopol*
Colour Sergeant Henry MacDONALD, Royal Sappers and Miners

20 April at *Sebastopol*
Corporal William James LENDRIM, Royal Sappers and Miners
(also 14 February and 11 April 1855 at Sebastopol)

22 April at *the Quarries, Sebastopol*
Private Joseph BRADSHAW, Rifle Brigade (Prince Consort's Own)

Private Robert HUMPSTON, Rifle Brigade (Prince Consort's Own)
Private Roderick McGREGOR, Rifle Brigade (Prince Consort's Own)

11 May at *Sebastopol*
Captain Thomas de Courcy HAMILTON, 68th (Durham) Light Infantry
Private John Byrne, 68th (Durham) Light Infantry

29 May at *Genitchi in the Sea of Azov*
Lieutenant Cecil William BUCKLEY, HMS *Miranda*, Royal Navy
(also 3 June 1855 at Taganrog in the Sea of Azov)
Lieutenant Hugh Talbot BURGOYNE, HMS *Swallow*, Royal Navy
Gunner John ROBARTS, HMS *Ardent*, Royal Navy

3 June at *Taganrog in the Sea of Azov*
Boatswain Henry COOPER, HMS *Miranda*, Royal Navy

6 June at *Sebastopol*
Sergeant George SYMONS, Royal Regiment of Artillery

7 June at *the Quarries, Sebastopol*
Bombardier Thomas WILKINSON, Royal Marine Artillery
Gunner Thomas ARTHUR, Royal Regiment of Artillery
(also 18 June 1855 at the Redan)
Captain Henry Mitchell JONES, 7th (Royal) Fusiliers
(see also 22 March 1855)
Private Matthew HUGHES, 7th (Royal) Fusiliers
(also 18 June 1855 at the Redan)

10 June at *Sebastopol*
Private John LYONS, 19th (1st Yorkshire, North Riding) Regiment

16 June at *Sebastopol*
Private John PROSSER, 1st (Royal) Regiment
(also 11 August at Sebastopol)

18 June at *the Great Redan (3rd Bastion) Sebastopol*
Lieutenant Henry James RABY, HMS *Wasp*, Royal Navy (Naval Brigade)

Captain of the Forecastle John (T.N.) TAYLOR, HMS *London*, Royal Navy (Naval Brigade)

Boatswain's Mate Henry CURTIS, HMS *Rodney*, Royal Navy (Naval Brigade)

Lieutenant Howard Craufurd ELPHINSTONE, Corps of Royal Engineers

Lieutenant Gerald GRAHAM, Corps of Royal Engineers

Colour Sergeant Peter LEITCH, Royal Sappers and Miners

Sapper John PERIE, Royal Sappers and Miners

Lieutenant William HOPE, 7th (Royal) Fusiliers

Corporal Felix Philip SMITH, 17th (Leicestershire) Regiment

Captain Thomas ESMONDE, 18th (Royal Irish) Regiment
(also 20 June 1855 at Sebastopol)

Private John Joseph SIMS, 34th (Cumberland) Regiment

Private John ALEXANDER, 90th (Perthshire) Light Infantry
(also 6 September 1855 at Sebastopol)
(see also: 20 September 1854 at the Alma; 5 November 1854 at Inkerman;
20 October and 5 December 1854 at Sebastopol; 22 March 1855 at Sebastopol;
and 7 June 1855 at the Quarries)

23 June at *Sebastopol*
Private Charles McCORRIE, 57th (West Middlesex) Regiment

3 July at *the Genitchi Straight in the Sea of Azov*
Seaman Joseph TREWAVAS, HMS *Beagle*, Royal Navy

13 July at *the Fort of Sveaborg in the Gulf of Finland*
Captain of the Mast George Henry INGOUVILLE, HMS *Arrogant*, Royal Navy

Lieutenant George Dare DOWELL, Royal Marine Artillery

15 July at *Careening Bay, Sebastopol Harbour*
Boatswain's Mate John SHEPPARD, HMS *St Jean D'Acre*, Royal Navy

21 July at *Sebastopol*
Corporal John ROSS, Royal Sappers and Miners
(also 23 August 1855 at Sebastopol, and 8 September 1855 at the Redan)

30 August at *Sebastopol*
Sergeant John COLEMAN, 97th (The Earl of Ulster's) Regiment

31 August at *Marionpol in the Sea of Azov*
Boatswain Joseph KELLAWAY, HMS *Wrangler*, Royal Navy

2 September at *Sebastopol*
Sergeant Alfred ABLETT, Grenadier Guards

6 September at *the Great Redan (3rd Bastion), Sebastopol*
Sergeant James CRAIG, Scots (Fusilier) Guards

8 September at *the Great Redan (3rd Bastion), Sebastopol*
Captain Gronow DAVIS, Royal Regiment of Artillery
Bombardier Daniel CAMBRIDGE, Royal Regiment of Artillery
Lieutenant Colonel Frederick Francis MAUDE, 3rd (East Kent) Regiment (The Buffs)
Private John CONNORS, 3rd (East Kent) Regiment (The Buffs)
Assistant Surgeon Thomas Egerton HALE, 7th (Royal) Fusiliers
Assistant Surgeon William Henry Thomas SYLVESTER, 23rd (Royal Welsh) Fusiliers
Corporal Robert SHIELDS, 23rd (Royal Welsh) Fusiliers
Sergeant Andrew MOYNIHAN, 90th (Perthshire) Light Infantry
Captain Charles Henry LUMLEY, 97th (The Earl of Ulster's) Regiment
(see also 20 September 1854 at the Alma)

September at *Sebastopol*
Private George STRONG, Coldstream Guards

17 September at *the Straights of Genitchi in the Sea of Azov*
Lieutenant George Fiott DAY, HMS *Recruit*, Royal Navy

29 September at *the Siege of Kars, Ottoman Empire*
Lieutenant Christopher Charles TEESDALE, Royal Regiment of Artillery

11 October at *Sivash in the Sea of Azov*
Commander John Edmund COMMERELL, HMS *Weser*, Royal Navy
Quartermaster William Thomas RICKARD, HMS *Weser*, Royal Navy

Research Sources and Further Reading

Ancestry.co.uk

army lists

Arthur, Max. *Symbol of Courage: The Men Behind the Medal*, 2004

Ashcroft, Michael. *Victoria Cross Heroes*, 2006

Bancroft, James W. *Devotion to Duty: Tributes to a Region's VCs*, 1990

Bancroft, James W. *Deeds of Valour: A Victorian Military and Naval History Trilogy*, 1994

Barham, John. *Journey Through the Crimean War*, n.d.

Beresford, Admiral, Lord Charles. *The Memoirs of Admiral Lord Charles Beresford*, 1914

Blackett, Captain Christopher Edward. *Crimean War Letters* at the *Cambridge University Library Special Collections*, 1854–5

Blake, R.L.V. 'Val' ffrench. *The Crimean War*, 1972

www.blennerhassettfamilytree.com

Blishen, Harry. *Letters from the Crimea*, 1863

Boulger, D.C. (ed.). *General Gordon's Letters from the Crimea, the Danube and Armenia*, 1854

British Newspaper Archive

Browne, James Alexander. *England's Artillerymen*, 1865

Burke's Peerage

Caldwell, George and Cooper, Robert. *Rifle Green in the Crimea*, 1994

Cambridge Chronicle, 9 December 1854

census returns, 1841–1911

Clifford VC, Henry Hugh. *His Letters and Sketches from the Crimea*, 1956

Conolly, T.W.J. *Roll of Officers of the Corps of Royal Engineers, from 1660 to 1898*, 1898

Conway, Sergeant Patrick, RA. *Royal Magazine*, 1905

Cook, Frank. *Casualty Roll for the Crimea, 1854–56*, 2011

Cope, Sir William H. *The History of the Rifle Brigade (Prince Consort's Own) Formerly the 95th*, 1877

Creagh VC, General, Sir O'Moore. *The VC and DSO, Volume One*, 1920

Crimean War Research Society

Crimean War Veterans in Western Australia

Crook, M.J. *The Evolution of the Victoria Cross*, 1975

War Correspondent, various, journal of the Crimean War Research Society

Daniels, Michael (danielvc.com). *The Life of Edward St John Daniel*

Delavoye, A.M. *Records of the 90th Regiment (Perthshire Volunteers)*, 1880

Dictionary of Welsh Biography

Doherty, Richard and Truesdale, David. *Irish Winners of the Victoria Cross*, 2000

Downer, Martyn. *The Queen's Knight*, 2008

Downham, John. *Heroes of Imkerman, 1854*, Lancashire Infantry Museum, n.d.

Elphinstone VC, Sir Howard Crawfurd. *The Siege of Sebastopol, 1854–55. Journal of the Operations Conducted by the Royal Engineers, Part 1: From the Invasion of the Crimea to the Close of the Winter Campaign, 1854–55*, 1859

Elton, Captain Frederick Cockayne. Fifty-two letters to members of his family during the Crimean War, 1854–6, held at the National Army Museum

FamilySearch

Fenton, Roger. *Letters from the Crimea*, 1855

Findmypast.co.uk

Fitzherbert, Cuthbert (ed.). *Henry Cifford VC: His Letters and Sketches from the Crimea*, 1956

Freemasonry Exhibition, the Library and Museum of, 2006

Gaine, Simon. *The Story of Sergeant William Coffey VC DCM*, 2005

Gowing, 7th Royal Fusiliers, Sergeant Major Timothy. *A Soldier's Experience* or *A Voice from the Ranks*, 1884

Grant, James. *British Battles on Land and Sea, Volume 3, 1827–1874*, 1877

Grehan, John. *The First VCs*, 2016

Gretton, Lieutenant Colonel G.M. *The Campaign and History of the Royal Irish Regiment, 1684–1902*, 1911

Hamley, General, Sir Edward Bruce. *The War in the Crimea*, 1891

Hampshire Record Office

Harvey, David. *Monuments to Courage*, 1999

Hibbert, Christopher. *The Destruction of Lord Raglan. A Tragedy of the Crimean War, 1854–55*, 1962

Huddie, Paul. *The Crimean War and Irish Society*, 2015

Illustrated London News, various, 1853–8

Ingleton, Roy. *Kent VCs*, 2011

Inverness Courier, 14 July 1911

Jocelyn, Colonel Julian R.J. *The History of the Royal Artillery (Crimean Period)*, 1911

Journal of the Victoria Cross Society, Brian Best (ed.), various

JWB Historical Library

Kelleher, J.P. *The Royal Fusiliers Recipients of the Victoria Cross*, 2010

Kent and Sussex Courier, 14 August 1914

Kerr, Paul. *The Crimean War*, 1997

Kinglake, A.W. *The Invasion of the Crimea*, 1887–8

Kirby, Henry L. and Walsh, R. Raymond. *Andrew Moynihan VC*, 1993

Knollys, Major William Wallingford. *The Victoria Cross in the Crimea. Deeds of Daring Library*, 1877

Lake, Colonel, Sir H.E. *Kars and Our Captivity in Russia*, 1856

Little, Matthew G. *The Royal Marines Victoria Crosses*, n.d.

Liverpool Daily Post, various

London Gazette, various, including the Victoria Cross citations of 24 February 1857; 5 May 1857; 25 September 1857 and 2 June 1858

London, Jack. *The People of the Abyss*, 1903

Loyd-Lindsay, H.S. *Lord Wantage VC KCB: a Memoir*, 1907

Lummis Files, held at the Imperial War Museum and the National Army Museum on behalf of the Military Historical Society

Lysons, Sir Daniel. *The Crimea from First to Last*, 1895

Mabel, Countess of Airlie. *With the Guards We Shall Go: A Guardsman's Letters in the Crimea, 1854–5*, 1933

McClintock, Mary Howard Elphinstone. *The Queen Thanks Sir Howard: The Life of Major-General Sir Howard Elphinstone, VC KCB CMG*, 1945

McLeod, Norman. *Good Words, Volume 11: Days in North India*, 1870

Manchester Guardian, various

Mawson, Michael Hargreave (ed.). *Eyewitness in the Crimea. The Crimean War Letters (1854–56) of Lieutenant-Colonel George Frederick Dallas*, 2001

Muddock, James Edward Preston. *For Valour, The VC*, 1895

Murphy, James. *Liverpool VCs*, 2008

Napier, Admiral, Sir Charles. *The History of the Baltic Campaign of 1854*, 1857

Napier, Gerald. *The Sapper VCs*, 1997

The National Archives, Crimean War Records

National Army Museum, including the Letters of Captain A M Earl of the 57th (West Middlesex) Regiment of Foot, 1854–57

Noakes, George. *A Historical Account of the Services of the 34th Regiment*, 1875

Nolan, Edward H. *The Illustrated History of the War against Russia*, 1857

Norfolk Chronicle, 11 September 1858

Norfolk News and *Norwich Gazette*, 24 July 1858

O'Malley, Corporal James. With *the Bengal Tigers in the Crimea. Recollections of a Soldier of the 17th Leicestershire Regiment during the Victorian Age*, 2012 (originally published as *The Life of James O'Malley*, 1893)

The New Oxford Dictionary of National Biography, 2004

Paget, Lord George. *The Light Cavalry Brigade in the Crimea*, 1881

Palmer, Alan. *The Banner of Battle*, 1987

Portsmouth History Centre

Quin, W.J. *'Heroes of the Crimea'*, *Melbourne Argus*, 20 June 1890

Ranken, W. Bayne (ed.). *Canada to the Crimea or Sketches of a Soldier's Life: From the Journals and Correspondence of the Late Major Ranken RE*, 1865

Reid, Douglas Arthur. *Memories of the Crimean War, January 1855 to June 1856*, 1911

Reilly CB, Captain W.E.M. *Account of the Artillery Operations Conducted by the Royal Artillery and Royal Naval Brigade Before Sebastopol in 1854–55*, 1856

Ross, Graham. *Scotland's Forgotten Valour*, 1995

Royal Collection Trust

Royle, Trevor. *The Great Crimean War, 1854–56*, 1999

Rundell, Anthony J. *Kars: Victory Into Defeat*, 2005

Russell, William Howard. *The British Expedition to the Crimea*, 1858

Russell, William Howard. *The Great War with Russia*, 1895

Sandwith, Dr Humphry. The *Narrative of the Siege of Kars*, 1858

Scotland's People

Scottish War Memorials Project

Scout Magazine, June 1909

Shannon, Stephen. *Beyond Praise: Durham Light Infantrymen Who Were Awarded the Victoria Cross*, 1998

Simpson, William. *The Sea of War in the East*, 1856

Sims, Anthony. *John J Sims: Bloomsbury to Sebastopol*, 2013

Smith, Brandon. *Portsea Island and the Victoria Cross: Portsmouth Burials*, n.d.

Smith, Cecil Woodham. *Florence Nightingale, 1820–1910*, 1950

Smith, Sergeant Major George Loy. *A Victorian RSM: From India to the Crimea*, 1987

Smith, Melvin Charles. *Awarded for Valour: A History of the Victoria Cross and the Evolution of British Heroism*, 2008

Southampton Central Library (Local Studies)

South African Military History Society

Spinks Catalogue, 22 April 2010

Springman, Michael. *Sharpshooters in the Crimea: The Letters of Captain Gerald Goodlake VC*, 2005

Sterling, Lieutenant Colonel Anthony. *The Story of the Highland Brigade in the Crimea*, 1895

Steward, W. Augustus. *From the Breasts of the Brave*, 1915

Steward, W. Augustus. *War Medals and Their History*, 1915

Strand Magazine, March 1891

Tameside Blue Plaque Scheme. *A Tribute to Men of Tameside Awarded the Victoria Cross*, 1995

Teesdale, Sir Christopher. Letters written to his father dated 30 September 1855 and November 1865

Tyrell, Henry. *The History of the War with Russia*, 1857

Usherwood, Charles. *Charles Usherwood's Service Journal*, 1852–6

Verney RN, Lieutenant Edmund Hope. *The Shannon's Brigade in India: Being Some Account of Sir William Peel's Naval Brigade in the Indian Campaign of 1857–58*, 1862

Vetch, Colonel R.H. (ed.). *Life, Letters, and Diaries of Lieutenant-General Sir Gerald Graham*, 1901

Victoria Cross Society

Victoria, Queen. *The Letters of Queen Victoria*, 3 vols, 1908

Wallace, Sir Christopher and Cassidy, Major Ron. *Focus on Courage: The 59 Victoria Crosses of the Royal Green Jackets*, 2006

Who Was Who, 1897–1916, 1920

Whitworth, Alan. *Yorkshire VCs*, n.d.

Willey, Harry. *Seaman James Gorman VC*, 2008

Williams, W. Alister. *Commandant of the Transvaal: The Life and Career of General Sir Hugh Rowlands VC KCB*, 2001

Williams, W. Alister. *Heart of a Dragon: The VCs of Wales and the Welsh Regiments, 1854–1902*, 2006

Winton John. *The Victoria Cross at Sea*, 2016

Wolseley, Garnet. *The Story of a Soldier's Life*, 1904

Wood VC, Sir Evelyn. *From Midshipman to Field Marshall, Volume One*, 1906

Woollright, Henry Herriot. *Records of the 77th (East Middlesex) Duke of Cambridge's Own Regiment of Foot*, 1907

Index

Regiments and Other Units

(In order of precedence)

British Locations

Miscellaneous